# COLLUSION

# COLLUSION

## HOW THE MEDIA
## STOLE
## THE 2012 ELECTION—AND HOW
## TO STOP THEM FROM DOING IT IN 2016

## L. BRENT BOZELL III
## & TIM GRAHAM

BROADSIDE BOOKS
*An Imprint of HarperCollinsPublishers*
www.broadsidebooks.net

HarperCollins books may be purchased for educational, business, or sales promotional use. For information, please e-mail the Special Markets Department at SPsales@harpercollins .com.

Broadside Books™ and the Broadside logo are trademarks of HarperCollins Publishers.

FIRST EDITION

*Designed by J. M. Wispe*

Library of Congress Cataloging-in-Publication Data has been applied for.

ISBN: 978-0-06-227472-4

13  14  15  16  17     DIX/RRD     10  9  8  7  6  5  4  3  2

To our anonymous benefactors—*we* know who you are.

# ACKNOWLEDGMENTS

Finding and organizing the flood of examples of media distortion and omission in this book requires far more than two people. It takes the careful daily record keeping of a whole news-analysis division at the Media Research Center. Brent Baker has directed the MRC's media-monitoring team for more than twenty-five years. Research Director Rich Noyes offered his insights, especially on Benghazi coverage and the avoidance of Obama's economic record. Deputy Research Director Geoff Dickens patiently read through every page of this book to keep us on track.

Our news-monitoring team includes NewsBusters Managing Editor Ken Shepherd and Senior Analyst Scott Whitlock, as well as Matthew Balan, Kyle Drennen, Matt Hadro, and Brad Wilmouth. Clay Waters of the MRC's TimesWatch project helped us expose the *New York Times*. We relied on research from interns Paul Bremmer, Alex Fitzsimmons, Kelly McGarey, Jeffrey Meyer, Ryan Robertson, and Matt Vespa.

We always require extensive use of the MRC video archive for a big book project, so our thanks to Michelle Humphrey.

And then there is Brent Bozell's assistant, the unflappable Melissa Lopez, who coordinates all things with the disposition of an angel.

We thank Adam Bellow and Eric Meyers at Broadside Books for their encouragement and guidance, as well as Jonathan Burnham,

Kathy Schneider, Trina Hunn, Joanna Pinsker, Tom Hopke Jr., and Stephanie Selah.

Tim Graham thanks his wife, Laura, and his children, Ben and Abby, and always thanks God for his parents, Jim and Ann Graham.

L. Brent Bozell III thanks his wife, Norma, for raising five children with sterling values, meaning not a one of them wishes to be a reporter.

# CONTENTS

# INTRODUCTION

# "The Best Campaign Team"

Mitt Romney thought he'd won. So did Paul Ryan. So did we.

With polls set to open in New Hampshire in mere hours, we were working the phones with John McLaughlin, of the McLaughlin Associates polling firm. I've known him for over thirty years. We cut our teeth together at the National Conservative Political Action Committee (NCPAC) in 1980, I in the fundraising operation, John working for the legendary Arthur Finkelstein, who did NCPAC's polling. McLaughlin has a reputation for being as good as anyone in the business. More importantly, he's impeccably honest.

We were on the phone putting finishing touches on some questions the Media Research Center was purchasing from his omnibus Election Night poll. Our desire was to determine the impact the media realized over the 2012 election process. More specifically: Did the public buy the media's "news" reporting during this cycle? Assuming Romney was the victor, would he have won the presidency had the public believed what it was receiving to be objective news reporting?

If the answer was in the negative, one had to ask the frightening question: Can free elections—democracy itself—survive a leftist political onslaught dishonestly packaged as objective news reporting?

I asked John to review with me the polling data for all "battleground" states. So he went to the RealClearPolitics.com website.

*Virginia*, I began. John walked me through the available media numbers for Northern Virginia v. the southern part of the state versus the mountain region versus the Norfolk/Tidewater area. *Conclusion?* I asked. *Romney.* We moved to the next state. *Florida?* Again the polling analysis, painstakingly. Panhandle, Palm Beach area. In between. *Conclusion? Romney.*

*Ohio? Romney. Wisconsin? Romney. North Carolina? Romney. New Mexico? Romney. New Hampshire? Romney. Colorado? Romney.* In state after state, after a discussion of polling data, voting trends, and other anecdotal information, the conclusion was unchanged: Romney. Only in Minnesota did McLaughlin hesitate. That state, he suggested, might be just too far out of reach. Give them all the red states and now add in all the battleground states and this was shaping up to be a certain Romney-Ryan victory and quite possibly, a landslide.

Virtually all the GOP-leaning pollsters and virtually all the GOP-leaning pundits (yes, including us) were in agreement. Even the ever-cautious Michael Barone, so learned about every voting backyard in America, was projecting a massive win for the Republicans. The problem was, all the Democratic-leaning pollsters, along with their Democratic-leaning pundits, were calling this one for Obama.

It wasn't unconvincing bravado coming from the Democratic pundits, unchallenged by media pollsters. Obama wasn't like a heavyweight champion who was pounded mercilessly but still smiles, shaking his head to deny the punch had hurt, but whose wobbled legs betray his battered condition. No, they were all confident in his corner. David Axelrod was laughing on national television, pledging to shave his trademark mustache if his boss lost, and his cohorts in the media were chuckling alongside him.

On Election Night the Axelrod lip hair was safe. Michigan. Pennsylvania. Wisconsin. New Hampshire. Minnesota. Florida. Virginia. Colorado. New Mexico. Iowa. One by one the battleground states reported, and one by one they lined up behind the incumbent. Only in North Carolina did the challenger persevere. By 11:30 P.M. there was Karl Rove, the personification of Republican Party politics, the man who raised hundreds of millions from GOP donors while pledging to deliver not just the White House but the Senate as well, desperately waving his hands on national television, the last man standing at the GOP's Little Bighorn, insisting Ohio was not lost.

What had (most) liberals known that (most) conservatives and Karl Rove had failed to grasp?

Yes, the Democrats' turnout machine was as spectacularly successful as the Republicans' was woefully nonexistent. It led the GOP to announce a post-election "autopsy" of their operations, which should have started with firing the idiot who further embarrassed the party by calling the exercise an autopsy.

That was not the concern for my colleague Tim Graham and me. Rather, it was the numbers themselves.

Throughout the campaign, particularly after Labor Day, when pollsters historically switch from the less-efficient "registered voter" to the more accurate "likely voter" formula, a debate raged between media pollsters who consistently found the incumbent enjoying a slight, but solid lead, and those mostly Republican leaners whose pollsters saw the opposite. Conservatives saw a liberal bias: the polling samples consistently were top-heavy with Democrats. Media pollsters defended the skewed samples as reflective of 2008 voting turnout. Republicans rejected this formulation, insisting the more recent 2010 results, which found significant GOP victories, triggered by superior GOP turnout was more accurate. In short, media pollsters saw Virginia as 2008 blue; GOP and conservative pollsters declared the commonwealth 2010 red.

Liberal media bias—that had to be the reason Obama was projected to prevail. But it wasn't. In the end, voter turnout did reflect the 2008 numbers. So the press pollsters were correct, objectively, impartially, truthfully correct.

Arguably it was the only thing about the 2012 elections where the media could be credited as being objective, impartial, and even, when it really counted, truthful.

PRESIDENT OBAMA climbed onstage in front of a raucous crowd in Chicago at 1:45 A.M. on Election Night to pay tribute to those who helped him win a second term. "To the best campaign team and volunteers in the history of politics!" Obama talked gauzily about young field organizers working their way through college, and military spouses sitting in a phone bank dialing away. He spent a lot of time talking about himself, too. He does that mercilessly.

But his praises for all the members of his campaign "family" failed to include his most powerful supporters. There was no love expressed at the lectern for the multimillion-dollar network anchors sitting patiently under the studio lights, preparing each day and night to launch another so-called newscast that would sell Obama and his talking points.

There were no warm words for newsmagazines that would so transparently honor him on their covers, or national newspapers that buried all the worst stories about him. If the "objective" press didn't want to maintain the myth of their nonpartisanship—a myth so easily apparent to anyone who wasn't a "low-information voter"—

Obama would have looked supremely rude by declaring his gratitude publicly.

Some things are better left alone.

The utter failure of Obama's policies and his resulting unpopularity (ratified in the 2010 midterm wave election) barely slowed down the media's reelection propaganda machine. No statistic like a trillion-dollar deficit or a high unemployment rate was going to shake their faith. No presidential candidate in the television era had received the rapturous acclaim that greeted Barack Obama in the Hope and Change election cycle of 2008. They were now invested in his reelection.

The second campaign couldn't be like the first one, where all the Hope and Change chatter painted a gauzy dream of the future. Reality had intruded. Obama promised recovery and delivered only stubborn economic stagnation. Obama promised to cut the deficit in half and instead created dizzying trillion-dollar deficits as far as the eye could see. Obama was handed a Nobel Peace Prize, but kept Guantanamo open and waged deadly drone attacks on terrorism suspects.

All this could have been—*should* have been—disillusioning for Obama's liberal supporters in the press. But so blinded were they by the light of their star that nothing, no fact, no statistic, no storm cloud, no controversy, no scandal—nothing was going to stop them. In 2012 they were doubling down. The national media relentlessly pushed for Obama's reelection with an undisguised affection for Obama-Biden "message discipline." There was an obvious collusion between the president's camp and the "objective" press.

In economics, "collusion" is defined as an agreement between parties to limit open competition by misrepresenting the independence of the relationship between them. The agreement may be set formally, or shared attitudinally. Either way, transparency is necessary but is instead denied. In a collusion, the parties may suppress evidence or even fabricate information to gain a competitive advantage and, ultimately, their economic objective.

This definition certainly fits the media, which utterly failed in 2012 to establish any independence from the Obama machine. While posturing as objective referees of news and information, they suppressed evidence that would mar Obama's personal character or political record, and they allowed the Democrats to invent and project information harmful to the Republicans. If all else failed, the media fabricated it themselves.

National reporters virtually begged their audience to share their desire to keep their man at the national helm. The media's president was a Celebrity President, a charismatic nonfiction TV character with Hollywood swagger. He defined hipness and modernity. And brilliance. And vision. He was History. He was, as Chris Matthews told us, *perfect*.

Mitt Romney's political machine (actually, political junk metal) was oblivious to all this, comfortable in the belief that an electorate searching for a National CEO, a Recovery President, would turn to the Man from Bain. It was a testimony to the singular ineptness of their effort that for the first time a presidential campaign chose to go into a prevent-defense crouch—while losing. When he wasn't being painted as an evil venture capitalist heartlessly stripping innocent Americans of hearth and home, Romney was presented as a pale and corny fifties sitcom dad like Ward Cleaver, someone never real enough to stop appearing in black-and-white.

The 2012 election can be easily cast as what the eighteenth-century English writer Samuel Johnson quipped about a second marriage— "the triumph of hope over experience." John Adams insisted that "facts are stubborn things," but that is now irrelevant. Politicians now are elected on something more slippery—a narrative. The official media-elite 2012 spin pitted a hardworking, compassionate president who was just beginning to show great promise against a soulless capitalist raider who wanted to eviscerate government programs for poor folks. The narrative sold. Voters like stories. Whether or not the official story bore any resemblance to the truth meant nothing to those projecting it.

In a post-election interview with *Politico*'s Mike Allen, campaign strategist Axelrod recounted telling Obama that the media elites hadn't been wrong when they spent much of the first two years of Obama's tenure "reporting" that the Tea Party people were extremists who would quickly ruin the Republican Party. "I said to the President the day after the midterm elections, I thought that the seeds of his re-election had been planted by that election," he remembered. "No Republican candidate was going to be able to get through that process without bowing to the force of the Tea Party and the social conservatives. And a number of very formidable candidates took a pass, in part because they recognized that."

Axelrod could say this because he had confidence that the "objective" media would be his echo chamber. The media coverage of Obama's reelection cycle neatly matched Axelrod's plan. Obama would not be judged based on a balanced and factual evaluation of his dismal record. It would be based on a liberal argument of inclusion— that even if Romney brought his vaunted recovery where Obama had failed, that prosperity would only benefit the "millionaires and billionaires" at the expense of "the people." It was also implied that the racially challenged Republicans, hobbled by their party's overwhelming whiteness, somehow didn't want nonwhite Americans to share in the coming cornucopia.

Axelrod told a crowd after the election at the University of Chicago, "The president's fundamental message was that we need not just to rebuild the economy, but needed to reclaim security. That fundamental compact that we thought of as the American Dream has been shredded." To liberals, welfare-state "security" and the American Dream are very tightly linked. Dependency, unlike recovery, could be guaranteed by government. Romney's vision of free-market solutions was dismissed as discredited top-down economics that benefited only the super-rich.

It was a message fully embraced and projected by the national press.

The media have always been liberal, certainly since TV news erupted in power and influence in the 1960s, but never have they shown such naked bias as they did in the 2012 election. It was unrestrained political agitation. So much of the broadcast networks, their cable counterparts, and the major establishment print media were out of control with a deliberate and unmistakable leftist agenda. The most usable facts about Obama were the positive facts. The most usable quotes about Obama were the positive quotes. The most compelling narratives about Obama were the endearingly personal narratives. The reverse held true for his opponent. Over the last quarter century we have closely monitored national political coverage, and we can say with authority that never has there been a more brazen and complete attempt by the liberal "news" media to decide the outcome of an election.

In 2004, then-*Newsweek* scribe Evan Thomas claimed that a media tilt toward John Kerry would be worth at least five (and "maybe fifteen") percentage points. In a race decided by less than four percentage points, can it be argued that the media's blatant salesmanship for Obama provided his margin of victory in 2012?

We believe the national press corps stole the election for Barack Obama in 2012, and will document the evidence in the pages that follow. We also believe that unless and until this blatant leftist disinformation effort is exposed and neutralized, Republicans—at least conservative Republicans—will not soon recapture the reins of power in this country.

Every conservative in America knows the liberal press has an agenda against them. What they cannot understand is why Republicans are so incapable of solving the problem. We share this frustration. We see the damage done daily, with virtually no GOP countermeasures, ever. Why not? There are several reasons.

*Ignorance.* Oh, they know there's a problem but they have no idea how serious it is. They take their news from Fox, or the *Washington Times.* Their radios are tuned to Rush Limbaugh, Sean Hannity and Mark Levin. Their favorite websites are Drudge, CNSNews, and Breitbart. The working assumption is that everyone else is there, too. Beyond the news media are the entertainment empires where far more mischief is created. Most Republicans are clueless. I once overheard a man ask the late Jeane Kirkpatrick, former ambassador to the United Nations and our very own force of nature, if she could ever handle watching Michael Moore's movie *Roger and Me.* The man stated with a knowing smile that he could *never* stomach the experience. "I already have, and so should you," she snapped. "You must always know what the enemy is doing."

*Arrogance.* A few years ago I was visiting with John Moody, then a senior vice president at the Fox News Channel, to talk about his network, which by now had risen to the top of the cable news business. I asked him, at what point did Republicans realize they had a venue that wasn't going to crucify them? I wanted to know. Moody's answer was immediate and emphatic: Democrats were comfortable with Fox far sooner than their counterparts simply because they understood the need to work with the press. When calling down to Washington in search of a GOP guest on Capitol Hill, or at the Bush White House, the Fox booker inevitably would be transferred to some press secretary with no authority to do more than take a message that would or wouldn't be returned by a senior staff member who—yawn—would or wouldn't be interested in delivering his boss. The Democrats? They booked the interview on the spot. Often the member of Congress jumped on the phone to facilitate the interview.

*Fear.* During the Bush years I was invited to Capitol Hill to meet with a select group of conservatives, from both parties, thoroughly frustrated and intimidated by the national news media over the issue that bound them—tax cuts. Any discussion along these lines invariably became a clarion call for "tax cuts for the greedy rich," when this was never their intent. They still carried the scars of the "Mediscare" campaign of 1995, when the press demolished the nascent Republican majority and buried the Contract with America by stating and repeating endlessly the falsehood that Republicans were abandoning the elderly (along with clean air and water, and the homeless, and the hungry, and blacks and Hispanics, and the children, the children, always the children). "What could they do?" they pleaded. Barring a better answer from me, their (unspoken) solution was to hide.

The answer, I tried to tell them, was otherwise, a three-part exercise. First, present your argument intelligently and cogently. Second, if your message is distorted by the press, give them the benefit of the doubt. Bring the offense to their attention, and give them the opportunity to correct it. Third, if they are in the wrong, and they refuse to correct the error, beat the hell out of them. Make *them* the issue. There was much chest-thumping in return as one by one they gave their speeches endorsing a declaration of war on the media. By and large that never happened. Instead they returned to fretting about what the media might do to them in response and they returned to the tall grass from whence they've not emerged.

That was then. We are in the midst of the most profound communications revolution in history, with extraordinary new opportunities presenting themselves to us, each one making the left-wing news media that much more irrelevant—if we're smart enough, and eager enough, and courageous enough to go there.

First it's critically important to understand the problem fully. Then it's important to correct it. What follows will address both.

# CHAPTER 1

## From Hope to Hatchets

### "He will have to kill Romney."

It is a dirty trick for the national media to decide who's playing dirty. Their support for liberal politicians verges on adoring. Conversely, because the media elite loathes most conservative politicians, almost anything goes in attacking them.

The first thing any conservative should tell his friends about the "news" business is this: reporters, editors, and anchormen are not those characters in your civics textbook, merely interested in telling you what happened in the world while you slept or while you were at work. They're not objective, impartial observers of a political system holding all politicians accountable. They are participants in the process.

The news business in the Obama era has been virtually indistinguishable from the Obama commercials, the official White House videos, and the campaign social-media messages. When they were "reporting" on Obama, reporters weren't offering a news story as much as they were advancing a narrative. They are in the narrative business.

In fact, it could be argued that today's campaign ads are more vetted for accuracy—and in fact, more accurate—than news reports. The 2012 cycle was loaded up with "nonpartisan" fact-checkers with liberal-media backgrounds frisking the candidates and their messages for accuracy. They weren't probing their fellow journalists for lies and inaccuracies. There is often only one difference between a candidate's vicious negative ad and an "investigative" news report: the undeserved patina of media "objectivity" and respectability.

Obama's Republican challengers could be viciously and personally attacked, and the media wouldn't paint the attackers as vicious—especially when they were among the attackers. Team Obama always believed Mitt Romney would be their opponent. In August 2011, *Politico* reported a "prominent Democratic strategist aligned with the White House" speaking bluntly: "Unless things change and Obama can run on accomplishments, he will have to kill Romney."[1]

Imagine the explosion had the Romney camp declared the need to kill Obama. Despite these words appearing in a liberal publication, and despite the Romney camp denouncing the quote as "disgraceful," the words "have to kill Romney" were completely ignored by the major media. They were ignored by the Associated Press, *The New York Times*, *The Washington Post*, and *USA Today*. This phrase wasn't quoted on ABC, CBS, NBC, NPR, PBS, or CNN. As usual, Fox News was the exception to the blackout. Oh wait, there was another. It was relayed once by *Last Word* host Lawrence O'Donnell on MSNBC. He enjoyed it as the "juiciest quote."[2]

The anonymous source was probably not someone like Axelrod, who would never concede Obama had no accomplishments. But it did reflect Team Obama's attitude toward the Republicans. The GOP contenders could all prepare for an historic campaign—defined as an historic level of mud-slinging, the tawdriest, flimsiest attacks of "investigative journalism," and bottom-scraping negative ads.

The architects of Obama's reelection campaign couldn't boast about any reelection mandate. The public was unimpressed by Obama's performance in his first term and reluctant to award him a second one. The Real Clear Politics average of the approval-rating polls in mid-September 2011 measured the president's approval rating at 43 percent approval, and 51 percent disapproval.[3] With these numbers, pundits could have measured his political coffin.

Instead, Axelrod would need to rely on a narrative that the Republicans were all too conservative to offer a serious challenge to Obama. He boasted afterward that he had told the president "the seeds of his re-election had been planted by that [2010] election. The Tea Party movement would need to be marginalized in order to drag all the GOP candidates down. He would need the national media to advance this narrative. In fact, the work was already under way.

Over the summer, the Tea Party wanted the Republicans to vote against increasing the debt limit, as a way to force the Democrats to limit spending. Opposition to Obama equaled hatred, even some form of jihad. *The New York Times* assembled an editorial-page tag team.

Columnist Thomas Friedman warned, "If sane Republicans do not stand up to this Hezbollah faction in their midst, the Tea Party will take the GOP on a suicide mission." Friedman later claimed on NBC that "there's a lot of Republicans who are starved for a candidate" who could debate Obama and attempt to be "as smart and mellifluous as the president."[4]

*Times* business columnist Joe Nocera claimed the country "watched in horror as the Tea Party Republicans waged jihad on the American people."[5] But columnist Maureen Dowd stood out from the crowd, sounding like she had swallowed a fistful of hallucinogenic drugs:

"Tea Party budget-slashers . . . were like cannibals, eating their own party and leaders alive. They were like vampires, draining the country's reputation, credit rating and compassion. They were like zombies, relentlessly and mindlessly coming back again and again to assault their unnerved victims, [Speaker of the House John] Boehner and President Obama. They were like the metallic beasts in *Alien* flashing mouths of teeth inside other mouths of teeth, bursting out of Boehner's stomach every time he came to a bouquet of microphones."[6]

*The New York Times* even published a book review by an Ohio State professor that equated the Tea Party with the Ku Klux Klan. "Imagine a political movement created in a moment of terrible anxiety, its origins shrouded in a peculiar combination of manipulation and grass-roots mobilization, its ranks dominated by Christian conservatives and self-proclaimed patriots, its agenda driven by its members' fervent embrace of nationalism, nativism and moral regeneration, with more than a whiff of racism wafting through it. No, not that movement." Opposing Obama—even if you were Herman Cain—demonstrated "more than a whiff of racism."

The candidates who jumped in didn't impress Axelrod. So during the primary season, the media elite treated the emerging Republican challengers as a field of nightmares, a group of pretenders and has-beens who could not be seriously hoping to defeat Obama. Republican debate audiences were criticized as "bloodthirsty" and demonstrating "bloodlust."[7]

There was no such thing as a loyal or honorable opposition. Instead, Obama critics were described as assassins. On MSNBC, Chris Matthews was asserting "the whole shebang, has been eliminate this guy's presidency. It's been personal, it's been about him, and it's about hatred. . . . 'We hate you, want to kill you—[dramatic pause] politically.'"[8]

## Republicans on the Chopping Block

From the start of the Republican race in 2011, every candidate who took the lead in the pre-primary polling was subjected to a beating. Even Sarah Palin was slimed in case she decided to run. Outbursts of "investigative journalism" erupted repeatedly against the GOP front-runner of the moment. Republican presidential campaigns were damaged or demolished, one by one.

PALIN. Governor Sarah Palin never declared she was running for president, but she frightened reporters by going on campaign-style bus tours to keep alive the notion that she just might run and her name in the headlines. Journalists feared the voters in Flyover Country might find her more culturally resonant than the globe-trotting sophisticate with the funny name that they preferred. Bill Maher told Piers Morgan on CNN he wouldn't put it past the Republicans. "Somewhere along the line they got on a short bus to Crazy Town, and if someone gets the nomination of one of the two major parties, especially in a bad economy, with a black president, yes, she could become president."[9]

Everyone was qualified to find Palin crazy—even Roseanne Barr. On CNN, she declared "[Palin is] a loon and I think she's kind of a traitor to this country. . . . Her followers are the dumbest people on Earth. . . . They can barely scare up a pulse. I'm serious." MSNBC host Martin Bashir had his own adjectives: "Vacuous, crass, and according to almost every biographer, vindictive too."

Author Joe McGinniss was roundly condemned by liberals as a

smear artist in 1993 for his Ted Kennedy book *The Last Brother*. It was an unreliable, unsubstantiated attack piece, they felt. But when McGinniss wrote *The Last Rogue*, a book attacking Palin, this same maligned scribe was given the red-carpet treatment on *Dateline NBC*. It didn't matter that Palin wasn't running for president. Just the chance that this "mama grizzly" might run inspired NBC's venomous portrayal.

McGinniss called Palin "[a]n utter fraud. An absolute and utter fraud." Rather than challenge that statement, his NBC interviewer, Savannah Guthrie, helpfully added: "You called her a tenth-grade mean girl." McGinniss insisted "those are kind words compared to a lot of what you would hear in Wasilla . . . the people who know her best like her least."

NBC needed no names or documents to prove any smear that McGinniss allegedly was repeating. Guthrie continued: "He accuses the famed hockey mom of using her children as props and reports she was not much of a mother at all." She was "virtually nonexistent as a mother," insisted McGinniss. Guthrie also helpfully relayed the unproven charge that Todd and Sarah Palin were "fighting incessantly and threatening divorce."

The Palins also used cocaine, according to the NBC manure-spreaders. Guthrie touted: "Another bombshell, McGinniss writes that both Todd and Sarah have used cocaine in the past, a claim that has not been verified. How do you substantiate something like that?" A far better, and more important question: Why was this unsubstantiated garbage being repeated on NBC? Are all unverified rumors accepted—if they are salacious enough, and the subject is a conservative?

Guthrie also helped champion McGinniss's claim that Palin slept with a pro basketball star: "McGinniss also quotes friends who speak of a sexual encounter Palin had with basketball star Glen Rice in 1987, while she was a sports reporter for a local Anchorage station, prior to her marriage." Proof of Sarah Heath's bed-hopping with bas-ketball stars at twenty-three? Who needs proof?

Then Guthrie wrapped up: "McGinniss portrays Palin as 'Hands Off' when it came to governing Alaska, but a ruthless political op-portunist who crushed her enemies and rarely lived up to the fiscal conservative image she championed." McGinniss said, "At best, she's a hypocrite. . . . At worst, she's a vindictive hypocrite." [10]

Ruthless opportunists . . . vindictive hypocrites who crush enemies—truer words were never spoken . . . if they were applied to the "news" manufacturers at NBC. Guthrie wasn't punished for this exercise in character assassination. She was promoted to her dream job as the cohost of *Today*.

BACHMANN. On July 11, 2011, as Michele Bachmann's popularity was growing (and about a month before she won the Iowa straw poll) ABC's *World News* touted a hidden-camera investigation of the clinic of her therapist husband, Marcus Bachmann. It was a "pray away the gay" scandal, they said. "We begin tonight with an ABC News investi-gation," oozed anchor Diane Sawyer. "Tea Party powerhouse Michele Bachmann has rocketed to the top of the Republican pack. Tonight, a closer look at the business she and her husband own back home in Minnesota. An outside group filmed undercover video inside the Bachmann's Christian counseling center. Bachmann's husband has said he does not try to turn gay people straight." [11] (The horror!) ABC (and then CNN, and then NBC) claimed otherwise.

But the hidden cameras of this "ABC News investigation" weren't sent in by ABC. They came from a radical homosexual lobby called "Truth Wins Out," a funny name for a group that had lied and faked its way into the Bachmann clinic. No one saw the conflict, apparently.

Mocking Bachmann was easy, and was never seen as sexist. On *The Tonight Show* with Jay Leno, MSNBC host Chris Matthews in-sisted, "I've always said she's in a trance. I mean, she looks like she's been hypnotized." Former *New York Times* executive editor Bill Keller couldn't stand religious sentiments on the campaign trail. "Rick Perry, Michele Bachmann and Rick Santorum are all affiliated with fervid subsets of evangelical Christianity, which has raised concerns about their respect for the separation of church and state, not to mention the separation of fact and fiction."

In August, *Newsweek* mocked Michele Bachmann on its cover, making her look pale and confused. Nutty. The headline said it all: "The Queen of Rage." The cover story by reporter Lois Romano threw mud. "Bachmann has become the living embodiment of the Tea Party. She and her allies have been called a maniacal gang of knife-wielding ideologues. That's hyperbole, of course. But the principled rigidity of her position has created some challenges for her campaign."

*"Obama and his allies are a maniacal gang of knife-wielding ideologues. That's hyperbole, of course."* Do you think any editor would ever allow that to stand?

Here's another typical, sneering sentence: "For now, Bachmann revels in the Iowa crowds, which don't fuss about the missing fine print behind her ideas, the perceived contradictions among them, or their radicalism." [12] *Newsweek* claims to loathe contradictions—as they write long, nasty editorials and then claim like complete hypocrites that they were publishing a "news" story.

The liberal website FunnyOrDie.com wrote alternative titles for the Bachmann cover picture, including "The Girl Next Door: Assuming You Live Next to an Insane Asylum" and "Zombies: Michele Bachmann Eats America's Young." [13]

PERRY. Governor Rick Perry looked like a strong contender when he entered the race in August, due to his booming success in the Texas economy and his ability to raise campaign cash. That's when reporters decided to portray him as the worst kind of cowboy bumpkin. ABC anchor Diane Sawyer called him the "human tornado," as reporter Jake Tapper added, "Democrats say that until Perry came along, they never thought they'd meet a candidate who made the other Republican candidates look responsible."[14] CBS ran a wild-haired cartoon image of Perry running with an exploding gun as they explained he believed in "America's right to bear arms—even in a speeding helicopter. Yes, he made it legal to hunt wild boar from the air. After all, he's the kind of governor who would shoot a coyote while he's out jogging."[15]

CNN commentator Jack Cafferty saw his ascent as the End of Brains. "Since Michele Bachmann won the Iowa straw poll and Rick Perry entered the race, these two have been sucking up most of the media's attention, mostly for saying stupid stuff. . . . That's a sad commentary on the state of our politics, isn't it? Here's the question: When it comes to presidential politics, why does America seem to be allergic to brains?"

But his days as front-runner were numbered as the big "investigative bombshell" arrived on October 2, when *The Washington Post* killed trees to report in earthshaking depth how the Rick Perry family had leased a hunting property where in 1983 or 1984, the N-word was found painted on a rock, and never mind it was the Rick Perry family that covered it with white paint. Reporter Stephanie McCrummen could conjure up a virtual Klan hood on Perry's head. "As recently as this summer, the slablike rock—lying flat, the name still faintly visible beneath a coat of white paint—remained by the gated entrance to the camp."

Near the end, she underlined it again: "In the photos, it was to the left of the gate. It was laid down flat. The exposed face was brushed clean of dirt. White paint, dried drippings visible, covered a word across the surface. An N and two G's were faintly visible."[16]

Three thousand words they spent on this.

The *Post* was throwing the biggest rock they could at a

Republican—racism, as in casual acquiescence to the N-word—
without telling the public who was behind the accusation. They
quoted seven sources, but six of them remained anonymous. Were
some Obama supporters or financial backers? Naturally, when some
readers protested, *Washington Post* ombudsman Patrick Pexton declared, "If the seven sources the *Post* relied on for this article are
truthful, then Perry is lying or is badly misinformed about when the
rock was painted." [17] Pexton also insisted that the Perry camp's failure
to protest more fiercely made him look guilty. Damned if you do,
damned if you don't.

Would the *Post* use six anonymous sources to push a three-
thousand-word story on the front page trashing Barack Obama for
something some people said anonymously that he did or said in the
1980s? Radio host Hugh Hewitt put it best: "It is a drive-by slander." [18]

Two days after the rock "scoop," a *Post* front-page article by Amy
Gardner found Perry's record on race was "complicated" . . . by the
facts. Perry "appointed the first African American to the state Supreme Court and later made him chief justice" and oh yes, "One
chief of staff and two of his general counsels have been African
American." But "minority legislators" complained he used "racially
tinged" tactics. Guess what was listed first? "Black lawmakers have
been particularly troubled by Perry's recent embrace of the Tea Party
movement."

CAIN. Herman Cain was exactly the kind of candidate liberals fear:
a successful, dynamic black Republican with a solid record of business success. Liberal journalists couldn't abide the idea that someone
of his ilk could ever pretend to be president. *Washington Post* writer
Tim Carman made him sound like a mobster: "One of his primary
credentials for the job involves his nearly miraculous healing of the
once-moribund Godfather's Pizza, as if America were a midgrade
Midwestern chain whose many problems could be solved with a few

deaths in the family (read: store closings) and a tough-talking thug in a pin-stripe suit and fedora."[19]

When Cain ascended to the top of the Republican polls, it wasn't proof that the Tea Party conservatives were suddenly or temporarily not racists. It was time for another "investigative" takedown. On the night of Halloween, the liberal newspaper *Politico* first reported that when Cain headed the National Restaurant Association, it settled two sex harassment lawsuits. Citing unnamed sources, *Politico* reported two unnamed women had alleged Cain was guilty of "conversations allegedly filled with innuendo or personal questions of a sexually suggestive nature," and also "descriptions of physical gestures that were not overtly sexual" but made women uncomfortable.[20]

"Another high-tech lynching," said Ann Coulter on Fox News.[21]

Even Stephen Engelberg, a former *New York Times* reporter at the investigative journalism shop ProPublica, found it underbaked. "If the facts as published were part of a memo to *Politico*'s editors they would amount to a first-rate tip on a story . . . in this case, it remains unclear whether this was merely a great tip or an actual bombshell."[22]

But the networks were thrilled. "This morning, bombshell blast," announced ABC's George Stephanopoulos hours after the story broke, reporting a "bimbo eruption" of the kind he used to keep out of the news for a paycheck from the Clintons. NBC's Matt Lauer gloated that Cain was "finding out the hard way about the attention that goes along with being a front-runner."[23]

In the first week of the scandal, ABC, CBS, and NBC combined for eighty-four stories on Herman Cain's alleged impropriety with women—before the media would or could identify an accuser with a name and a face.[24] By contrast, eight days into Bill Clinton's sexual harassment scandals with publicly identified accusers Paula Jones and Kathleen Willey and adding even the rape allegation of Juanita Broaddrick, there were eight reports on the three named Clinton accusers combined.[25]

The network story count was almost 100 before a real name emerged, a television avalanche. The networks hurled 117 stories at Cain in the first ten days. Not only that, ABC's Brian Ross suggested Cain's backers were thugs, since one accuser "hired a security team to guard her home outside Washington." Ross added that the accusers might appear together "so they can all tell their stories of Herman Cain, with the sense of safety in numbers." [26]

On November 28, Ginger White told WAGA, the Fox affiliate in Atlanta, that she had a thirteen-year adulterous affair with Cain. All three networks reported it almost simultaneously with the Atlanta story. This is not the way allegations against a Democrat are handled. Ginger White makes an adultery charge against Cain and she's on the *NBC Nightly News* within hours. But when Juanita Broaddrick in a 1999 *Dateline NBC* interview accused Bill Clinton of raping her, then-anchor Tom Brokaw never allowed one single second of her voice to break into his evening newscast. [27]

If only Herman Cain were a Democrat. By the next morning, Cain was dismissed as a political corpse, or a ghost. On ABC, anchor Robin Roberts suggestively asked, "Do [White's] shocking revelations spell doom for his troubled campaign?" On CBS, political analyst John Dickerson proclaimed, "It's hard to see how he comes back from this. . . . At the worst, it's a death blow to the campaign." But NBC's Chuck Todd was the most colorful, citing movies: "Now we're in sort of *The Sixth Sense* mode. Everybody knows this candidacy is basically dead except the campaign." [28]

One day later, Ginger White gave an interview to George Stephanopoulos, a man who would have shredded her reputation and kept her off television if she had claimed an affair with Clinton. The ABC host gloated over Cain's impending doom: "Will our interview spell the end of the one-time front-runner's presidential bid?" [29]

Stephanopoulos was so brazen that he dismissed Cain on character grounds: "There are just too many questions about his honesty, his judgment, his experience, his organization. Even if he stays in [the race], he's not going to be a factor."[30] This from the former official spokesman for Bill Clinton.

Collectively, the media sounded like Yul Brynner playing Pharaoh Ramses in *The Ten Commandments*, shouting, "So let it be written! So let it be done!" Cain soon withdrew.

GINGRICH. Many conservative voters loved the smarts of Newt Gingrich, and loved the way Newt fired away at liberal-media debate moderators—not to mention the idea of him aggressively debating Obama. But seemingly all liberal journalists still carried their 1990s loathing of Gingrich around. NBC anchor Brian Williams announced one night: "The Newt Gingrich that a lot of folks will remember from his speakership days back in the '90s was back on display making statements about controversial issues that left some of his critics slack-jawed."

Chris Matthews recklessly smeared Newt Gingrich, saying, "He looks like a car bomber. . . . He looks like he loves torturing."[31] With a complete lack of awareness of his own incivility, Matthews accused Newt of polluting the civil discourse. "Ever since he appeared on the national scene, politics has been nastier, more feral, too often uglier."[32]

Matthews also declared Gingrich was "a political killer, a gun for hire. . . . That's why they're offering up their partisan souls, why they're ready to bow down before this false god of hatred."

Reporters endlessly cited Gingrich's personal "baggage" in his personal life and public remarks as an impossible obstacle to overcome. Somehow the "baggage" gets lost when the media bellhops are writing about Democrats.

Then again came the Gingrich "investigative bombshell." On the January 19 *Nightline*, days before Gingrich won the South Carolina primary, ABC anchor Terry Moran oozed, "Tonight on *Nightline*, breaking her silence. In an exclusive TV interview, one of presidential hopeful Newt Gingrich's ex-wives speaks out, questioning his moral fitness to be president." Not only was he cheating on her with the woman who would become his third wife, "he was asking for an open marriage."

Brian Ross eagerly prompted ex-wife Marianne Gingrich to tell all: "You know his secrets. You know his skeletons." He boasted to viewers that his scoop could be seen as a "January surprise" to whack Gingrich. Ross implied he shouldn't be considered a conservative, not with his background: "And now, as a candidate for president, Gingrich regularly expounds on family values and the sanctity of marriage between a man and a woman." [33]

What a difference four years makes, especially if the candidate belongs to the other party. At this point in the 2008 campaign, on January 4, Ross was disparaging character attacks on the Democratic contenders. "At grocery store checkout lines, there have been *National Enquirer* headlines, claiming a love child scandal involves Senator John Edwards or a member of his staff, forcing Edwards to issue a strong public denial." Edwards insisted on ABC: "The story's false. It's completely untrue and ridiculous." [34] Ross didn't investigate Edwards for "bombshells" and "skeletons." Ross provided him a national platform to profess his innocence to millions of viewers.

SANTORUM. In November, MSNBC host Rachel Maddow of 2011 laughed at the idea that anyone would ever vote for dark horse former senator Rick Santorum. "Nobody's going to vote for Rick Santorum, come on," Maddow declared, reminding her audience that thanks to far-left sex columnist Dan Savage, when you Google-searched for Santorum, you would find a vulgar definition for the fluid aftermath of anal sex. [35]

MSNBC host Martin Bashir reached for historical smears. "In reviewing his book, *It Takes a Family*, one writer said, 'Mr. Santorum has one of the finest minds of the 13th century.' But I'm not so sure. If you listen carefully to Rick Santorum, he sounds more like Stalin than Pope Innocent III."

Santorum reminded former top *New York Times* editor Bill Keller of a radical fundamentalist: "Remember earlier in the campaign when Newt Gingrich was worrying everyone about Sharia law: the Muslims were going to impose Sharia law in America? Sometimes Santorum sounds like he's creeping up on a Christian version of Sharia law."

On January 16, a few days before Santorum's victory in the Iowa caucuses was belatedly announced, the usual "investigative bomb-shell" landed. *Newsweek* (on its *Daily Beast* website) decided it was "news" to report on Mrs. Santorum's ancient dating history in a piece titled "Before Karen Met Rick." Yes, *before the couple ever met.* The author was Nancy Hass, who a few months before had written a val-entine to radical feminist pioneer Gloria Steinem, announcing that Michele Bachmann and Sarah Palin "wouldn't be riling up the Tea Party faithful had Steinem not paved their way out of the kitchen."[36]

Hass wrote that Karen Santorum, the "ultra-pro-life wife," had a dirty secret. "Her live-in partner through most of her 20s was Tom Allen, a Pittsburgh obstetrician and abortion provider 40 years older than she, who remains an outspoken crusader for reproductive rights and liberal ideals. Dr. Allen has known Mrs. Santorum, born Karen Garver, her entire life: he delivered her in 1960." The article featured a picture of young Garver posing with her much older boyfriend as he lounged in a hammock.[37]

It is impossible to imagine a greater personal attack on an in-nocent wife, and a blameless candidate, than this. Even the networks were a little queasy over this twenty-four-year-old story about a can-didate's spouse. CBS brought up the relationship in an interview with Mrs. Santorum in March, forcing her to admit, "I did go through a phase of life where I wasn't living the way I should have been." NBC jumped right on it, though. On the January 21 *Today*, NBC's Michael Isikoff (a *Newsweek* alum) checked the box: "*Newsweek* reported that before she married Santorum, she had a six-year live-in relationship with a Pittsburgh abortion doctor forty years her senior."

In the same story, Isikoff also noted Gingrich's second wife going on ABC and making her "open marriage" allegation. He concluded with the odd suggestion that these personal attacks and ugliness weren't generated by the "objective" media: "All this, political analysts say, is unusual, even by the rough-and-tumble standards of Southern politics. . . . With polls pointing to a close result tonight in South Carolina, personal attacks show no signs of abating as the GOP race continues."[38]

Can you imagine *Newsweek* plotting a hard-hitting investigation of who Michelle Obama dated before Barack? Or who Barack dated before Michelle? Did Mrs. Obama have sex with other men before Barack? Did she have affairs with married men? Those questions would be considered beyond the pale, a repugnant violation of privacy. But somehow, all those niceties did not apply to Mrs. Santorum before she even knew her husband.

At the end of 2004, *Newsweek* proclaimed the arrival of Senator-elect Barack Obama with Jonathan Alter's cover story titled "The Audacity of Hope." In the same issue, there was also a profile of Santorum by Howard Fineman. The contrast was stunning, even by *Newsweek*'s obnoxious standards.[39]

Obama was introduced to the country as the "incredibly pragmatic" soul of civility who is "uniquely qualified to nudge the country toward the color purple" (merging the red states and blue states). He was all about "embracing our hybrid origins and transcending our often narrow-minded past." But Santorum was consistently described with violent undertones. His career was a "bruising crusade" supported by anti-abortion "shock troops." He was a "cultural militant," and a "heat-seeking missile" with a "combatively devout approach."

The photos framing the stories told the tale all by themselves. Obama was shown on a Chicago rooftop with the caption "Skywalker." Santorum was shown in his office next to his picture of "Roman Catholic martyr Thomas More." Captured on his office TV was a Fox News Channel graphic about schools excluding Christ from Christmas. The caption was "Bully Pulpit." No coincidence.

In other pictures, Obama was seen interacting with staff, backslapping with John Kerry, practicing a speech next to Michelle, and kissing his three-year-old daughter, Sasha (to a caption titled "Family Man"). In the only other picture accompanying his profile, Santorum was pictured in the darkened frame of his office door, with the caption underlining his admission that he smoked pot in the 1970s, but adding he is now "in the front ranks of the new faith-based GOP." *Newsweek* had no room for Obama's self-described pot-smoking and cocaine-snorting in their early valentine . . . and no room to acknowledge Santorum was a "family man" with six children.

While Mrs. Santorum was pounded for her ancient romances in 2012, *Newsweek* lauded Michelle Obama in 2004 as a Harvard-trained lawyer with an "innovative nonprofit that provides leadership development." After two of Obama's potential 2004 Senate rivals—Republican Jack Ryan and Democrat Blair Hull—were energetically removed from Obama's path by the gumshoes at the *Chicago Tribune* suing for (and then spilling) their divorce records—Michelle was Obama's character witness. "People always ask, 'What's he got in the closet?' Well, we've been married 13 years, and I'd be shocked if there was some deep, dark secret."

For starters, *Newsweek* could have found the nutty reverend that married them.

Alter even helpfully reported that Mrs. Obama "goes so far as to say" her husband wasn't even a politician. He "is not a politician first and foremost. He's a community activist exploring the viability of politics to make change." Perhaps the most transparently phony thing any reporter could ever write about the news media's "rising star" of liberalism was that he somehow wasn't a politician—a Chicago pol, riding on a shiny rocket of media hype. But Republicans? "Politician" was about the nicest thing said about them.

# CHAPTER 2

# You're Our Mr. Clean

## Obama, "remarkably free of scandal."

There's a corollary to the idea that the first media dirty trick is adjudicating who is dirty. To say the media's rules for what constitutes a scandal are incredibly elastic is an understatement. Journalists who tut-tutted, then declared Herman Cain's campaign deceased for charges of sexual misbehavior were singing a much different tune just thirteen years before. Then faced with far more substantial reports about Bill Clinton's womanizing, they performed great feats of acrobatic journalism telling America we needed to move on.

The double standard could apply to just about anything. They could even treat hurricanes under Democrats as natural disasters and under Republicans as an unethical and racist fiasco. NBC's Brian Williams lectured to Jon Stewart about Hurricane Katrina and how much better the Bush response would have been "if this had been Nantucket."[1] Obama could do a photo-op at Sandy Hook Elementary, then ignore the catastrophe, and still he was viewed as the savior.

An important component in the construction of the image of

perpetually shiny and flawless Obama was the declaration that he had never dirtied himself in the ethical scrapes and scandals that bother and bewilder earthly politicians. The narrative was preposterous, but delivered with a straight face.

On July 17, 2012, *Hardball* host Chris Matthews was in his usual lather on MSNBC, denouncing the "crapola" and "crazy yahoo talk" from Michele Bachmann, Jim DeMint, and Newt Gingrich, as they insisted in turn that Obama was a radical, anti-business, anti-American, and hostile to the Constitution. Those conservative critiques were defensible if not true on all counts.

Matthews couldn't concede even that these charges were grounded in reality. Instead, he addressed them with all the ferocity of someone who's livid that anyone would dare speak against the Great Leader, that anyone would so rebelliously challenge the media cult of personality. "This guy's done everything right! He's raised his family right! He's fought his way all the way to the top of the *Harvard Law Review*, in a blind test becomes head of the *Review*, the top editor there. Everything he's done is clean as a whistle! He's never not only broken any law, he's never done anything wrong! He's the perfect father, the perfect husband, the perfect American!"[2]

This is not journalism. It's the very opposite of journalism. Instead of observing the world as it is and describing it, warts and all, Matthews chose to ignore truth and instead flailed away at Obama's critics, insisting that Obama had no failures, no scandals, no imperfections of any kind. Obama is not just the omnicompetent Alpha and Omega of American politics, but the very essence of goodness. Saintly, even.

Naturally, like a predictable liberal, Matthews concluded these attacks on Obama's radical policy views were . . . racial. Obama was perfect, "and all they do is trash the guy. And it's impossible for me to believe they would have said the same thing about a Walter Mondale or a Jimmy Carter or a Bill Clinton. There's an ethnic piece to this." This "ethnic piece" complaint wasn't lodged by Matthews when his fellow liberals were hunting for scandals in the Justice Department under George W. Bush's friend and U.S. attorney general Alberto Gonzales. Or Clarence Thomas. Or Allen West. Or Herman Cain. Or any Republican of color.

Matthews was not the only pseudo-journalist shredding the rules of his own profession by pushing this zero-scandal myth. On October 27, 2011, former *Newsweek* senior editor Jonathan Alter wrote a column for Bloomberg News headlined "Obama Miracle Is White House Free of Scandal." Alter began: "President Barack Obama goes into the 2012 [campaign] with a weak economy that may doom his reelection. But he has one asset that hasn't received much attention: He's honest." Whether Alter was giggling when he typed those words is unclear.

Alter even bragged: "According to a metric created by political scientist Brendan Nyhan, Obama set a record earlier this month for most days without a scandal of any president since 1977."[3] Nyhan's methodology insisted that a president doesn't have a scandal until there is "a front-page *Washington Post* story focused on a scandal that describes it as such in the reporter's own voice," by using the S-word, as in "the Fast and Furious scandal."

This little trick neatly grants all the power in defining what is or is not a scandal to the Washington media elite. Congress can launch investigations, hold hearings, or otherwise make real news, but journalists hold all the power. It's a scandal when *they* say it's a scandal. Their perpetual pose of ignorance has also helped to keep the Obama scandals from entering the satire stream of late-night comedy shows.

This notion of a scandal-free Obama also emerged occasionally from the print press, the people alleged to obsess about the boring details. *Washington Post* editorialist Jonathan Capehart boasted to

NBC viewers on the October 29, 2011, *Today* program: "We're look-ing at the GOP looking to scratch, trying to find a scandal in an ad-ministration that is remarkably free of scandal."[4]

On June 24, 2012, *Post* columnist Dana Milbank appeared on CNN and acted utterly perplexed at complaints about the media's aggressive scandal avoidance. "I think to say the media isn't interested in scandal is preposterous. We love scandal. I love scandal. That's the thing that really drives us," Milbank chortled. "It's not an ideological thing. I think the media would love to have an Obama scandal to cover."[5]

Clearly, Milbank hadn't checked in with Matthews and Alter. Still, the results were the same: no coverage of scandals. Milbank's *Post* columns brought comfort to Team Obama on Solyndra (one column was headlined "A solar pariah had Republican parents, too") and Fast and Furious ("The Republicans may be furious, but this political scandal is going nowhere—fast").[6]

## Skipping Fast and Furious

In 2009, under Barack Obama and Attorney General Eric Holder, the Bureau of Alcohol, Tobacco, Firearms, and Explosives launched "Op-eration Fast and Furious," which allowed licensed gun dealers to sell weapons to illegal straw buyers. Obama's team was hoping to track the guns to Mexican drug cartel leaders, with the hope of following the guns as they were transferred to higher-level traffickers and key figures in Mexican cartels, with the expectation that this would lead to arrests.

But it all went terribly wrong. Mexican gangs shot and killed Bor-der Patrol agent Brian Terry in 2010 (as well as hundreds of Mexican citizens) with guns the ATF allowed to "walk."

A reporter on one network recognized this story as important news. On the February 23, 2011, *CBS Evening News*, Sharyl Attkisson declared : "December 14, 2010: the place, a dangerous smuggling route in Arizona, not far from the border. A special tactical border squad was on patrol when gunfire broke out and agent Brian Terry, shown here in a training exercise, was killed. . . . The assault rifles found at the murder, similar to these, were traced back to a U.S. gun shop. Where they came from and how they got there is a scandal so large, some insiders say it surpasses the shootout at Ruby Ridge and the deadly siege at Waco."[7]

How could this story *not* be news?

On March 23, 2011, three months after Terry's death, President Obama appeared on Univision and spoke about the controversy. He said that neither he nor Attorney General Holder authorized Fast and Furious. He also stated, "There may be a situation here in which a serious mistake was made, and if that's the case, then we'll find out and we'll hold somebody accountable."

Why did it take so long for the president to respond, and why did he think he could play innocent in this scandal?

Because most of the media aren't in the Obama accountability business. While Attkisson was an outlier, with twenty-nine stories on CBS unspooling the scandal, ABC and NBC stayed virtually silent for many months, even as Holder admitted he had misled Congress about when he learned of Fast and Furious, thus also making his boss a dupe, or a liar. So much for scandal-free.

ABC had aired only one brief, on the June 15, 2011, *Good Morning America*. In a bizarre turn, ABC White House correspondent Jake Tapper asked Obama about Fast and Furious in October 2011, but ABC refused to allow any soundbite on that subject to appear on *Nightline*, *World News*, or *Good Morning America* (which all played clips of the interview).

Instead, on *Nightline*, ABC found time to air Tapper and the president playfully discussing children's books and the greatness of

Dr. Seuss. Tapper said, "At the school where we spoke, the president showed off his personal knowledge of children's books." Obama asked Tapper whom he liked in that field. "I'm a big Dr. Seuss guy," said Tapper. "You can't beat Dr. Seuss," agreed the president.[8]

ABC really knows how to make Democrat presidents sweat.

Even Holder's admission on November 8, 2011, that—oops—he may have misled Congress in a May 3 hearing didn't wake ABC and NBC out of their long nap of self-censorship. In May, Holder told Congress he'd learned of Fast and Furious just "a few weeks" beforehand. In November, he admitted "I probably could've said 'a couple of months.'" In fact, he admitted that Senator Charles Grassley (R-IA) had handed him letters in person on the matter in late January. Obama answered Tapper in the unaired ABC interview: "This is not something we were aware of in the White House. And the attorney general, it turns out, wasn't aware of it either."

On the November 8, 2011, *CBS Evening News,* Sharyl Attkisson focused on another deception, this time that Holder claimed in February there was no gun-walking. Holder bizarrely claimed under GOP questioning that the Department of Justice's letter was somehow not false, just inaccurate: "What I said is it contains inaccurate information. . . . I don't want to quibble with you, but 'false,' I think, implies people making a decision to deceive."[9] He was back to the-meaning-of-what-is-is spin.

Why would reporters fail to report on a public official saying it's not a falsehood if it was allegedly *unintentionally* false? Is this the way Bush-whacking journalists treated the case for war in Iraq?

NBC aired absolutely nothing on their morning and evening newscasts. NBC arrived on the story on June 12, 2012—546 days after Agent Terry's shooting. On June 20, the House voted to hold the attorney general in contempt of Congress for failure to provide documents, which caused shameless *NBC Nightly News* anchor Brian

Williams to begin his program by trying to shame someone else: "Washington has blown up into a caustic partisan fight. . . . And for those not following the complexities of all of it, it just looks like more of our broken politics and vicious fights now out in the open."[10]

Williams seemed perturbed that someone would push him to cover this scandal. "Those not following the complexities of all of it" could be defined as anyone who relied on NBC for news on the Obama administration.

To be fair, Chris Hansen, on the April 17, 2011, edition of NBC's magazine show *Dateline*, briefly mentioned that the ATF "as part of an undercover operation, actually allowed hundreds of guns to be smuggled to the Mexican drug cartels." However, Hansen never linked Obama or Holder to the operation or even mentioned Terry's death or name. How could they *not* be part of the story? They were the story.

NBC's failure to mention Terry's name is particularly galling considering that his mother, Josephine, repeatedly demanded Holder apologize for her son's death. After a February 2, 2012, hearing she called Attorney General Holder a "coward politician." Josephine Terry would not be granted one iota of the saint/celebrity status that the networks gave George W. Bush—harassing "peace mom" Cindy Sheehan, whom CBS's Bill Plante called "the red-hot symbol of opposition to the war" and a "magnet for the anti-war movement."[11]

Only CBS put Mrs. Terry onscreen, in a story on *The Early Show* on November 9, 2011: "Brian loved his country. Brian was a true Marine. He was a true American. When Brian was a Marine, he used to always say, you never leave a man behind. And, I think they are leaving my son behind. That's what I think. And I know that would be a disgrace to him."[12]

Even CBS developed cold feet about this scandal as the primaries began. Their first *CBS Evening News* report of 2012 didn't come until

June 20—when Mitt Romney made it an issue. *CBS This Morning* only offered one full story in the first half of the year, on February 3. Sharyl Attkisson had been given other assignments.

## No Heat on Holder

The networks offered no brickbats for Attorney General Holder. He submitted himself to zero network TV interviews over the last two and a half years of the first term. But Holder did grant an interview on April 27, 2012, to NPR legal reporter Carrie Johnson. NPR *All Things Considered* anchor Robert Siegel announced "a rare and personal glimpse of the man." Johnson began by observing Holder walk quickly into the Clinton Presidential Library in Little Rock, Arkansas, where she was granted the interview: "Eric Holder is looking back on the arc of his career. After nearly thirty years of government service, he's achieved his highest goal."

NPR listeners were supposed to get a thrill up their legs during rush hour because Holder was attorney general. "The attorney general lingered, wordless over footage of Mr. Clinton's campaign speeches. He had more to say in front of an exhibit of the Little Rock Nine. They were black schoolchildren who tried to integrate Central High School here in 1957, only to be met by violent mobs and soldiers blocking the door." Holder solemnly proclaimed: "These are the folks who make, you know, Barack Obama possible, Eric Holder possible."

The program may be called *All Things Considered*, but one thing wasn't. In the entire seven-minute, thirty-nine-second story, there was absolutely no mention of Fast and Furious. Holder proclaimed, "I serve a president who is among other things a great lawyer. And he spends a great deal of time, great deal of interest focused on the Justice Department, which is a good thing—most of the time." [13] But neither one of them could be blamed for fumbling Fast and Furious? Neither could be challenged to take ownership of what they launched?

There were more important matters to cover. Johnson wasted time ribbing Holder about the Justice Department suing Apple: "So you're hoping you're still on a first-name basis with the guy at the Apple store?" Holder replied they were still happy to see him.

The networks had a chance to revisit Fast and Furious in September. On the 20th, two high-ranking Justice Department officials resigned over the scandal, but as usual, only Attkisson at CBS reported on that. The next day, Obama appeared on the Spanish-language channel Univision for a town-hall interview. Anchor Jorge Ramos asked Obama if Holder shouldn't have known about Fast and Furious, and if not, "shouldn't you fire him?"

Obama's reply was misleading on multiple levels. "I think it's important for us to understand that the Fast and Furious program was a field-initiated program begun under the previous administration." No, it wasn't. While the Bush administration had a version of this, Fast and Furious began in the fall of 2009.

So was *this* now news ? Obama had just pulled a Nixon. The networks noted the Univision interview but ignored Fast and Furious, focusing instead on "tough questions" about the attack on the consulate in Libya, and on the hot concern from the left-wing Democrat base over how (suddenly pandering) Obama admitted his greatest failure of his first term was not fighting harder to pass "immigration reform." Ramos even showed up on ABC's *This Week* roundtable a few days later, and no one brought up Fast and Furious. Again they homed in on the need for amnesty for illegal immigrants.

At the end of September, Univision produced a devastating investigative bombshell on Fast and Furious. Gerardo Reyes and Santiago Wills reported, "Indirectly, the United States government played a role in the massacre" of fourteen Mexican teenagers in a one-story house by "supplying some of the firearms" used in a vicious cartel massacre.[15] In all, Univision claimed that they found fifty-seven additional U.S. government-provided weapons that Congress had not identified.

The same news media that leaped into panic and outrage over mass shootings in Aurora (and after the election, in Newtown) found nothing interesting in fourteen Mexican teens being gunned down with weapons supplied through the Justice Department. They said nothing.

All this was quite a contrast to 2007, when the networks were loaded with hyperbole on the allegedly massive scandal of a smattering of U.S. attorneys fired by the Bush Justice Department. Then–Attorney General Alberto Gonzales—the first Latino attorney general of the United States—tried to put out the blazing story by appearing on five morning-news shows on the same day: March 14, 2007. There were no shootings, no murders. Yet somehow it was worse.

Gonzales was asked forty-two questions by the TV interviewers—and ten of them were repeating demands that he resign, including on the Fox News Channel.[16] NBC's Matt Lauer read from *Washington Post* columnist Ruth Marcus, who accused Gonzales of being "an absentee landlord, chronically clueless." By July 24, 2007, ABC News anchor Chris Cuomo—son of ultraliberal former New York governor Mario Cuomo, and brother of current governor Andrew Cuomo—bluntly asked, "Is Alberto Gonzales out of a job at end of business today?" Cuomo wanted the attorney general professionally whacked, and a month later, got his wish. Gonzales resigned.

Five years later, no one in the media demanded Eric Holder resign. No one even demanded Holder show up at a TV studio for an interview to explain his department's scandalous behavior.

Meanwhile, the Obama Justice Department was working hand in glove with liberal media "watchdogs" to intimidate Attkisson and other outlets like Fox News from covering this story. On September 18, 2012, *Daily Caller* reporter Matthew Boyle uncovered collusion between the Justice Department and the liberal group Media Matters for America, including e-mails back and forth coordinating attacks on conservative media and politicians to contain the damage on Fast and Furious.

For example, in an e-mail on July 8, 2011, Media Matters blogger Matt Gertz wrote to Justice Department spokeswoman Tracy Schmaler asking for her help "debunking what I think is a conservative media myth about Operation Fast and Furious." Gertz told Schmaler that "Xochitl directed me to you as the person to talk to." Gertz was referring to Xochitl Hinojosa, a Justice Department spokeswoman—and former Media Matters staffer.[17]

Another example was a January 31, 2012, e-mail chain titled "per our conversation," in which Schmaler and Gertz were cooperating on an article attacking Representative Darrell Issa (R-CA), chairman of the House Government Reform and Oversight Committee. Schmaler sent Gertz two paragraphs of text from Issa's comments during a House Judiciary Committee hearing on December 8, 2011. Schmaler underlined a portion of the text in those paragraphs in which Issa discussed the differences between Fast and Furious and programs that resembled it in the George W. Bush years. Just hours after Schmaler sent Gertz those blocks of text, they appeared in a Media Matters article titled "Rep. Issa Ties Himself in Fast and Furious Knots."

This kind of partisan media collusion obliterated the old saw that the Justice Department is supposed to be the least partisan outpost in all the cabinet. Only Fox News found this story of collusion worth reporting.

When the networks take months and even years to acknowledge a Democratic scandal exists, it also helps to keep the scandal from entering the satire stream of late-night comedy shows. Obama was a recipient of that journalistic largesse. But when he hosted the White

House Correspondents Association dinner on February 2, 2012, ABC late-night host Jimmy Kimmel mocked Obama from the left: "Even some of your Democrats think you're a pushover, Mr. President. . . . They would like to see you stick to your guns and if you don't have any guns, they would like to see you ask Eric Holder to get some for you."[18]

"It's hard to make fun of Obama in general because he's a cool character," Jimmy Kimmel told Reuters going in, insisting that "outside of his ears, there's not a whole lot" to joke about.[19]


## The "Green Jobs" Vanish with Solyndra


On the campaign trail in 2008, Barack Obama painted a picture of five million new "green jobs" created over the next decade, generated by federal government loans of $15 billion annually. The national media have been very generous in evaluating that promise: Reuters said the jobs have been "slow to sprout."[20] That puts it mildly.

*The Washington Post* to its credit crunched the numbers in September 2011: instead of creating 65,000 jobs, as promised, the $38 billion loan program, which included Solyndra, could only claim 3,545 new jobs, a fraction of a fraction of the presidential promise. But no one on TV was willing to acknowledge this failure, because network coverage of the "green jobs" concept had tilted overwhelmingly in Obama's favor. "We have gotten the message. Green-collar jobs are the wave of the future," cohost Diane Sawyer cheered on ABC's *Good Morning America* on April 15, 2009. MRC's Business and Media Institute found that out of fifty-two network stories that mentioned the administration's "green jobs" program, only four of them (8 percent) bothered to include any critics at all.[21] Not one tilted against the administration.

California-based Solyndra was the first solar company to be awarded a loan from the Department of Energy under President Obama, a cool $535 million in March 2009. Two years later, on August 31, 2011, Solyndra declared bankruptcy and suspended all production, laying off 1,100 employees and sticking the taxpayers with the bill.

Was this news? In the first two months of 2002, the Big Three networks reported a stunning 198 stories on the bankruptcy of Enron, a Houston-based energy company. Enron CEO Ken Lay had been to the Clinton White House, but the networks zoomed in on George W. Bush. They underlined that Bush nicknamed Lay "Kenny Boy." Democrats denounced George W. Bush's "Enronomics" and "Enronizing" of Social Security. In the two months after its August 31 bankruptcy filing, ABC, CBS, and NBC filed a grand total of fifteen stories on Solyndra.[22]

That's an Enron-to-Solyndra comparison of more than 13 to 1. Worse, from the end of that period (Halloween 2011) to Election Day, the networks offered only nine more stories (and six of them were simple anchor-read briefs). The last full story came from CBS on January 13, 2012, ten months before the election. In the election year, there was less evening-newscast time on this scandal than a two-minute commercial break.

"I think the media would love to have an Obama scandal to cover," the *Post*'s Dana Milbank told us. Never were more vacuous words ever spoken.

Only ABC (on the October 3, 2011 *World News*) ever ran footage of George Stephanopoulos asking President Obama about Solyndra, despite Obama's casual dismissal about the company's failure. "Do you regret that?" he was asked. Obama said no, that America needed to subsidize "green energy" so American companies "at least have a shot," and blithely admitted "Solyndras would happen." Stephanopoulos followed up: "And you were getting warnings not to back that company up, not to visit?" Obama shot back with annoyance: "Well, you know, hindsight is always 20/20."[23]

On October 7, the same Obama administration that pledged to be the most transparent ever engaged in a late-Friday document dump. The pile included e-mails showing a top Obama fundraiser and Energy Department official, Steven Spinner—who had supposedly recused himself from Solyndra's loan application because his wife worked at a law firm representing the solar energy company—persistently pushing his colleagues to approve the deal.

Spinner sent e-mails demanding to know: "Any word on OMB? I have the O.V.P. [Office of the Vice President] and W.H. [White House] breathing down my neck on this. . . . How hard is this? What is he waiting for?"[24]

Even though these e-mails were sensational enough to make it onto the front page of *The New York Times*, the networks never found a moment over the long Columbus Day weekend to mention it, never mind investigate the story themselves, just as they skipped the earlier news that Jonathan Silver, who ran the Energy Department loan program that handed more than $500 million in taxpayer money to Solyndra, had resigned.

"Don't ever send an email on DOE email with a personal email addresses," Silver wrote on August 21, 2011, from his personal account to another program official's private account. "That makes them subpoenable."[25] There's nothing innocent in that sentence. Any reporter worth his weight would pound on that lead.

*The Washington Post* reported then that "Silver repeatedly communicated about internal and sensitive loan decisions via his personal email, the newly released records show, and more than a dozen other Energy Department staff members used their personal email to discuss decisions involving taxpayer-funded loans as well." That was it.

This was a pervasive problem in the Obama administration. Jim Messina, Obama's 2012 campaign manager, used his private AOL account during his time in the White House to make deals with Big Pharma lobbyists to support Obamacare, where they agreed to buy $150 million in ads and lobby for his bill's enactment.[26] This was non-news, but the idea that Alaska governor Sarah Palin used her private e-mail for any public business? That registered as a major scandal to the national press in 2011, when reporters pored over twenty-four thousand Palin e-mails they obtained.

To get traction on the Solyndra scandal, Mitt Romney even made a surprise visit to stand in front of the empty Solyndra headquarters on May 31, 2012. Still, no reaction. The networks only mentioned it in passing, offering no stories explaining Romney's backdrop. CBS reporter Jan Crawford asked Mitt Romney one solitary Solyndra question on *CBS This Morning* on June 1.

When two Solyndra executives took the Fifth Amendment before Congress in September, ABC and NBC skipped that news, too, while CBS offered about twenty-five seconds of coverage. Once he was named Romney's running mate, Representative Paul Ryan briefly mentioned Solyndra in at least two network interviews as an example of "crony capitalism and corporate welfare" by Obama. But the networks weren't following up.

In the vice presidential debate, when Ryan was denouncing the "stimulus" for including "$90 billion in green pork to campaign contributors and special interest groups," Joe Biden interrupted in midsentence, as did the debate moderator, ABC's Martha Raddatz, who quickly handed the floor to Biden.[27] They did not want that audience to hear a word about Solyndra.

As former *Newsweek* editor Jonathan Alter predicted in his Obama-miracle article: "Although it's possible that the Solyndra LLC story will become a classic feeding frenzy, don't bet on it. Providing $535 million in loan guarantees to a solar-panel maker that goes bankrupt was dumb, but so far not criminal or even unethical on the part of the administration." [28]

Liberal journalists couldn't even locate anything unethical in awarding campaign donors with federal loan money for a company already in grave danger of collapse. It was a bad call when *McLaughlin Group* host John McLaughlin ended a show in August with this last sentence: "I predict that this will become damaging to Barack Obama's reelection." [29]

## Down the Drain with MF Global

On Halloween 2011, MF Global Holdings filed for bankruptcy with a shady mystery: some $1.6 billion was missing from their customers' accounts. Financial analysts blamed the company's CEO, Jon Corzine, a former Democratic U.S. senator and governor of New Jersey, who became the center of an FBI investigation. One TV reporter underlined that this could be a major political problem for President Obama.

Corzine was "one of the leading Wall Street fundraisers for President Obama's campaign and suggested to investors that he might take a top administration post if the President were re-elected. . . . His new legal troubles, sparked by the bankruptcy filing of his investment firm, MF Global, could complicate the President's efforts to raise money from the financial community given Corzine's central role in those efforts. A recent list of top 'bundlers' or elite fundraisers released by Obama's campaign listed Corzine in the highest category—reporting that he had raised more than $500,000 for the campaign." [30]

That TV reporter was Michael Isikoff of NBC News—but his reporting never made it to television. (You'd have to find it on MSNBC. com.) In the upside-down world of Obama "news" judgment, that "leading Wall Street fundraiser for Obama" part seemed to make it *less* newsworthy for NBC and the rest, when it should have made it more so.

Eventually, after several months, the story drew just a few minutes of coverage—six full stories and sixteen anchor briefs on ABC, CBS, and NBC—so it wasn't censored. But nowhere, not once, in this small set of stories was there a single, solitary *whisper* of the name "Obama."

In fact, Jon Corzine's party affiliation was only mentioned once, when Kelly O'Donnell noted it in her December 8, 2011, report for the *NBC Nightly News*. "A fallen Wall Street CEO, personally rich and politically well-connected . . . New Jersey's former Democratic Governor and U.S. Senator Jon Corzine under oath . . . and under fire," O'Donnell announced.[31] NBC was the only network to notice months later that Corzine may have lied to Congress. Lying to Congress drew only yawns.

ABC's only full story came on the same evening on *World News*. David Muir announced "a former political heavyweight under fire tonight. Jon Corzine, once a U.S. Senator and governor of New Jersey, forced to explain himself to small, everyday investors today. He was testifying on Capitol Hill, saying he has no idea where their billion dollars in investment money went."

On *CBS Evening News*, the network sent correspondent Cynthia Bowers to talk to customers whose money was lost. She asked one man: "So if you could run into Jon Corzine today, what would you say to him?" The man replied: "It would be a bad day for Jon Corzine."[32]

*New York Post* columnist (and former CNN and Fox anchor) Terry Keenan added, "In what may be the 2011 prize for chutzpah, Corzine made it a point that he would not press for $12.1 million in severance payments from what is now a corpse of a company. Gee, thanks, Jon."[33]

Corzine and MF Global escaped with no federal criminal charges, and liberal journalists who insisted that Mitt Romney would be too friendly to Wall Street didn't care. They were too focused on Romney's tenure at Bain Capital. A few days after the election, Republicans on the House Financial Services Committee issued a report blaming Corzine for the MF Global debacle.[34] Even then, the networks didn't care.

A recent Gallup survey concluded that almost 80 percent of those surveyed do not have confidence in television news.[35] Part of that distrust comes from ideological bias, and part of it comes from the media's ratings-conscious addiction to human-interest stories and celebrity coverage. Those two trends can combine, and demonstrate a media more intensely covering fluff than the stuff of scandal.

As the nonpartisan Tyndall Report found, networks racked up 171 minutes of royal-wedding coverage and 111 minutes of the Michael Jackson wrongful-death trial on the evening news in 2011.[36] Obama scandal news—and hence, any notion the media act as a watchdog or a check on government, during an election year, no less—was nowhere to be found in Tyndall's list of top stories.

# CHAPTER 3

# Barack Hollywood Obama

The billion-dollar campaign goes populist.

The most effortless dirty trick in the liberal-media playbook in 2012 was painting Mitt Romney anywhere and everywhere as an uptight white gazillionaire, a man who was running for president to boost the profits and ego of his own social class. What really took chutzpah was the other half of the equation: boosting Barack Obama as a populist as he hobnobbed with the richest and most famous elites in Hollywood. Anonymous rich people make better villains than some of the most beloved names in show business.

No pollster ever asks the public if they believe Beyoncé "understands the problems of people like you." In a very real way, it doesn't matter. She's a performer, not a political leader. But in American culture, Hollywood is the closest we'll come to royalty, and where royalty parks its endorsement somehow means something, just as so many Hollywood stars sheers ignorance means nothing. Stars like Beyoncé somehow added glamour and hipness to Obama's aura, transforming his aloof and detached personality into instant populism. And the *Entertainment Tonight* audience willingly, insatiably swallowed the bait.

In keeping with the Obama, "Man of the People" persona, the Obama-Biden campaign was sending its own donors slick "personal" e-mails about how just a tiny three-dollar donation could buy you dinner with the Obamas. This one came with the president's signature attached:

*Friend—*

*It's not all that often that Michelle and I get to host a casual meal with friends.*

*That's one of the reasons we're both excited about the upcoming dinner with three supporters and your guests.*

*It's the first one we've ever done like this together, and we'd love to have you and whoever you choose to join us.*

*Chip in $3 or whatever you can today—and you'll automatically be entered to be one of our dinner guests.*

Okay, hokey. Staged. Thoroughly staged. But that's politics, and Obama does politics better than anyone. Big deal. But then came the truth-mangling: "We don't take a dime from D.C. lobbyists or special-interest PACs—never have and never will. Instead, we believe in the kind of politics that gives everyone a seat at the table—so we're literally offering these seats at dinner to folks who are willing to step forward and be a part of it."[1]

It was a bold-face lie. Obama has taken untold millions from lobbyists. This is a perfect illustration of how the media couldn't even hold Obama to his own (and their own) liberal ideals. The Romney campaign had no ban on lobbyist donations. It's only the anti-capitalist, Bill Moyers–loving hard-liners in the Democratic base who want to somehow remove the lobbying industry from politics.

So in the same way that Republicans are seen by media liberals as much more hypocritical when they commit adultery, so too phony lobbyist-donation bans and campaign finance scandals should fall much harder on Democrats.

But they don't.

Team Obama defined "lobbyist" with all the sleazy legalistic finesse of Bill Clinton defining "sexual relations." By their definition, if you didn't register as a lobbyist with the federal government, you weren't a lobbyist. Take, for example, David Cohen, the executive vice president for Comcast, which acquired NBC Universal by spreading its influence around the Obama administration in the first term. Cohen was described in the papers as Comcast's "chief of lobbying," but he wasn't registered. He was an Obama bundler, and raised $1.2 million when the president attended a fundraiser at Cohen's glitzy Philadelphia home in June 2011 with about 120 attendees giving at least $10,000.[2] But Obama hasn't taken a dime from lobbyists, "never have and never will."

At the end of 2011, Ed Morrissey at the Hot Air blog mocked the outrage of Obama staffers that they would be typecast as infatuated with big bucks. "You know, nothing says *classy* in a presidential campaign like having to bleep out a word from the national campaign manager in a *prepared video*."[3] Campaign manager Jim Messina told supporters it was "bullshit" that Obama will run a "billion-dollar campaign." Messina sent an e-mail to supporters insisting: "This campaign is funded almost exclusively by more than a million grassroots supporters giving what they can afford—$3 and $10 donations have powered us from the start.... We do not and will not have a billion-dollar war chest."

Fast-forward to the website *Politico* on October 25, 2012: "Team Obama raises $1 billion."[4] Reporters Kenneth Vogel and Dan Berman relayed that "Chicago pushed back against the $1 billion figure, saying it really should be $988 million because Obama did not officially declare his candidacy for reelection until April 2011," as if the Obama gang wasn't raising money before then.

Perhaps the most "out of touch" millionaires and billionaires threatening the "common folks" narrative were the entertainment elites in Hollywood and Manhattan. They often had the most elevated—and publicly expressed—opinion of Obama. After the election, on the Soul Train Awards on November 25, actor Jamie Foxx let his adoration hang out: "First of all, give an honor to God, and our lord and savior Barack Obama!"[5]

Barbra Streisand was almost as absurd, claiming on the *Huffington Post* on September 18, 2012, "Compared to George W. Bush and Ronald Reagan, Obama has been more fiscally conservative than any other president in recent history, with the exception of President Bill Clinton."[6] Who has time to notice those unprecedented trillion-dollar deficits? No one in the media raised an eyebrow at that howler.

After the election cycle was over, the Center for Responsive Politics reported that 220 "celebrity" donors had given Obama's campaign $744,857, while only 18 comparable "celebrity" donors gave Romney a total of $60,750.[7] That's a more than 12-to-1 financial disparity.

Through 2011 and 2012, Obama outraised Romney from what the Center called the "TV/Movies/Music" industry, by nearly 5 to 1, with Obama raising $6.39 million to Romney's $1.27 million. These numbers exclude the entertainment industry bundlers who collect money from friends, relatives, and business associates and combine it into one gift. Obama bundlers throwing splashy events included not just movie moguls like Jeffrey Katzenberg and Harvey Weinstein. There was imperious *Vogue* magazine editor Anna Wintour—who inspired the novel and movie *The Devil Wears Prada*—as well as *Glee* creator Ryan Murphy and rock singer Gwen Stefani. Now the Hollywood-generated contributions were in the tens of millions of dollars—and still there was more.

## Bill Maher, Super Flack

These figures did not count how Obama's Super PAC "Priorities USA" reveled in three very large Hollywood donations: $2 million from DreamWorks mogul Jeffrey Katzenberg, $1 million from actor Morgan Freeman, and $1 million from Bill Maher, the toxic, atheist bomb-thrower with his weekly *Real Time* show on HBO. Maher didn't just give at "the office" by trashing Republicans on pay-cable TV. He brought a large check onstage during a standup comedy performance in San Jose on February 23—and none of the networks cared.[8] They could ask if Donald Trump was going to embarrass and distract from Romney, but they wouldn't make that connection with a bigot like Maher and Obama.

Just days before, all three networks rang the national alarm bells over how "far to the right" Republicans were tilting when Santorum Super PAC backer Foster Friess had repeated a very old, and equally innocent, joke about Bayer aspirin being used as birth control. Nobody would warn about the Democrats being stuck with a hard-edged atheist image for standing with God-hating Bill Maher, the guy honored for saying "religion must die for humanity to live." But *this* assault on humanity by Friess must be denounced!

On *CBS This Morning*, cohost Charlie Rose demanded that Santorum defend himself over the Friess joke.[9] Nobody at CBS asked Obama about Maher, including Charlie Rose. Indeed, it was worse than that still. A few weeks later, *CBS This Morning* cohost Erica Hill reported that "comedian Bill Maher writes in the op-ed page of *The New York Times*, we've become too sensitive in referring to this year's nasty political campaign. Maher writes, quote, 'When did we get into our heads that we have the right never to hear anything we don't like?'"

The news media were not just shutting out conservative speech or tough questions they didn't like, they were questioning the very right to hear conservative speech.

CBS did not report it when Fox News analyst Kirsten Powers and her friend Penny Lee wrote a letter to the editor published in the *Times* replying to Maher: "We're both women who have worked in Democratic politics and the media for decades and find Bill Maher's misogynist treatment of women candidates deeply disturbing. While others have been held to account for their sexism, Mr. Maher remains unrepentant for his attacks on women in public life. . . . Our message to Mr. Maher and his ilk is: Please *start* apologizing." [10] (Italics theirs)

Maher could start an apology tour by reflecting on all the conservative people he's joked about should be dead.

There's Rush Limbaugh: "Why couldn't he have croaked from [OxyContin] instead of Heath Ledger?"

Dick Cheney when he was vice president: "I'm just saying if he did die, other people—more people would live. That's a fact."

Glenn Beck, when he was a Fox News host: "When we see crazy, senseless deaths like this, we can only ask why, why, why couldn't it have been Glenn Beck?"

Sarah Palin: "Sarah Palin screaming about death panels? You know what, Sarah, if we were killing off useless people, you'd be the first to know."

And Rush Limbaugh again: "Do it [repeal Don't Ask, Don't Tell] because it will make Rush Limbaugh explode like a bag full of meat dropped from a helicopter. Do it because it will make Sarah Palin 'go rogue' in her pants."

Then there was Karl Rove, after Romney lost: "It was a little Hitler's bunker, wasn't it? I wanted to rush in with a cyanide capsule there."

Incredibly, in May, ABC's George Stephanopoulos claimed on his Sunday show *This Week* (over Laura Ingraham's scoffing) that "the President's been held accountable for Bill Maher." [11] In September,

Maher became the star of a strange segment on NBC's *Rock Center* that attacked not Maher, but Maher's critics, including media watchdogs.

We were a bunch of lowlife "gaffe-seekers." Ted Koppel announced, "Comedian Bill Maher has always been a favorite target of Bozell's, but especially since he made a one-million-dollar contribution to a Super PAC supporting Barack Obama." Koppel conjured up the vision of busybodies at groups like the Media Research Center "sitting there with headsets . . . watching television sets . . . waiting for someone to make a misstep." Maher replied: "Gaffe seekers." Koppel injected: "Any little gaffe they can find." [12]

This amazing indictment came after more than a year of liberals leaping on any gaffe or pseudo-gaffe from Republican candidates (and even their donors!) that sounded too conservative, too religious, too Republican, or too rough on Obama. Koppel didn't run any of Maher's gaffes, of course, just one joke: "I love this generation of Republicans. Their approach to a woman's body is the same as their approach to the economy. They have no idea how it works, but they're eager to screw with it anyway."

This was Maher's way of mocking monogamous, married Republicans with children, as opposed to his lifestyle as a childless, lecherous Playboy Mansion regular. Could you label it a joke? Surely. Wishing the deaths of Limbaugh, Cheney, Beck, Palin, and Rove isn't funny. It's a good deal more serious than a "gaffe," too. But it isn't *news*, not to Koppel.

Koppel and the other network stars couldn't even note that this millionaire Maher was beloved by HBO and the rest of the media elite for trashing common Americans in Flyover Country as mouth-breathing idiots. In a *Newsweek* story honoring Maher as a testament to the American Dream, Lloyd Grove noted he "lives like a Reagan Republican in a shining city on a hill—actually a large estate in a rarefied aerie of Beverly Hills." [13] Then Grove told a story of how the uncommonly generous Bill Maher drove his $120,000 electric Tesla roadster downtown and bought Occupy Los Angeles protesters a hundred pairs of dry socks. What a philanthropist! That must have set him back about the cost of dinner at Spago.

The Democrats wanted their candidate to be seen as the embodiment of the "99 Percent." In truth, Obama was the personification of, by, and for the exclusive and ultimate One Percent—the super-rich and super-famous.

## Occupy My Heart and Soul

Obama relentlessly attended fundraisers with the Hollywood glitz elite. There was no fear he'd be hounded and accused by fellow liberals in the press because these mansion events with movie moguls and stars are a violation of the left's "Occupy Wall Street" vibe. That short-lived, lawless, and violent protest movement was presented with all the salesmanship and mendacity that only a colluding media can provide.

It served a purpose—making liberalism look populist—and as such it was glorified. But the optics weren't helping. Visuals of violence, of filth, of public urination and defecation by foul-mouthed punks—none of this helped.

The liberal media's apparent ignorance didn't help much, either. ABC *World News* anchor Diane Sawyer looked like a complete idiot by proclaiming this temporary movement had "spread to more than 250 American cities, more than a thousand countries—every continent but Antarctica." That only overstated the number of countries by about eight hundred. Sawyer would later "correct" herself by claiming "more than a thousand *cities* around the world—every continent but Antarctica." [14] That was still exaggerating. If three hoboes showed up with tagboard signs in a town square, that would be included in the ABC count.

When the Occupy movement burst on the scene, in just the first eleven days of October 2011 ABC, CBS and NBC flooded their morning and evening newscasts with a whopping thirty-three full stories or interview segments on the protesters.[15] That was more TV coverage in eleven days than the Tea Party drew in its first nine months swarming in the capital and other cities. By the end of October, the number of stories climbed to eighty-one. A staggering 190 soundbites (80 percent) were given to those who were in favor of the Occupiers; only 10 soundbites (four percent) featured those who were critical of the movement, a 19-to-1 tilt.[16]

Throughout the weeks of Occupy protest coverage, network anchors and reporters largely avoided the question of how this movement's violence and radicalism might affect President Obama and the Democrats at the polls. They only used the word "liberal" once, and never "radical" or "left-wing." Instead of considering this movement as a political drag, on October 16, NBC's David Gregory touted that these encampments were "going to dovetail nicely into a big message that the President's selling, which is that the wealthy should pay more."

*NBC Nightly News* anchor Brian Williams led off one newscast: "We begin tonight with what has become by any measure a pretty massive protest movement." In the first week of coverage, Williams already decided they had more staying power than the Tea Party. It "could well turn out to be the protest of this current era." When it faded away after being evicted by big-city Democrat mayors, the anchors turned down their volume buttons on the topic without acknowledging how emphatically they had oversold it.

To demonstrate their slogan that "We Are the 99 Percent," these protesters staged a "Millionaires March" in New York City, parading to the homes of wealthy citizens such as Fox News owner Rupert Murdoch and Tea Party funder David Koch. But Occupy organizers conveniently ignored the massive wealth of celebrities within their own ranks—super-rich Hollywood leftists like Michael Moore. On CNN, Moore disingenuously denied that he qualified financially to be in the dreaded "one percent," as conservative bloggers displayed his multimillionaire's lakeshore mansion in northwestern Michigan.[17]

The Occupiers never showed up to protest Brian Williams (or his two General Electric CEO neighbors) outside his apartment in the glass-encased Bloomberg Tower in midtown Manhattan, thirty-four stories above the tony restaurant Le Cirque. They somehow avoided Diane Sawyer's homes with film director Mike Nichols, including the Fifth Avenue penthouse they bought from Robert Redford for $11 million. The whole movement was a smelly Potemkin village of propaganda.

## Obama Boogies Down to Tinseltown

In late September, just days before "Occupy Wall Street" became the latest media fad among liberals, President Obama landed in Southern California for three events: one at the ritzy La Jolla home of Elizabeth and Mason Phelps; a gay event at the House of Blues in West Hollywood with ABC *Modern Family* star and gay activist Jesse Tyler Ferguson; and then a $17,900-a-plate dinner with one hundred top Hollywood bigwigs at Fig & Olive restaurant on Melrose Place, including Jack Black, Judd Apatow, Quincy Jones, Danny DeVito, and Rhea Perlman.[18] This was Hollywood's One Percent, wealthier and far more famous than most of Romney's corporate one-percenters. So how was Obama not at least as elitist as Romney?

On October 24, 2011, Obama warned guests at a $35,800-a-person

Hollywood fundraiser (including actor Will Smith and former NBA star Magic Johnson) stating that "[t]he election will not be as sexy as the first one." In 2008, "everybody loved the Hope posters and all that, but this time, we've got to grind it out a little bit."[19] The same night, Obama grinded it out at a $5,000-per-ticket fundraiser at the home of Melanie Griffith and Antonio Banderas.

On the twenty-fifth, *The Hollywood Reporter* relayed the president had a "secret meeting" with "some of Hollywood's power players," including studio mogul Harvey Weinstein, *Modern Family* creator Steve Levitan, Atlantic Records chairman Craig Kallman, actor and onetime Obama White House staffer Kal Penn, and others. It was reported to be a "casual affair with 'influencers' who could help the president's reelection campaign."[20]

Then he flew to San Francisco for a $7,500-a-head fundraiser with entertainment by mellow pop singer Jack Johnson. Interestingly, about a hundred protesters from Occupy Wall Street and other leftist causes like medical marijuana and "peace" marred the event—they apparently were not buying this populist nonsense—but the national media didn't notice. Only Fox News reported how the *San Francisco Chronicle* published a surprising staff editorial protesting the tight leash on the media, using the darkest left-wing bugaboo, Nixon: "If anything, there's almost a Nixonian quality to the level of control, paranoia, and lack of credibility this White House has demonstrated on the issue of media access to President Obama's fundraisers."[21]

But the Obama-loving media, always slashing the unfavorable news out of their scripts, ignored this. That morning, NBC news reader Tamron Hall reported only that the president "continues his West Coast swing with a fund-raiser tonight in San Francisco. On Monday in Las Vegas, he unveiled his plan to help struggling home-owners modify their mortgages and avert foreclosure."[22] Obama the Populist marched on.

* * *

On the next morning came a doozy. After showing clips of Obama joking around with Jay Leno, NBC *Today* cohost Ann Curry somehow turned this glitz-elite fundraising venture into a populist campaign in a question to David Gregory: "Why is the president making this populist effort now out West, on Leno, reaching out to college graduates, and will it give him the momentum he needs?" Gregory reassured her Obama was leading every Republican contender.[23]

In mid-February, Obama attended a $35,800-a-person fundraiser at the home of Bradley Bell, who produces the CBS soap opera *The Bold and the Beautiful*, with more middle-class guests having an option to attend a Foo Fighters concert in Bell's backyard early in the day for $250. The location was in the Holmby Hills, which local real estate agents tout as "perhaps the most spectacular and luxurious in all of Beverly Hills."

Again, there were Occupy protesters, this time at Will Rogers Memorial Park. The Patch.com website in Beverly Hills quoted the outrage of Nicole Steiner of Occupy Los Angeles: "That money could be spent far better on the human needs of the 99 percent instead of allowing one-percenters to buy a dinner with the president." Steiner complained that for the nearly $36,000 donors were bringing to Obama they could buy dinners for seventeen thousand people at area food banks.[24] A story for an Internet blog—okay. A national television or print story? Forget it.

On *CBS This Morning*, reporter Bill Plante obediently omitted the CBS-soap-mogul details: "His Republican rivals are continuing their long drawn-out battle much to the delight of the President's campaign folks. And the President today heads out to do a little fundraising. Now, this comes just a week after his campaign reversed course and said that it would encourage those large unlimited donations to a Super PAC."[25] Then Plante added that the White House was delighted with the latest CBS poll numbers.

"A little fundraising." That's like saying Michelle does "a little vacationing."

That evening, NBC anchor Brian Williams put more emphasis on Obama's attempt to link himself with economic success stories: "President Obama was in the Midwest today, as well, visiting a Master Lock plant in Wisconsin that has brought some overseas jobs back to the United States. The president pitched his ideas for tax cuts for manufacturing businesses and penalties for companies that move jobs out of the country." The glitzy fundraisers were a tiny footnote, an afterthought: "Tonight he's on a fundraising tour of the West Coast, eight separate events from L.A. to Seattle." [26]

On May 10, the Obama campaign raised $15 million in a fundraiser at George Clooney's mansion. This occasion drew network attention, but it wasn't negative. ABC's Jake Tapper called it "Starmageddon." [27] NBC anchor Brian Williams said Obama hoped "to capitalize on the history he made yesterday" by announcing his support for gay marriage. [28]

Over on CBS, reporter Bill Whitaker turned the event around on Romney: "A-list actors and producers arrived in style," he announced, and interviewed director Rob Reiner. "He says Hollywood progressives who helped put Mr. Obama in the White House, grew disillusioned with him for too often buckling under Republican pressure—but turned off by the hard-right rhetoric of Republican Mitt Romney, and turned on by the President's endorsement of same-sex marriage, Hollywood's excitement has been rekindled." [29]

It's amazing that TV reporters can let Hollywood liberals attack moderates like Mitt Romney as the "hard right." Where does that put Rob Reiner on the American ideological spectrum? This denounce-the-extremes tactic was a habit of Reiner's: on *HBO's Real Time with Bill Maher* in 2010, he complained, "My fear is that the Tea Party gets a charismatic leader, because all they're selling is fear and anger and that's all Hitler sold." [30]

The CBS morning show also ran a clip from *The Daily Show*, in which Jon Stewart asked if the mood was positive at Clooney's house. Jason Jones replied: "Has it been positive? President Obama is at a giant Hollywood party the night after he came out for gay marriage. This is like going to Israel after you kill Hitler."[31]

That evening, CBS anchor Scott Pelley was joyous: "Well, there are no money troubles in the presidential race. Last night President Obama raised a record $15 million at a fund-raiser at the Los Angeles home of actor George Clooney." All this came in the same news cycle in which Romney was fending off the prep school anti-gay/bullying/haircut non-story published by *The Washington Post*. Any elitist overtones of Clooney's event were lost in the shuffle.[32]

On June 6, a Beverly Hills fundraiser drew famous faces from CBS: Les Moonves, the company CEO, and his second wife, Julie Chen, who was a CBS morning news host from 1999 to 2010. Moonves told a reporter for the *Los Angeles Times* of his respect for Obama, who he said "has shown great leadership"—by bringing his support for gay marriage out of the closet.

Moonves stated "I run a news division. I've given no money to any candidate," which is misleading at best. He made a very public appearance at a fundraiser for the DNC's LGBT Leadership Council, although it's unclear exactly whether he or his network made the DNC donation. He didn't contribute directly. But the DNC certainly gave to candidates. Then Moonves dared to admit the obvious: "Ultimately, journalism has changed . . . partisanship is very much a part of journalism now."[33]

Moonves was acknowledging reality, for once. His industry was in the Obama-reelection business.

Just for yuks, Byron York of the *Washington Examiner* asked CBS spokesman Dana McClintock whether Moonves was referring to CBS News. McClintock sent back a four-word response: "No he was not."[34] Obviously, CBS newscasts didn't report its own boss was clinking glasses with the president in Beverly Hills.

Later that night, Obama moved on to a $25,000-a-head event at the nearby home of *Glee* creator Ryan Murphy and his "fiancé," David Miller. Murphy was the "pioneering" TV producer who stated he wanted his legacy to be that he "made it possible for somebody on broadcast television to do a rear-entry [sex] scene" on national TV. The Obama fans attending included movie stars Julia Roberts and Reese Witherspoon, *Glee* star Jane Lynch, and HBO's president of programming, Michael Lombardo.

The media also avoided the European phase of Obama's fund-raising campaign, which began in Paris on July 4 with a reception organized by various fundraising heavy-hitters. Independence Day fundraisers in Paris—somehow the irony of that wasn't noticed. The Obama campaign also hosted events in Geneva, Switzerland, in August as part of their "European outreach effort." George Clooney headlined a fundraiser there for Americans Abroad for Obama that raised an estimated $625,000.

The Associated Press reported without any ironic overtones that Obama "says Clooney is low-maintenance and doesn't take advantage of their friendship. He says Clooney keeps his distance so Mr. Obama won't be criticized for hanging out with Hollywood celebrities."[35]

## Mild-Mannered with Manhattan Moneybags

The New York–based national media also went radio-silent on Obama while he raised millions just blocks away from their studios in Manhattan. For days, the media elites incessantly reminded the little people that Obama suavely sang six words of Al Green's soul classic "Let's Stay Together." That came at the Apollo Theatre in one of several Big Apple fundraisers. The *Today* show hyped Obama as "Crooner-in-Chief" onscreen, as weatherman Al Roker oozed "he could be on *The Voice*." News anchor Natalie Morales added, "Sign him up."[36]

That same night, Obama held a $35,800-per-ticket fundraiser at the Upper East Side brownstone of director Spike Lee, who was infamous in the Bush era for suggesting, in a reckless conspiracy-theory HBO documentary, that the federal government dynamited the levees to drown black people in New Orleans after Hurricane Katrina. Obama patronized the director by claiming his wife and he went on their first date to see Lee's movie *Do the Right Thing*, which ends with a fiery race riot.

All the networks skipped that event, and even *The New York Times* barely mentioned it at the very bottom of its story on Obama's travels that day, even though *Times* reporter Jackie Calmes was present at Lee's place on behalf of other media outlets in the White House reporter pool.

But on July 9, Mitt Romney held a fundraiser out on Long Island, in the Hamptons, and suddenly the class-war negativity was unleashed. Michael Moynihan, a summer substitute for Jennifer Rubin at the "Right Turn" blog for *The Washington Post*, noticed an aggressive anti-Romney trend.[37]

The Associated Press argued "Romney may have unintentionally helped the Obama campaign. Mercedes, Bentleys—and, in one case, a candy red 2013 Ferrari Spider crowded into a series of closed-door Romney fundraisers" in the "weekend playground" of the Wall Street elite.

*The New York Times* also spotted "a line of gleaming Bentleys, Porsches and Mercedes-Benzes waiting to deposit guests paying up to $25,000 a head" who dined on "prosciutto-covered melon balls." The *Los Angeles Times* noted a "line of Range Rovers, BMWs, Porsche roadsters and one gleaming cherry red Ferrari."

AP spoke with an investment banker who "chewed a cigar in his black Range Rover." The AP also distributed a photo of leftist protesters "from MoveOn.org, the Occupy Movement and the Long Island Progressive" with a banner that read "Mitt Romney Has a Koch Problem." [38] Obama admitted snorting coke, but he never suffered a Coke Problem.

*The New York Times* also carried a photo of the protesters with the "Koch problem" banner and began its story: "A woman in a blue chiffon dress poked her head out of a black Range Rover here on Sunday afternoon and yelled to an aide to Mitt Romney. 'Is there a VIP entrance? We are VIP!'" The fundraising lunch was held at Ron Perelman's house. "Widely described as the largest estate in East Hampton, when last advertised in the early 1990s, the house was said to have 40 rooms, 9 fireplaces and a mile of frontage on Georgica Pond." [39]

The *Los Angeles Times* insisted without an ounce of disdain that the MoveOn and Occupy protesters "posed with a flag in the style of the Marines at Iwo Jima." [40]

It wasn't the same when Obama had two New York fundraisers less than a week later on June 15 with stylist actress Sarah Jessica Parker and *Vogue* magazine editor and diva Anna Wintour.

*The New York Times* didn't mention anyone's Bentleys or real estate values in a story simply headlined "Obama Visits New York for Star-Studded Fundraisers." [41] Two days later, Wintour was puffed in a *Times* piece headlined "Power Is Always In Vogue." [42] The *Los Angeles Times* offered no story.

The networks were indifferent. CBS barely noticed at all (with one brief mention of Parker and Wintour on *CBS This Morning* on June 15 in their quick-edit "Eye Opener" feature). NBC passed it along a few times, as Chuck Todd breezily reported on that same morning, "Well, it wasn't quite Bieber fever last night at Sarah Jessica Parker's house, but the president again found himself rubbing elbows with a bunch of celebrities as he tries to rake in as much cash as he can at a couple of fundraisers last night."[43]

Only ABC's Jake Tapper and Terry Moran briefly broke the mold and audibly pondered that the images might not look good in hard economic times. Previewing the events on the June 4 *Nightline*—airing in the East at 11:35 P.M.—Moran said "there just seems to be something tone deaf about the Obama campaign's decision at the very moment unemployment is again on the rise to enlist Madame Wintour as one of the hostesses of his fundraiser."[44]

Unlike their anti-Romney piece, the AP turned the Obama fundraisers into a debate. They quoted Obama spokesman Jay Carney firing back about the super-rich events: "Two words. Donald Trump. Next question?" AP acknowledged "Obama has surrounded himself with blockbuster names lately . . . who make more in one year than most people do in a lifetime," but coolness had to be acknowledged: "Obama played basketball with a Batman (Clooney) and a Spider-man (Tobey Maguire), all in one game."

The story also included this Obama quote to his donors: "You're the tie-breaker. You're the ultimate arbiter of which direction this country goes."[45] Liberal journalists hate the idea that super-rich capitalists are the "ultimate arbiters" of the country's direction—but not so for super-rich actors and fashion magazine editors.

The trend resurfaced on September 18 with a $40,000-a-plate dinner for one hundred people at rap star and former drug dealer Jay-Z's 40/40 Club in Manhattan. *The New York Times* couldn't even put this story in the paper. Online, their report began, "On a day when Mitt Romney's videotaped remarks at a Republican fund-raiser dominated the campaign, President Obama attended two fund-raisers of his own in New York City, one hosted by the music super-couple Beyoncé Knowles and Jay-Z."

They let Obama lecture Romney on populism, reporting that Obama appeared on the Letterman show on CBS and argued, "My expectation is, if you want to be president, you've got to work for everybody, not just for some." Later, he added, "What I think people want to make sure of is, you're not writing off a big chunk of the country." [46]

The *Times* did not report on Jay-Z's prize attraction. His nightclub features a champagne tower of 350 bottles of $300-a-bottle Armand de Brignac Brut Gold, worth $105,000. [47] Try imagining Obama and Jay-Z in front of that spectacle while Obama tells Letterman you can't just work for the rich people.

AP shamelessly distributed a story headlined "Obama: As President You Represent Entire Country." Matthew Daly reported: "Rebuking Mitt Romney, President Barack Obama said Tuesday that Americans are not 'victims' and that voters want to make sure that their president is 'not writing off big chunks of the country.'" [48] With zero sense of irony, Daly began a perfunctory recap of the Jay-Z fundraiser at paragraph 16, with no word of a champagne tower. ABC, CBS, and NBC never mentioned this clash of opulence and "populism."

Obama could campaign comfortably in the knowledge that he didn't really have to worry that the press would report the screaming contradiction between his mansion-hopping opportunism and his left-wing anticapitalist ideals. As Jason Mattera concluded in his book *Hollywood Hypocrites*, Obama's celebrity backers are "the perfect embodiment of all that is wrong with the Left's ideas and policies. Not only do their progressive ideas fail, but they are so bankrupt that even their loudest adherents live lives that stand in direct opposition to their ideology." [49]

# CHAPTER 4

# The Audacity of Myth

Obama sounded "like great fiction"—and that's what he wrote.

The media's sneakiest dirty trick in the book is bias by omission, because it is so hard to find, when journalists decide "what the people don't know won't hurt them," or more precisely, "what the people don't know won't hurt our candidate."

Back in 1992, CBS correspondent Betsy Aaron made a blunt statement at a journalists' conference. "The largest opinion is what we leave out," she said. "I mean, it sounds simplistic, but I always say worry about what you're not seeing. What you are seeing, you can really criticize, because you're smart and have opinions. But if we don't tell you anything and leave whole areas uncovered, that's the danger."[1]

In Barack Obama's case this omission emerged in 2012 over his biographical narrative: his 1995 memoir *Dreams from My Father*, which became a huge bestseller as he prepared to run for president and enriched him with an estimated $1.3 million in royalties (not to mention almost $4 million for his campaign book *The Audacity of Hope*), and that's just through 2007.[2]

Reporters loved this book. In an October 23, 2006, cover story in *Time* magazine, Joe Klein oozed about Obama's parentage: "He told the story in brilliant, painful detail in his first book, *Dreams from My Father*, which may be the best-written memoir ever produced by an American politician."[3]

Chris Matthews was even more effusive, to the point of slobbery, on MSNBC, which is to say, typical. The book was "unique because he's a politician and not since U.S. Grant has a politician written his own book, and that is refreshing." It was great literature. "It's almost like Mark Twain. It's so American, it's so textured. It's so, almost sounding like great fiction because it reads like us. It's picturesque. Is that the right word, 'picturesque'? I think it's got that quality."[4]

Matthews was exactly right. It sounded like great fiction because so much of it was fictionalized. The warning was right there in the preface to his 1995 memoir, where Barack Obama admitted the chapters to come were taking liberties with the truth: "Although much of this book is based on contemporaneous journals or the oral histories of my family, the dialogue is necessarily an approximation of what was actually said or relayed to me." Even the people weren't entirely real: "For the sake of compression, some of the characters that appear are composites of people I've known, and some events appear out of precise chronology."[5]

Ask a journalist if he supports the notion of a president whose life story is one part mythology, like George Washington and the cherry tree. Some media people have been stunned when they are told of this paragraph, as if they never read this book, or skipped the preface. But that has never nicked the larger legend that's been created. The nation's so-called guardians of factual accuracy don't even expect honesty from Obama on *his own life story*.

Liberal journalists—especially hacks like Matthews at MSNBC—

routinely disparage conservatives for the "birthers" and their conspiracy theories that Obama couldn't be president because he wasn't born in the United States. They enjoyed the circus around Donald Trump's demands for Obama's birth certificate as proof that conservatives can't accept a black man as president. When Romney clinched the Republican nomination in late May, NBC's Matt Lauer wondered on the *Today* show, "will his ongoing relationship with Donald Trump overshadow his big moment? As Trump plays the birther card once again."[6]

But the public should see the entire national media as a pack of "mythers"—people who blithely accepted Obama's concocted life story without challenging the factual reliability of any of it. It should be called *Fever Dreams from My Father*. Or *Day Dreams From My Father*. Anything to underscore that this should *not* be seen as a biography.

Instead, Obama was *honored* for his narrative-mangling skill. In 2008, *New York Times* reporter Janny Scott oozed, "Senator Obama understands as well as any politician the power of a well-told story. He has risen in politics less on his track record than on his telling of his life story—a tale he has packaged into two hugely successful books that have helped make him a mega-best-selling, two-time Grammy-winning millionaire front-runner for the Democratic presidential nomination at age 46."[7]

Liberals occasionally tried to preserve a fraction of their dignity as journalists with a few uncomfortable facts. But they were quiet about it.

For example, on July 13, 2011, in a story published on page 16, *New York Times* reporter Kevin Sack explained, "The White House on Wednesday declined to challenge an account in a new book that suggests that President Obama, in his campaign to overhaul American health care, mischaracterized a central anecdote about his mother's deathbed dispute with her insurance company."

The headline said the book "challenges" the Obama story, and in the story they used the word "mischaracterized." It was a whole lot more misleading than that.

That new book was titled *A Singular Woman: The Untold Story of Barack Obama's Mother*. The author was Janny Scott, the same *Times* reporter who was so impressed with Obama's storytelling in 2008. But she found holes in the narrative. Scott quoted from correspondence from Obama's mother, Ann Dunham, to assert that the 1995 dispute concerned a Cigna disability insurance policy. Her actual health insurer had reimbursed most of her medical expenses without argument. The *Times* noted that although candidate Obama often suggested Dunham "was denied health coverage because of a pre-existing condition, it appears from her correspondence that she was only denied disability coverage."[8]

So he was lying. Indeed, reporters could have held Obama accountable for lying repeatedly on his way to his first presidential victory and beyond, obscenely using his own deceased mother as a prop:

- He lied to an entire stadium of supporters in his August 28, 2008, convention speech. "As someone who watched my mother argue with insurance companies while she lay in bed dying of cancer," he announced, "I will make certain those companies stop discriminating against those who are sick and need care the most."

- The same lie was repeated in the October 7, 2008, presidential debate, carried live from coast to coast by all the networks, like the convention speech. "For my mother to die of cancer at the age of 53 and have to spend the last months of her life in a hospital room, arguing with insurance companies because they're saying that this may be a preexisting condition and they don't have to pay her treatment, there's something fundamentally wrong about that."

- He lied as president in a town-hall-style meeting in Portsmouth, New Hampshire, in August 2009. "I will never forget my own mother, as she fought cancer in her final months, having to worry about whether her insurance would refuse to pay for her treatment."

Obama also mentioned her in a 2007 campaign TV ad: "In those last painful months, she was more worried about paying her medical bills than getting well. I hear stories like hers every day."

Kevin Sack of the *Times* turned to liberal Harvard professor Robert Blendon to pronounce the obvious: if Obama's phony story line had been discovered during the 2008 campaign, "people would have considered it a significant error." But it was not an error. It was a bald-faced lie, repeated over and over.

Blendon added: "I just took for granted that it was a pre-existing condition health insurance issue." So did the entire American news media.

But the suppressing media not only failed to find this deception in 2008. They ignored it when it was exposed in 2011. Network coverage of this new jaw-dropper on ABC, CBS, and NBC? Zero in 2011, and zero in 2012.

This suppression of Janny Scott's most damaging anecdote was even true for the *Times* itself. When the paper first ran an excerpt of her book in their Sunday magazine on April 24, 2011, it came with a cover photo of Barack as a preschooler in a pirate costume standing by his mother. The article was a flowery bouquet of prose about "the stout, pale-skinned woman in sturdy sandals, standing squarely a half-step ahead of the lithe, darker-skinned figure to her left. His elastic-band body bespoke discipline, even asceticism . . . he had the studied casualness of a catalog model, in khakis, at home in the viewfinder." [9]

This is the same set of newspapers and networks that had devoted multiple heavy-breathing stories to "correcting" noncandidate Sarah Palin's historical knowledge of Paul Revere or mocking Michele Bachmann for confusing the birthplace of John Wayne. But Obama didn't stumble, and wasn't confused. He lied repeatedly about his mother—a shameless, pandering appeal to emotion, using his mother to enact socialized health care, and the media—how can we deny this?—deliberately abetted that dishonesty.

After Obama was safely reelected, David Axelrod insisted that the voters prized Obama's authenticity and disdained Mitt Romney's apparent plasticity. "Barack Obama's very authentic. They knew what drove him. They were comfortable with him." [10] Authenticity was hardly Obama's strong suit, but how could voters know otherwise when the national media were censoring news?

## Obama's "Composite" White Women

David Maraniss of *The Washington Post* was another reporter flying all over the world trying to separate the real Obama from the phony memoir of *Dreams*—but in the friendliest possible way. Maraniss told *Vanity Fair* that Obama's memoir had value despite its pack of lies: "I say that his memoir is a remarkably insightful exploration of his internal struggle, but should not be read as rigorous factual history. It is not, and the president knew that when he wrote it and knows it now." [11]

This was a bombshell. Maraniss had spent months exploring Obama's past and held a prestigious editor's post at the dominant paper in the nation's capital, and was overseeing campaign coverage as Obama faced a difficult reelection. But the bombshell never exploded.

In mid-June, his book *Barack Obama: The Story* came out. On June 5, deep inside the paper, *New York Times* reviewer Michiko Kakutani noticed several factual problems with Obama's memoir. She called the book a "forensic deconstruction" of Obama.[12]

For example, Obama wrote about "a woman in New York that I loved." But while the physical description of this character closely resembles a white Obama girlfriend named Genevieve Cook, Maraniss wrote Obama "distorted her attitudes and some of their experiences, emphasizing his sense that they came from different worlds." Maraniss relayed that during an interview at the White House on November 10, 2011, Obama acknowledged his description of his New York girlfriend was actually a "compression" of events "that occurred at separate times with several different girlfriends."[13]

Obama didn't just dump his old girlfriends. He then added insult to injury by blurring them into a fictional composite. If a memoir can't be honest about something as trivial as " a woman in New York that I loved," how can it be considered accurate with matters that are profound?

The glossy magazine *Vanity Fair* published an excerpt from Maraniss but didn't focus very seriously on the "compression." They were fascinated by excerpts from Cook's diary, and letters Obama wrote to another white girlfriend, Alex McNear. On May 2, ABC anchor Diane Sawyer swooned as she quoted Obama's letters, and pretended it was somehow a "peril" for ABC to discover them and praise them.

"One of the perils of being President: Everything you ever wrote will become public. And today, Barack Obama, age 22—long before he met Michelle—new letters and diary entries revealed in *Vanity Fair* from a biography out soon," Sawyer announced.

"He had college girlfriends, two women . . . Genevieve Cook and Alex McNear. And in a love letter to McNear, the President writes adoringly about life in New York. Quote, 'Moments trip gently along over here. Snow caps the bushes in unexpected ways. Birds shoot and spin like balls of sound. My feet hum over the dry walks.' Oh, we were all so romantic when we were young. The book relies on a trove of letters and journal entries that Obama and his friends created during the 1980s." [14]

So much for "peril." Sawyer and ABC never showed the slightest interest in Obama compressing and mangling his college sweethearts in his book.

There was more distortion. One weekend, Cook and Obama took a bus to her stepfather's country estate in Norfolk, Connecticut. He described it this way: "The family knew every inch of the land. They knew how the hills had formed, how the glacial drifts had created the lake, the names of the earliest white settlers—their ancestors—and before that, the names of the Indians who'd once hunted the land." Obama's point was "I realized that our two worlds were as distant from each other as Kenya is from Germany," and "I was the one who knew how to live as an outsider."

This Obama passage had one factual error: the estate didn't belong to Cook's father, but to her stepfather, Phil Jessup. That can be overlooked as an innocent mistake. Less innocent: Cook complained to Maraniss that the notion that the Jessups had been among the earliest white settlers and that they knew the names of the Indians was a "gross exaggeration." Cook also felt Obama misled readers in that she felt just as alienated from the place—and the old-money establishment—as Obama claimed he did, and then, "The ironic thing . . . is he moved through the corridors of power in a far more comfortable way than I ever would have." [15]

Obama also told a story about taking a girlfriend to a "very angry play" by a black playwright and she came out "talking about why black people were angry all the time. I said it was a matter of remembering—nobody asks why Jews remember the Holocaust, I think I said—and she said that's different, and I said it wasn't, and she said that anger was just a dead end. And we had a big fight, right in front of the theater."

Again, Maraniss reported, "None of this happened with Genevieve." She said they attended the theater just once together, to see the British actress Billie Whitelaw performing from the work of the Irish playwright Samuel Beckett. The one time they were in the midst of a black audience was a trip to the movies in Brooklyn to see Eddie Murphy in *Beverly Hills Cop*. Cook told Maraniss, "I was the only white person in the audience," and "It was such a wonderful, uplifting, mind-blowing experience."

There was no fight. There was no crying in the car (neither person had a car). There was no scene where Obama's girlfriend asked about angry black people.

Maraniss asked Obama about this at the White House. Obama acknowledged the scene did not happen with Cook. "That was not her," he said. "That was an example of compression. I thought that was a useful theme to make about sort of the interactions I had in the relationship. And so that occupies, what, two paragraphs in the book? My attitude was it would be dishonest for me not to touch on that at all." [16]

Stop. Rewind. He's saying "it would be dishonest of me" *not* to make up a story about a black-white lovers' quarrel? To Obama, real life was merely raw material for manufacturing the "larger truth" of his mythology. His story was false—period.

In another stunning passage from the same chapter of the Maraniss book, a passage that *Vanity Fair* did not excerpt—perhaps because it wasn't about Obama's love life—Obama describes his brief tenure after graduation from Columbia at a place called Business International, which produced newsletters and updates for corporations seeking to do business abroad. Obama boasted, "I had my own office, my own secretary, money in the bank. Sometimes, coming out of an interview with Japanese financiers or German bond traders, I would catch my reflection in the elevator doors—see myself in a suit and tie, a briefcase in my hand—and for a split second, I would imagine myself as a captain of industry, barking out orders, closing the deal, before I remembered who it was that I wanted to be and felt pangs of guilt for my lack of resolve."

Maraniss found these recollections were "seen as distortions and misrepresentations by many of the people who had worked with him." They said Obama had no secretary, and his office was the size of a cubicle, barely large enough to fit a desk. The dress code was informal and people in his position rarely wore suits. "He dressed like a college kid," said his supervisor Lou Celi.

Ralph Diaz, the company's vice president for publications, thought Obama was embellishing his role for dramatic effect "in a book that reads more like a novel." He said "Obama worked at a very, very low position there. . . . The part about seeing his reflection in the elevator doors? There were no reflections there. . . . He was not in this high, talking-to-Swiss-bankers kind of role. He was in the back rooms checking things on the phone."

Another colleague characterized it with equal distaste: "He re-tells the story as the temptation of Christ . . . the young idealistic would-be community organizer who gets a nice suit and barely escapes moving into the big mansion with the white folks." [17]

In an interview with *Vanity Fair*, Maraniss admitted that he bent his usual rules to make his interview with the president more advantageous. What's the harm in a little collusion?

"I did something I rarely do: I gave him a copy of the introduction to the book so he would understand its parameters. I also gave him the table of contents, knowing that some of the chapter titles, such as 'Genevieve and the Veil,' would mean something to him but not to his staff. The interview was scheduled for 45 minutes. It went on for more than an hour and a half. He answered all of my questions, sometimes took issue with my interpretations, but was fairly forthright."[18]

Here's how he was forthright. When Maraniss was interviewed on NBC's *Today* on June 18, 2012, substitute host David Gregory noted, "You point out inconsistencies. You talk with greater depth and detail about his pot smoking as a young person. You unearth letters from former, you know, loves. Genevieve Cook. How did he react to all of that?"

Maraniss: "Well, he's a writer himself. When I first interviewed him, he said, 'David, your introduction'—[which] I let him read—'is interesting, but you called my book fiction.' And I said, 'No, Mr. President, I complimented it. I called it literature.' There's a big difference between memoir and biography. And it wasn't that I was trying to fact-check everything that he wrote in his biography, but I just wanted to get the story right. So, he didn't—he didn't really fight with me about it. But it was an interesting conversation."

In the book's introduction, after he praised *Dreams* as "unusually insightful," Maraniss wrote that "it is important to say it falls into the realm of literature, and not of history and autobiography, and should not be read as a rigorously factual account."[19]

Gregory asked, "Was he forthcoming about these additional details?" Maraniss understood Gregory's roundabout inquiry and said Obama didn't put up a fight to the charge he'd mangled his own life story:

"In most cases he said, you're probably right. You know, a lot of the mythology of the family was passed along to him that he didn't check. Like, that his step-grandfather in Indonesia he thought died fighting the Dutch in the anti-colonial war. In fact, the man died of a heart attack falling off an ottoman changing the drapes in his living room. You know, that sort of story is something that the president did not check. And when I told him the reality of so many of those things he said, you're probably right."[20]

These "journalists" were tying themselves into pretzels to avoid calling this a fabrication.

Maraniss faced a tension between his self-perceived role as a historian versus his role as a journalist. The historian wanted to present with some objectivity and detachment a reliable record for the ages. The journalist living in the present was much more circumspect about his findings.

## The Punahou Hoops Scoop

Here's the most remarkable discovery of media omissions on Obama's behalf: *The Washington Post,* the journalistic home base of Maraniss, never touched on the memoir lies. *All these passages on Obama's self-made mythology were never republished in the newspaper.*

The *Post* ran massive exposés trying to ruin first Rick Perry, then Mitt Romney, but published nothing about Obama's blatant myth-making. Instead, on June 5, the *Post* published a rave review of the Maraniss tome on the front page of the Style section, headlined "A masterful portrait of a guarded politician."

Shamelessly, *Post* reviewer author T. J. Stiles oozed, "Every biographer knows how difficult it is to render an actual human being with the depth of a fictional character. . . . A character should be capable of surprises without seeming inauthentic or arbitrary." [21] But Stiles never mentioned Maraniss exposing Obama's fictionalizations. He even wrote Maraniss "makes the fringe skepticism of Obama's birthplace seem even more ridiculous, if possible," but utterly ignored how the *Post* editor found Obama lied about his mother's almost-immediate departure for the homeland after his birth.

What did Maraniss think of this whitewash? Maraniss didn't mind. He linked to the rave review on Twitter, with the words: "TJ Stiles says 'no review can convey this book's breadth and depth,' but his review of Obama: The Story not 2 shabby." [22] Not shabby? Stiles had ignored the most damaging part of the book's depth.

After running very large investigative pieces on the front page trashing Rick Perry and Mitt Romney, Maraniss and the *Post* provided the perfect contrast of anti-Republican bile with pro-Obama goo. The only Maraniss book excerpt appearing in the newspaper was placed at the top of the Sunday sports section on June 11. The 5,500-word excerpt carried the headline "President Obama's Love for Basketball Can be Traced Back to His High School Team." The story took up two whole pages inside the sports section. [23]

The *Post* apparently found nothing about Obama's life more illuminating or substantive for readers than repeating that Obama loved basketball—about which Maraniss had also written syrupy passages in 2008. As always with Maraniss, it was all about lovingly toying with Obama's racial identities:

"To say that President Obama loves basketball understates the role of the sport in his life," the excerpt began. "He has been devoted to the game for 40 years now, ever since the father he did not know and never saw again gave him his first ball during a brief Christmastime visit. Basketball is central to his self identity. It is global yet American-born, much like him. It is where he found a place of comfort, a family, a mode of expression, a connection from his past to his future. With foundation roots in the Kansas of his white forebears, basketball was also the city game, helping him find his way toward blackness, his introduction to an African American culture that was distant to him when he was young, yet his by birthright."

All this because Obama likes basketball.

Strangely, the excerpt wrapped up with Maraniss laboring to suggest Obama's use of marijuana in high school was very typical for the Disco Era. "If there is a representative teenager's life, Barry Obama lived a version of it in Hawaii in the late 1970s. Several things stood out—he went to a prestigious school, he lived with his grandparents, his father was gone, his mother was infrequently present, he was a *hapa* black in a place where most people were a lighter shade of brown—and those traits helped shape his particular character, but they did not make his life odd or mysterious. He smoked pot with his Choom Gang and goofed around outside the classroom, where he came across as smart and mature if not notably studious, but the central activity of his high school life was basketball."

The "choom" in "Choom Gang" was a verb meaning to smoke pot. Maraniss found Obama was an enthusiastic pot smoker, but it was mentioned in passing in the *Post.* This paragraph was lifted out of a chapter that began with Maraniss reporting the future president and his friends believed in "TA," or "total absorption," as in "[w]asting good bud smoke was not tolerated." Barry championed "roof hits," that when they were pot-smoking in the car, all the windows had to be rolled up, and when the pot was gone, they tilted their heads upward to suck in the last bit of smoke from the ceiling. Barry was also known for "intercepting" the rotating joint.[24]

Try not to be shocked. Those evocative details were left out of the 5,500-word basketball excerpt.

Maraniss and the *Post* also milked the hoops angle to sell Obama in 2008. As might be expected, a Nexis search of the words "Obama" and "Punahou" brings out mostly laudatory references to his high school basketball career. The seven stories in the sample offered zero criticisms of young Obama, but plenty of oozing sympathy for his fatherless plight. Here are the headlines, to give you a flavor:

1. "A Rusty Toyota, a Mean Jump Shot, Good Ears" (Outlook section collection of positive quotes from friends and classmates, February 11, 2007)

2. "The Ghost of a Father" (December 14, 2007)

3. "BARACK OBAMA WAS DRAWN TO BASKETBALL AS A KID, AND HE HAS NEVER LET IT GO" (same day, December 14, 2007)

4. "For Obama, the Sport Is Much More than a Game" (Sports, April 16, 2008)

5. "Though Obama Had to Leave to Find Himself, It Is Hawaii That Made His Rise Possible," by David Maraniss (August 24, 2008)

6. "Obama Visits Grandma Who Was His 'Rock'; Candidate Hopes She Will See Election Day" (October 25, 2008)

7. "What School Sports Taught These Political Contenders" (Sports, October 30, 2008)

That last story before the election, by Preston Williams, made sure to throw in some negativity toward opponent John McCain: "Obama was sometimes called 'Barry Obomber,' even though the left-handed small forward was known more for his long arms and quick first step on slashes to the basket than for his shooting touch. He favored a street-ball style; Coach Chris McLachlin preached fundamentals."[25]

But for the Republican, "McCain, a self-described rabble-rouser at Episcopal, at the time an all-male boarding school, was one of the smaller boys on campus—he wrestled in the 127-pound class as a senior. But he was also one of the feistiest, earning such nicknames as 'McNasty' and 'The Punk.'"

In 2008 as in 2012, the *Post* would strongly suggest the Republican challenger was a teenaged bully.

## Slouching Toward Selma

There's another example that demonstrated that the major media never cared about Obama's reckless disregard for the truth, especially when he was pandering to black voters. Maraniss reported that Obama's account of being separated from his father when he was two was "received myth, not the truth." Maraniss explained Obama's father was "married in name only. Within a month of the day Barry came home from the hospital, he and his mother were long gone from Honolulu," as Ann Dunham returned to the mainland to attend the University of Washington.

In Obama's mythical version, "the family breach did not occur until 1963, when his father left the island. That version of events is inaccurate in two ways. The date: his father had gone from Hawaii in June 1962, less than a year after Barry was born, not 1963. And the order: it was his mother who left Hawaii first." [26]

No one reported on this, or questioned Maraniss about it, never mind questioning Obama himself. Five years before, on March 4, 2007, Obama made a speech saluting the 1965 civil rights march in Selma, Alabama, and claimed his parents were inspired by Selma before he was born. "There was something stirring across the country because of what happened in Selma, Alabama, because some folks are willing to march across a bridge. So they got together and Barack Obama Jr. was born. So don't tell me I don't have a claim on Selma, Alabama. Don't tell me I'm not coming home when I come to Selma, Alabama." [27]

This is a pretty bizarre claim for a man who was born in Hawaii and whose parents never had a real marriage, and were literally on different continents by the time of the Selma march of 1965. Selma didn't bring his parents together; they were officially divorced in 1964, and Obama's father left Harvard in 1964 and returned to Kenya with another white American woman, named Ruth Baker, and they married there in 1964. His mother married Lolo Soetoro in 1965. The real story in no way resembled Obama's mythical narrative that Selma inspired two people to fall in love and conceive a future president.

Obama had no claim on Selma, Alabama.

Obama was never mocked for his shameless attempts at burnishing his legend. NBC anchor Brian Williams could devote attention on three straight nights in June 2011 to how noncandidate Sarah Palin's account of Paul Revere's ride allegedly "differs with history," [28] but with candidate Obama in Selma, NBC's Andrea Mitchell used this uncorrected clip: "Don't tell me I don't have a claim on Selma, Alabama. Don't tell me I'm not coming home when I come to Selma, Alabama."

On ABC, John Cochran said Obama "seemed to address accusations that he is not black enough because of his mixed ancestry," and used the same clip. ABC's Jake Tapper repeated the tactic in the morning, adding some gush: "Obama's eloquent piety is seldom received better than in a church full of Democrats, especially black ones."

On CBS, correspondent Gloria Borger at least made a small nod to reality, without correcting Obama. "In March of 1965, Barack Obama was just three years old. Even so, he says, he's still the product of Selma." [29] Then came a clip of Obama: "This is the site of my conception. I am the fruits of your labor. I am the offspring of the movement."

*CBS This Morning* offered a warm anniversary story from Selma on March 4, 2012, but no one explored Obama's absurd claims of 2007. On the day of Obama's second inauguration, the *Post* published a special inaugural section, where *Post* reporter Wil Haygood highlighted quotes from Obama's Selma speech again—including "My very existence might not have been possible had it not been for some of the folks here today"— a claim now clearly debunked. It was only one of several "cultural touchstones related to African-American history" greeting Obama's second term, like the anniversary of the Emancipation Proclamation and the new movie on Lincoln.[30]

## Daily Fake Campaign Anecdotes

Obama has never stopped using poetic license when telling his life story. So where are the reporters to point out where he doesn't tell the truth? Let's take just one typical Obama stump speech, on July 5, 2012, in Sandusky, Ohio, and identify the fibs and stretches. They're not hard to find.

There are tall tales about his ancestors. He claimed, as he has many times, "My grandfather fought in Patton's army." In 2009, AP's Nancy Benac noted that the president's grandfather, Stanley Dunham, was in a supply and maintenance company, not in combat. That's noble work, but "fought in Patton's army" implies something else. Moreover, Benac reported Dunham's company was assigned to Patton's army for two months in 1945, and then quoted Obama's own self-boosting memoir: "Gramps returned from the war never having seen real combat." Why was Benac alone in exploring this blatant exaggeration?

There were also myths about Obama's campaigns. Obama bizarrely told the crowd in Sandusky that "back in 2008, everybody said we couldn't do it because we were outspent, we weren't favored." Did Obama mean in the primary race? By a slim margin, he outraised Hillary Clinton, who was the early favorite. But this spin is comical if it refers to the general election, where Obama outraised McCain $779 million to $347 million.

Then Obama added: "That first race that I ran as a state senator, Michelle and I, we were going around knocking on doors, passing out leaflets. Nobody gave us a shot. Everybody said, 'Nobody can pronounce your name, how are you going to win?'" But Obama *ran unopposed* in 1996 in both the primary and the general election.[31]

At first, state senator Alice Palmer urged Obama to replace her since she was going to run for Congress. But she lost that race to Jesse Jackson Jr. and then turned around to seek reelection. In a burst of Chicago-style politics, Obama removed *three* primary opponents (including Palmer) from the ballot by challenging their signatures. A bitter Palmer refused to endorse Obama in the primary or the fall election. To the gut-punchers in Chicago, it meant Obama had arrived. But none of the networks have ever breathed Palmer's name.

Obama's years in the Illinois Senate, from 1997 through 2004, were a part of his life story the national media never found interesting. It was a bit shocking that CBS reporter Steve Kroft would pile up five friendly interviews with Obama on *60 Minutes* before the 2008 election, and two more right after the victory, and yet completely, shamelessly avoid Obama's record in Illinois. It might seem less surprising that his Chicago past didn't come up in the seven interviews Obama gave to Kroft since becoming president. Kroft has never asked about his radical Chicago friends like the Pentagon bomber Bill Ayers and his anti-American minister Jeremiah Wright.[32]

It's not really unusual for CBS to catch up on ancient controversies in a presidential reelection campaign . . . or at least it wasn't when the president was George W. Bush. In 2004, CBS spent untold hours, days, weeks, months, chasing a story about George Bush and the Alabama Air National Guard in 1973 because that was important. But Obama palling around with terrorists, associating with hate-mongers? No one at *60 Minutes* cared what Obama did when he was in his mid-twenties. He was "finding himself."

The liberal assumption was that everything on George W. Bush's résumé was handed to this lightweight by Daddy. This is never a problem when your last name is Kennedy, only if you're an Old Money Republican. Obama, on their other hand, was their poster child, their heavyweight champion—sympathetic, cosmopolitan, progressive, racially mixed, and eternally conflicted about it. Every prize and privilege handed to Obama—including a contract to write a semi-fictional memoir fresh out of Harvard Law School—was somehow owed to him, a small fraction of America's racial sins being cleansed.

Steve Kroft did find one Obama scandal figure back on April 23, 2008—Tony Rezko, a Syrian-born housing developer, when he was on trial for corruption in Chicago. But CBS never mentioned Obama in the piece. Instead, Kroft was doing a story on how the Bush administration was implicitly allowing corruption in Iraq, and how the former Iraqi electricity commissioner's name came up in Rezko's corruption trial.[33]

Kroft mustered no mention of Rezko's contributing and bundling hundreds of thousands of dollars in campaign financing for Obama, or his scandalous help in helping the Obamas as they bought a fancy six-thousand-square foot Georgian Revival house with seven bathrooms for $1.65 million in June 2005. (Rezko's wife, Rita, bought an adjoining parcel to the Obamas for $625,000, and both sales closed on the same day.) At the time, Rezko was already being investigated for bribery and fraud. Obama later told the *Chicago Tribune* the deal was "boneheaded," but the national media weren't repeating that.

The Rezko scandal even emerged again during the Republican primary season. On November 22, 2011, as the networks were pounding away on Herman Cain's treatment of women, Rezko was sentenced to ten and a half years of prison time for corruption and extortion. ABC, CBS, NBC, MSNBC, NPR, and PBS said absolutely nothing. CNN offered one sentence to Rezko on this day, as John King ironically announced the "news you need to know."

*USA Today* and *The Washington Post* both reported the news briefly inside their papers, listing Rezko in their headlines as an ally of corrupt governor Rod Blagojevich—not Obama. The Associated

Press headline also touted "Blago ally Rezko." Obama's name came up just once, in paragraph 21.[34]

This was merely the latest proof that even on the most personal matters, Barack Obama could count on the media to act like another set of corrupt business partners. Team Obama could make fun of John McCain's seven homes or Mitt Romney's car elevator and chuckle in the knowledge that Obama's "news" buddies would never mention his Rezko-assisted home purchase. After all, he was perfect.

# CHAPTER 5

# Richie Rich Romney

Don't vote for a "predatory capitalist" stereotype.

Have you ever noticed the media's dirty trick about multimillionaires in politics? If you're a Democrat named Kennedy or Rockefeller, who inherited millions, or have a habit of marrying women with millions (think John Kerry), or made your millions chasing ambulances (Edwards), it couldn't possibly put a wrinkle in your populist image. As long as you favor every redistribution scheme that the Ivy League economists can muster, your riches aren't disqualifying. They can even add glamour to your aura.

But if you're a Republican with a gleam in your eye toward tax cuts and deregulation, then it doesn't matter whether you're Old Money or New Money or even No Money. You will be deemed an "economic royalist," as Franklin Roosevelt put it.

When ABC anchor Diane Sawyer interviewed Mitt Romney on April 17, 2012, she casually announced "the Obama campaign is working overtime to paint the portrait of a man whose riches have put him out of touch." She then offered Romney the Obama spin:

"The speaking fees, the Cadillacs, the story out now that there's an elevator for your cars in the new house you're planning in La Jolla. Are you too rich to relate?"[1]

There's an obvious answer that Romney did not give. "Diane, you make $12 million a year. The ritzy Manhattan penthouse, the wealthy movie director husband, the estate on Martha's Vineyard. Does that make you too rich and elitist to relate to your audience?"

Romney's actual answer wasn't bad. "We don't divide America based upon success and wealth and other dimensions of that nature. We're one nation under God. We come together. This is a time when people of different backgrounds and experiences need to come together."

The Obamas, like most liberals, loved to talk a good game about national unity, but in the political wars, talk is cheap. They have always preferred, and benefited from, the divide-and-conquer basics of class warfare. In his post-election interview at the University of Chicago, Obama strategist David Axelrod expressed amazement that Romney and his campaign team never sold his life story aggressively. "I don't think they fleshed him out enough," he said. "People need to know who you are, they need to be comfortable with who you are. . . . Whatever message you build has to be built around your biography, and it has to be compelling."

Obama had a biography that journalists never failed to recount and find compelling, even if, as we've discussed, so much of it was the president's own mangled memoir myths and stump-speech whoppers, augmented by apple-polishers like Chris Matthews who found him perfect in every way.

Axelrod and Team Obama obviously preferred to have Obama evaluated as a compelling historical figure, and not so much as a policy architect. They wanted him painted as above the grubby fray of everyday politics. Obama's policies were always secondary, and necessarily so, given their abject failure. Even policy statements could be better understood as empathetic personal poses for the lower- and middle-class voters that said "I understand you, I'm like you . . . unlike that out-of-touch Richie Rich over there with his car elevator."

Axelrod professed amazement that Romney spent at least 90 percent of his primary money on negative ads against his Republican opponents instead of defining himself. After he won the primary, "we thought the first thing they would do would be to do that, and just create a stronger sense among the American people of just who he was." Axelrod was happy that Romney skipped it: "That of course left an opening for him to be defined around some of his business practices that have become well-known now."[2]

Team Obama knew what it was doing. Team Bain Capital didn't have a clue. The Obama campaign and its "unaffiliated" Super PACs were merciless in attacking Romney as the worst kind of financial assassin and tax cheat. Reporters covering the campaign didn't protest. They did not like Romney. He lacked personal warmth. His way of speaking was too crisp and efficient, his hair too tidy. He was a soulless robot. Romney felt compelled to add the word "human" to his campaign speeches, but it did no good. He was a rich Republican capitalist. Strike One, Strike Two, and Strike Three.

For example, on July 17, the very same day that Chris Matthews described Obama on *Hardball* in utopian terms as "the perfect father, the perfect husband, the perfect American," on the very same channel *New York Times* columnist Charles Blow offered MSNBC's dystopian take on former Massachusetts governor Mitt Romney on *The Last Word*. Romney would abandon every liberal position he ever took in Boston to win the White House—as if Obama had never flip-flopped on anything in 2008, or once he was inaugurated—so he had no soul.

"This is the kind of man that Mitt Romney is. This man does not have a soul. If you opened up, you know, his chest, there's probably a gold ticking watch in there and not even a heart. This is not a person.

This is just a robot who will do whatever it takes, whatever he's told to do, to make it to the White House. And he will take whatever push in the back from whatever nasty person is pushing him and move him further in that direction."[3]

The media staunchly resisted any attempt to humanize Romney because it didn't help Obama. In both of his two campaigns for president, Mitt Romney told the heartwarming story of closing down Bain Capital in 1996 to hunt for the missing daughter of a coworker, fourteen-year-old Melissa Gay, who disappeared after going to a "rave party" and was found the next day. That story even was published that year in *The New York Times*—although Mitt Romney's name wasn't mentioned, just Bain Capital.[4] But her name hasn't been mentioned in the *Times* since then. Her name never came up in either election on ABC, CBS, CNN, MSNBC, or NBC. Republicans like Romney have to pay for *advertisements* to make themselves look human. The networks did that on a daily basis for Obama, free of charge.

## The Haircut Bully

In May, after the media had helped eliminate all Romney's conservative challengers, it was Romney's turn to be the object of an attack piece. With exquisite timing, *The Washington Post* suddenly found their latest "investigative" hit piece on Republicans.

Reporter Jason Horowitz penned a 5,400-word "expose," a bombshell. Mitt Romney may have pinned a boy down and cut his hair in 1965. *Nineteen sixty-five.* That's almost a half century ago. Even if every detail in this hit piece was accurate—and they weren't—how is it relevant? The same journalists who couldn't find anything relevant in the mistresses Bill Clinton or John Edwards were "romancing" in the risky present of their presidential campaigns could somehow find something more compelling—a haircut—in the yellowed past of Mitt Romney's high school career. The *Post* carried several full pages of breathless prose under the big headline "Romney's pranks could go too far." [5]

The *Post* reported that Romney's Cranbrook schoolmate John Lauber was "perpetually teased for his nonconformity and presumed homosexuality," and that he screamed for help as a brutish Romney held him down and forcibly hacked off his hair. Another student, David Seed, told the *Post* he ran into Lauber three decades later at an airport and apologized for not doing more to help him. Seed claimed Lauber said, "It was horrible. . . . It's something I have thought about a lot since then." The paper recounted another incident in which Romney allegedly once shouted "atta girl" to a different student at the all-boys' school who, years later, came out as gay.

This story was neatly paired with President Obama announcing the end of his completely insincere opposition to gay marriage. Even centrist *Post* columnist Kathleen Parker could see the way the major media wanted this to unfold: "One, Barack Obama is an evolutionary, 21st-century hero who supports equality for all. Two, Mitt Romney is a gay-bashing bully mired in the previous century who also supports a war on women and, oh yeah, hates dogs." [6]

So what did the alleged victim of the Romney rampage have to say? The family of John Lauber, who died of liver cancer in 2004, issued a statement saying "the portrayal of John is factually incorrect and we are aggrieved that he would be used to further a political agenda." One sister said, "If he were still alive today, he would be furious" about the story. [7] Yet none of this slowed down the *Post* one bit, nor kept everyone else in the national media from rushing to repeat the story.

ABC anchor Diane Sawyer hyperbolically found a firestorm in this tiny tale: "Five of Romney's former classmates have come forward to tell the same story, accusations creating a firestorm and Romney is forced to respond."[8] CNN anchor Soledad O'Brien called it a "pretty harrowing story" from the *Post*. "They talked to several people who recall with great detail and what sounds like a tremendous sense of guilt about that attack on this kid."[9]

"Creating a firestorm." The media create it, and then announce it's created.

After readers complained, *Post* ombudsman Patrick Pexton touted this "scoop" as a "deeply reported story" that "holds up to scrutiny." They claimed the paper "received no specific complaint of inaccuracy from the Lauber family." Note the word-parsing. The Lauber family certainly did complain. But it wasn't a *specific* complaint, so it didn't count. Pexton then turned to national editor Kevin Merida, who insisted, "We stand by the story. It's a full portrait. It's the story of Mitt Romney's years at Cranbrook. . . . Our intention with this story and future stories about both Mitt Romney and President Obama is to give people the fullest possible portrait of the men who are running for president."[10]

Pexton did not explain to readers that Merida is no objective editor. He is a black journalist who wrote a critical biography of Clarence Thomas, called *Supreme Discomfort*, and penned captions for a coffee-table book for Obama-loving liberals titled *Obama: The Historic Campaign in Photographs*. He was named the *Post*'s national editor during the Obama transition. When *Washingtonian* magazine asked him at the time how he would run the national desk, he said, "We're witnessing the rebirth of the country. We have to ask ourselves, 'What did we produce to help people understand the moment of great change?'"[11] It would be safe to assume he didn't want the "moment of great change" to be ended by a President Romney. After the election, Merida was promoted to managing editor, the number-two job.

This story was certainly not a "full portrait," as Merida claimed. It was a hit piece that helped liberal journalists, talkers, and bloggers assault Romney as someone who "tortured gay kids" for fun. Leftists like Joan Walsh of Salon.com had a field day. Her story was titled "Mitt the Prep-School Sadist."

Pexton admitted the *Post* timed this story precisely to echo on the day after President Obama's big pro-gay announcement. They actually waited a day longer than planned to let Obama have the front page to himself when he was being "historic." Merida told Pexton they didn't want the bully story clashing with the Thursday Obama-now-favors-gay-marriage story. In truth, they wanted each story to dominate the front page, not share it. So the Romney hit piece was published online late Thursday morning and was splashed on the front page on Friday.

The "reader's advocate" agreed with this politicized news judgment, implying the *Post* rushed the piece a little once they heard Obama's "history" was coming. "Do I think *The Post* took advantage of the timing? Yes. Vice President Biden had telegraphed the president's position on gay marriage just days earlier," Pexton allowed. "If I were an editor I might have sped it up a little, too, to take advantage of the national discussion on gay marriage. Does that mean *Post* editors are timing stories with the White House? I hope not, and I doubt that is the case."

*Post* executive editor Marcus Brauchli eventually sent an outraged e-mail to Pexton (which was posted online) strongly denying any hint of collusion, declaring "there was no collusion or coordination between *The Post* and the White House over the Romney story. The notion is 'absurd and the implication is outrageous,'" Brauchli relayed. Pexton added, "I believe him, and based on my time here in the past 14 months I have not seen this kind of collusion or coordination."

Merida made the amazing claim that the story had to be rushed because they are a "competitive news organization." But that never moved the *Post* to action when its investigators worked on the Clinton sex scandals. In 1994 the *Post* delayed for three months the story of Paula Jones claiming sexual harassment, until Clinton hired a defense lawyer. They published the Juanita Broaddrick rape story only after the Clinton impeachment trial had concluded and the president's tenure was safe. They are experienced practitioners of politicized story timing.

The *Post* knows full well that they never did this kind of "investigation" of Barack Obama in 2008. Take Obama's admissions in his memoirs of teenaged marijuana and cocaine use. Did the *Post* send a reporter to find out from Obama's classmates how often he used illegal drugs, and where he purchased them? And did he in turn distribute them?

No. The *Post* tried to assert these troublesome admissions wouldn't matter. In a front-page story published on January 3, 2007, five weeks before he announced he was running, they rushed to the story—a year before the first primary election—and then failed to investigate if Obama's memoirs were accurate.

Reporter Lois Romano's story was headlined "Effect of Obama's Candor Remains to Be Seen; Senator Admitted Trying Cocaine in a Memoir Written 11 Years Ago." It took Romano twenty-four paragraphs to include the actual passage from *Dreams from My Father*: "Pot had helped, and booze; maybe a little blow when you could afford it. Not smack, though."

"Presidential aspirants tend to write more sanitized books for use as campaign tools," Romano claimed. Then she dismissed it as a potential cause of damage: "Obama's partisan opponents and experts said it is too early to know whether the admissions will be a liability because the public seems to be enthusiastically embracing his openness at this point."[12]

Do you think that if Romney had written in a memoir openly professing that he bullied kids in high school, the media would report "the public seems to be enthusiastically embracing his openness"? As for the openness, it was very limited. White House spokesman Robert Gibbs tried to spin it as a positive that Obama admitted cocaine use: "I believe what the country is looking for is someone who is open, honest and candid about themselves rather than someone who seems endlessly driven by polls or focus groups." The next sentence in the Romano story undercut the embracing-openness narrative: "Gibbs said yesterday that Obama was not available for an interview." [13]

## Romney and the Dog on the Roof

While stories like Obama's drug use were smothered in his first campaign for president and were considered forgotten in 2012, liberal journalists continued to embarrass Romney on old stories that emerged in his first presidential campaign. In 2007, *Boston Globe* reporter Neil Swidey reported that on a family vacation in 1983, Romney had put his Irish setter, Seamus, in a cartop carrier for a trip to Canada. The dog was apparently frightened enough to suffer from diarrhea, which rolled down the back window. Romney then pulled over to a gas station, cleaned the dog off with a hose, and put him back on top and drove on.

It was a profoundly *nothing* story, but that of course doesn't matter. The Obama people loved it, and would tweak Romney with it. On January 30, 2012, Obama strategist David Axelrod drew a wave of Internet attention when he tweeted a photo of Obama riding inside his car with his dog Bo with the caption, "How loving owners transport their dogs." CNN's Political Ticker blog wrote it up under the title "Axelrod's tweet worse than his bite." [14]

Predictably, some liberal journalists descended into wretched excess. On the January 13, 2012 edition of the public-radio show *On the Media*, distributed across America by NPR, host Bob Garfield interviewed Swidey. "So back in 2007, you surely knew that this story would not be taken only at face value, that it would mutate," Garfield declared, "and it would be used as ammunition by those who would portray Mitt Romney as the Michael Vick of presidential candidates. It still wound up as your lede. You feel any compunction about that at this stage?" [15]

The better question is why Garfield didn't have any compunction comparing Romney's alleged mistreatment of a pet with Michael Vick, who pled guilty to hanging or drowning six to eight dogs. Garfield's program boasts about its own civility on its website: "While maintaining the civility and fairness that are the hallmarks of public radio, *OTM* tackles sticky issues with a frankness and transparency that has built trust with listeners." [16] This would be true if your listeners were limited to liberals who loved this story like David Axelrod did.

No one embraced this story more feverishly than *New York Times* columnist Gail Collins, who served as the paper's editorial page editor for most of the Bush years. Collins worshipped Obama so much that she wrote a column just before Thanksgiving in 2008 with this request: "Thanksgiving is next week, and President Bush could make it a really special holiday by resigning. Seriously." [17] Like many other journalists, Collins was so desperately pro-Obama she wanted him inaugurated in November.

How obsessed as this woman with the silly dog story? Clay Waters of the TimesWatch blog counted that since her first 2007 column on the anecdote, headlined "Haunted by Seamus," Collins had mentioned "Crategate" in twenty-eight columns from 2007 through November 2011. "Every column that mentioned Romney during that span has included the dog story." [18]

The pattern continued from December 2011 through Election Day, with another thirty columns pounding away at the story. On January 3, Collins urged New Hampshire voters to write in the dog: "Did I ever mention that Romney once drove to Canada with the family Irish setter strapped to the roof of the car? The dog's name was Seamus. New Hampshire Republicans, if you can't think of anybody to vote for on Tuesday, consider writing in the name Seamus when you go to the polls. Maybe we can start a boomlet. Makes as much sense as the Newt Gingrich moment." [19]

Collins wrote a whole column on the subject headlined "Dogging Mitt Romney" on March 8. "People, does any of this sound appealing? Elect Mitt Romney and he will take the nation on the road to the future. Some of us will be stuck on the roof. The rest of us will be inside singing camp songs and waiting for the day when the master plan lets us stop to visit the bathroom. Plus, anybody who screws up on the way to the future gets the hose." [20]

CBS and David Letterman liked this story, too, so Collins appeared with late night's most devoted Obama fan on March 20. Letterman told Collins he adored her obsession: "I so loved the fact that this happened to this guy, and I loved the fact that you more than any single journalist that I know, has promoted it. Tell us how you know about it." When she described it, Letterman added, "I mean, as silly as this all might be, I'm told that later upon arriving in Toronto, the dog left, hitchhiked back, he had somebody, took him over the border, and they never saw him again." Collins added to the joke: "He asked for amnesty."

Then Letterman grew angry and said People for the Ethical Treatment of Animals wanted to shut down his "Stupid Pet Tricks" segments. "Now why haven't they been up Mitt's nose about the dog episode?" he demanded.

Letterman admitted that he certainly can't say he hasn't shown poor judgment in his personal life—having reckless sex at the office with the staff like he's Bill Clinton—but insisted this was different because he wasn't running for president. As for Romney, "This is a guy in the Oval Office, the most powerful position in the world, he's a guy we want with crystal-clear judgment, maybe shaded a little bit one way or the other, but by God we don't want a guy deciding 'Let's put the dog on the roof and drive to Canada.' I mean, I'm right about something there." Collins added, "There was a survey done this week in which I think most Americans said they would rather not have a dog on the roof under any circumstances."

Letterman asked the Seamus-obsessive journalist if this was important. "But am I on to something here about this suggests a greater wrinkle of the fabric than just something stupid he did on vacation?" Of course, she replied. "I think pet transport is not a major issue probably in the campaign. But there is something about it, it's sort of like Imelda Marcos and the 2,700 shoes, it just kind of tweaks some feeling people have about Mitt Romney right now, that does make them kind of, you know, 'What was he thinking?'"

Letterman shot back: "Well, yeah, tweaked, but I'd like to see the guy arrested." [21]

In April, Jim Treacher of the *Daily Caller* pulled out a story from Obama's memoir, *Dreams from My Father*, which told of his first months in Indonesia with new stepfather Lolo Soetoro. "With Lolo, I learned how to eat small green chili peppers raw with dinner (plenty of rice), and, away from the dinner table, I was introduced to dog meat (tough), snake meat (tougher), and roasted grasshopper (crunchy)." [22]

Romney misplaces dogs. Obama eats them. How can the former be news—big news—and the latter not be any news at all? To this argument, Collins lamely replied that "eating dog meat when you are a child in Indonesia is not the same thing as driving to Canada with the family Irish setter strapped to the roof of the car when you are 36." [23] That's true. In one case, the dog is dead. Or as Treacher put it, "Say what you want about Romney, but at least he only put a dog on the roof of his car, not the roof of his mouth."

## Romney Versus the "Complicit News Media"

*The New York Times* didn't just crusade for Obama on the editorial page. Two days after Collins appeared with Letterman, in the midst of 8.2 percent unemployment and four-dollar-a-gallon gas prices, the *Times* printed a front-page story headlined "Obama Seizes Chance to Score As an Everyman." The paper stooped to giving Obama and Axelrod credit for exploiting the *Times* along with the rest of the "news" media.

Political reporter Mark Leibovich proclaimed how "Mr. Obama's team has proven effective in exploiting each gaffe" Romney made. He reported that Axelrod's Seamus-mocking Twitter post came a few days after the president's reelection campaign created a "Pet Lovers for Obama" group on Facebook. Leibovich was also strangely impressed that Axelrod mocked Romney's clumsy claim that "the trees are the right height" in Michigan (Axelrod's tweet: "So Mitt wins Guam, where the Sea Hibiscus are just the right height!").[24]

Leibovich even slavishly paid tribute to Axelrod on Twitter: "@davidaxelrod you ate your tweeties today, Axe. Impressed."

The story grew weird as Leibovich quoted "Romney loyalist" Mike Murphy complaining about pro-Obama bias: "How hard is it to cash a lottery ticket?" Leibovich wrote that Murphy "added that Mr. Obama had benefited from a complicit news media that loves to point out Mr. Romney's perceived screw-ups. This in turn makes the Romney campaign—and candidate—overly self-conscious, prompting more gaffes." Murphy said, "I think Governor Romney knows that he's now trying to feed a dog that's trained to bite him." The *Times* surely appreciated another chance to push Romney as hostile to dogs.

Leibovich's story and pictures all sold Obama as a man of the people, touting the president's NCAA basketball tourney talk and his hot-dog chomping at a game alongside British prime minister David

Cameron: "It is the latest iteration of the Obama-Just-Folks offensive, and one that coincides—not by accident—with some particularly clumsy efforts by the Republican front-runner, Mitt Romney, to shed the stereotypical airs of a super-rich guy." [25]

Inside, there were large photos of Obama at the basketball game with the prime minister. Only in media-elite circles is it considered a "just-folks offensive" to fly Air Force One to Kentucky with the British prime minister for a photo op at a basketball game. Obama loves basketball! Who knew?

We were told about Obama boasting he knew about Jeremy Lin of the New York Knicks before the rest of the sports world did. Leibovich forwarded Axelrod making fun of Romney's decision to avoid making NCAA picks. "They asked Mitt if he was filling out his brackets," Axelrod had tweeted, "and he said, 'No I have my accountants to do that.'" They also thoughtfully included a photo of Obama crouching down for a face-to-face meeting with his dog Bo.

The *Times* even made hay with Romney's Mormon devotion to alcohol abstinence. "While office seekers always strain to be the proverbial 'candidate you'd rather have a beer with'—and such contests will never favor a teetotaling Mormon—the president has been laying it on as thick as the Guinness he sipped at a Washington bar on St. Patrick's Day."

Then they turned to the wives: "Michelle Obama went on the *Late Show with David Letterman* on Monday and reminded everyone she went shopping at Target last year (Mr. Letterman helpfully flashed a photo of the outing). It goes without saying that Target is not the kind of store one might envision, say, Ann Romney pulling up to in one of the Cadillacs that her husband says she drives. Or that the Obamas have been playing up their folksiness at a time when Mr. Romney has proven rather butterfingered with his common touch."

The *Times* failed to note that neither the Associated Press nor the White House would comment on how exactly it came to pass that

AP photographer Charles Dharapak was the only news photographer present at the Target store just south of the Pentagon in Alexandria, Virginia, to capture Mrs. Obama's strange shopping excursion.

"All I can say is that it was the result of good source work on his part," AP spokesman Paul Colford said, declining to elaborate on the sources or the work involved. This was a brush-off, not an answer.

*Washington Post* media reporter Paul Farhi explained what the *Times* ignored—that conservative media had been "sniping" at Mrs. Obama "when she appeared at a fundraiser in New York wearing $40,000 worth of borrowed diamond jewelry," so the Target run looked like a political stunt, and one way to make it look less political was to get the AP involved. If the White House itself issued a photograph of the First Lady at Target, the media would be reluctant to spread it around. But if it emerged from the nation's preeminent wire service, then it would be "news." Farhi implied this stunt also required the corporate cooperation of Target, which usually refuses any attempt at news photographs inside its stores.[26]

NBC best demonstrated its servility in one of its regular Michelle-boosting *Today* segments. A soundbite was featured of *Post* gossip columnist Amy Argetsinger touting the "wow factor" of the First Lady going to the discount department store. Later, NBC's Kelly O'Donnell declared: "Doing ordinary things in tough economic times can be good for a public image." A soundbite followed from left-wing *Huffington Post* politics editor Howard Fineman: "It's great PR for them, because they can say, 'Look, on this trip and others, we know what's going on outside the gates of the White House.'"[27]

It's great PR because the "news" media so shamelessly bought into it. Journalists favored Obama so shamelessly that his transparent manipulation *of* them was praised *by* them as proof of his political skill.

## Ann and the Horse

Mitt Romney's wife, Ann, was the kind of aspiring First Lady that liberal journalists cannot fathom: the stay-at-home mom. Feminists say they believe in women making choices, but cannot understand why they would ever make the choice to stay home. Unless—aha!—they are the greedy rich. Now, Michelle Obama could wear $42,000 in diamond bracelets or $500 sneakers from hip fashion designers and draw a pass. It didn't hurt John Kerry to have a wife as wealthy as Teresa Heinz Kerry in 2004. They were liberals and therefore automatic heroines with a right to their wealth, and media swoons were mandatory. Ann Romney, like Cindy McCain in 2008, would be mocked for her money.

Fox News analyst Juan Williams displayed this contempt after Mrs. Romney spoke at the Republican convention: She "looked to me like a corporate wife. . . . The stories she told about struggles—ah, it's hard for me to believe. I mean, she's a very rich woman. And I know that, and America knows that."[28]

Hollywood displayed this contempt, too. As Comedy Central roasted the "legendary" pig Roseanne Barr in August, actress Katey Sagal joked: "Roseanne, I feel honored that you and I broke new ground as TV moms who didn't cook, didn't clean, and didn't make any money. In the '90s that made you a bad mom, but today it makes you Mitt Romney's wife."[29] Neither woman was in a lower tax bracket than Ann Romney.

This hostility came through loud and clear when the media took exception to Mrs. Romney's affection for horses and her involvement in the Olympic equestrian competition known as dressage. This is clearly an enthusiasm for people of wealth, in political terms the very opposite of a populist chomping on pork rinds at the rodeo. Wealthy liberal anchormen and comedians and newspaper editors socked it to the Romneys without any reservation.

Leading the horse-whipping was *The New York Times,* which published a 2,300-word front-page Sunday story on May 26 by Trip Gabriel that reminded everyone that the Romneys are really, really rich. The headline: "In Rarefied Sport, a View of the Romneys' World." The Republican nominee's wife was involved in dressage, "in which horses costing up to seven figures execute pirouettes and other dancelike moves for riders wearing tails and top hats."[30]

Just as with Gail Collins and David Letterman, liberal comedy and journalism worked in tandem. Trip Gabriel whacked Romney by quoting the fake-conservative comedian Stephen Colbert, who "ribbed the sport's fussy, elitist image." In a June 17 story, he quoted Colbert's attack: "The image of Romney as a privileged princeling ends today, because now Mitt is just your average blue-collar fan of dressage."

Gabriel warned, "As millions tune in to the Olympics in prime time this summer, just before Mr. Romney will be reintroducing himself to the nation at the Republican convention, viewers are likely to see 'up close and personal' segments on NBC about the Romneys and dressage, a sport of six-figure horses and $1,000 saddles. The Romneys declared a loss of $77,000 on their 2010 tax returns for the share in the care and feeding of Rafalca."

Gabriel wrote the Romneys didn't really want to talk about this because they "may also have been wary of the kind of fallout that came after Mr. Romney's mention of the 'couple of Cadillacs' his wife owned and the disclosure of plans for a car elevator in the family's $9 million beach house in California, which prompted criticism that Mr. Romney was out of touch with average Americans." He concluded by painting Mrs. Romney as "she mingled casually outside and in the V.I.P. tent, where the dress code included white pants for men and women, with various breeds of small dogs as popular accessories." [31]

This Thurston Howell III routine came from the family newspaper handed down to Arthur "Pinch" Sulzberger Jr., and from a reporter with the first name of "Trip." As a reader might suspect, Gabriel was actually born with the name Bertram Gabriel III, in 1955, and attended Phillips Academy in Andover, Massachusetts, and Middlebury College in Vermont, where he earned a bachelor's degree in philosophy. His father, Bertram Gabriel Jr., was a real estate developer in Santa Fe, and before that was president of Gabriel Brothers Inc., a New York toy company.[32] Before covering politics for the *Times,* Gabriel was an editor for what *The New Republic* dismissed as the paper's "luxury porn" sections, the ones dedicated to the tastes of conspicuous consumers whose idea of a cheap timepiece is an $890 watch from Prada.[33]

It's nice to know that *The New York Times* is looking out for the little guy.

## "Imagine the Neighbor from Hell"

The *Times* stooped low enough to survey Romney's neighbors at his new vacation home in suburban San Diego. Political reporter Michael Barbaro rounded up the liberals in a splashy Home section feature titled "The Candidate Next Door." The accompanying text box established the theme: "On a cul-de-sac in La Jolla, residents are not happy about their new neighbor's renovation plans—or his entourage."

Barbaro began: "On Dunemere Drive, it seems as if just about everyone has a gripe against the owners of No. 311. . . . Bellyaching over the arrival of an irritating new neighbor is a suburban cliché, as elemental to the life on America's Wisteria Lanes as fastidiously edged lawns and Sunday afternoon barbecues." But this time, it was Romney, whose presence was "deeply polarizing."

Romney was crass enough to want to expand his home to fit more children and grandchildren, and "many of the residents of this exclusive tract in La Jolla say they are rankled by what they see from their decks and patios as the Romneys' blindness to their impact on the neighborhood. And personal politics is fueling their frustration as much as anything else, several days of interviews with about a dozen residents suggest." [34]

When liberals are unhappy, their disgruntled partisanship only makes them more newsworthy. "It turns out that Mr. Romney—who has likened President Obama's policies to socialism, called for cutting back on federal funding to PBS and wants to outlaw same-sex marriage—has moved into a neighborhood that evokes *Modern Family* far more than *All in the Family*. (There are six gay households within a three-block radius of his house, neighbors said.)"

The stars of the story (with two photos, one on the front page of the section, and one inside) were Randy Clark and Tom Maddox, who wanted to organize an Obama fundraiser in the neighborhood just to stick it to the new neighbor. The inside caption was a doozy: "CONCERNED: Randy Clark, right and Tom Maddox are among those who say they want to protect the tight-knit neighborhood." From Republicans, apparently.

They weren't alone. James Geiger was half of another gay couple. Barbaro added, "Chatting with Mr. Maddox and Mr. Clark a few weekends ago, Mr. Geiger playfully proposed hanging a gay-pride flag from the Italian stone pine tree in his yard 'so that Romney's motorcade has to drive under it.'"

There were more Democrat neighbors to interview. Mark Quint hated the "McMansions" that were being built, like Romney's. "The only thing he wants small is government and taxes," Mr. Quint said. "He likes big houses, big families and big religion."

Barbaro added, "For partisan candor it was hard to top Karen Webber, who lives several blocks away and dislikes the heightened security measures. 'If this were Obama,' she said, standing near bright orange barriers restricting access to Dunemere, 'I'd probably be fine with it.'"

This story suggests a good slogan for *The New York Times*: All the "partisan candor" that's fit to print.

Anti–"big religion" Quint helped spread the story that the intolerant Romneys—think "uptight Mormons"—discouraged pot smoking on the beach. "A young man in town recalled that Mr. Romney confronted him as he smoked marijuana and drank on the beach last summer, demanding that he stop."

MSNBC's Lawrence O'Donnell lunged at this story hours later and interviewed Maddox and Clark. "Imagine the neighbor from Hell," he unsubtly began. Both neighbors touted the "freedom to marry" whoever you want. "We look at our family [as] no different than he and Ann," Tom Maddox declared. O'Donnell wanted to get back to trashing Romney, bringing up the *Times* claim that Romney admonished pot smokers on the beach: "It looks like he's a candidate for Neighborhood Watch there. Are the neighbors talking about this Romney as Local Cop stuff?" Clark admitted, "Well, we do joke about that."[35]

When the primary season ended, *Washington Post* political writer Chris Cillizza suggested Romney's general-election strategy should start with getting a "positive first introduction" to voters through the liberal media because "only the national media can provide that megaphone and serve as a sort of validator for him."[36]

How hard did he laugh after he wrote that?

# CHAPTER 6

# The War on the Religious Right

Outdated haters don't deserve to be heard.

In every electoral cycle since 1980, when the Reaganites demonstrated their hold on the Republican Party by expunging from the party platform's support for the feminist Equal Rights Amendment to the Constitution, coloring the Republicans as extremists on the "social issues" has been a favorite media dirty trick.

Anyone following the tone of the news media at home might be puzzled at this treatment of the ideological spectrum. The conservative position is automatically "far right," and the liberal position is always moderate. Conservatives are out of the mainstream, extremists usually. Liberals are the essence of common sense. This constantly tells the audience that they must aspire to be a good liberal.

Opposing abortion for any reason is a fanatical extreme. Supporting abortion for any reason is somehow firmly in the mainstream. Opposing the clamor for "gay marriage" and other items on the LGBT agenda isn't just extreme and outdated, but carries the flavor of "hate speech." Favoring everything on that agenda makes you the

Wave of the Future. Opposing untrammeled immigration or asking when the "affirmative discrimination" of ongoing racial quotas is no longer needed is extreme, and racist to boot. Favoring them is the only way to embrace the dreams of the American people.

To follow the Obama campaign narrative, Romney and the Republicans weren't just losing an appeal to women. They were conducting a "War on Women." They weren't just having trouble attracting minorities in competing with the first black president. They were badly disguised crypto-racists.

Obama strategist David Axelrod felt that women and minorities were the key to the president's reelection. In his post-election remarks at the University of Chicago, he explained, "Our country's becoming more diverse. That every election, that diversity becomes more prominent, more Latino voters represented, African-American voters. Women voters would vote in larger numbers than men, and often in a different way.

"We mapped out a plan, a strategy, to make the case strongly to those constituencies that while Governor Romney was separating himself in many ways from those constituencies. We worked very hard to develop and burnish our support there, which was strong to start with."

Romney was "separating himself" from women and minority voters? That was coded language for shoring up his conservative pro-life base by trying to make everyone forget his pro-abortion stance when he ran statewide in Massachusetts. "Mitt Romney made a series of Faustian bargains" to get the nomination, Axelrod said, as if the Democrats had no corresponding liberal base to please. The Republican "gravitational pull was against immigration reform, was against choice [abortion], gay marriage"; they "were running against the demographic and social trend." [1]

This was the political agenda of a well-oiled and radicalized political machine. It was and continues to be the worldview of our national "news" media. It is impossible to locate where leftist political activism ends and journalism begins. It is one and the same.

The results of the 2012 election caused a wave of liberal triumphalism about how the growing diversity of America's population would spell doom for the White Male Republican Party. The favorite sport of liberal journalists might be Pin the Tail of Racism, Sexism, and Homophobia on the Elephant.

For women voters, in the Axelrod narrative, the 2010 wave election, both in the House and in the states, ushered in social conservatives who would push back against the abortion lobby, especially for government support for Planned Parenthood, by far the nation's largest corporate provider of abortions.

For the press it was no different. The media's feminist mindmeld with Planned Parenthood was demonstrated, for example, by the abortion conglomerate's 2011 "Maggie Awards for Media Excellence," honoring the most pro-abortion reporters. The ceremony was hosted by Liane Hansen, an anchor for twenty-two years for NPR's *Weekend Edition Sunday.*

Hansen proclaimed her fervor toward abortion: "As a reporter, I am committed to journalistic excellence, and I am also deeply invested in the protection of women's reproductive health care. I am delighted to be able to honor my colleagues who share both commitments. Through their intelligent investigative work, they have educated the American public and lawmakers alike on these important issues."[2]

She wasn't the only journalist "deeply invested" in abortion. A House investigation into Planned Parenthood business improprieties spurred the Susan G. Komen Foundation to announce on February 1, 2012, that it would no longer be donating to the abortion giant. The outrage boiled over as ABC, CBS, and NBC rushed to play defense. Over the course of about sixty hours, the Big Three emphasized the controversy with thirteen morning and evening news stories on how "women's groups" spurred "outrage and disappointment engulfing the Internet." The soundbite count was loaded: 76 percent of the quotes came from supporters of Planned Parenthood. Only eleven clips or statements came from Komen representatives or their new (very temporary) pro-life allies.[3]

On ABC's *World News* on February 2, correspondent Claire Shipman concluded that the apparent outrage at the breast cancer charity "shows the passion in this country among women on the issue of women's health care, access to services. I think we're going to hear a lot more of that over this campaign year."

Shipman surely knew about what to expect in the coming campaign talking points. Her husband is White House press secretary Jay Carney.

Within days, Komen snapped like a toothpick, reinstalling its Planned Parenthood donations and accepting the resignation of its pro-life vice president, Karen Handel, who was blamed for this "mistake." After the abortion giant crushed Komen on the PR front, MSNBC host Lawrence O'Donnell saluted Planned Parenthood boss Cecile Richards in a tone of deep reverence. "You now have my nomination for America's ambassador to the United Nations," he oozed to her. "Your artful diplomacy and how you have handled yourself in this relationship with your former partner who is now again your partner, the Komen foundation, has been something to behold."[4]

This was classic liberal back-scratching. O'Donnell was one of the "deeply invested" liberal hacks whom NPR's Liane Hansen honored with a "Maggie Award" in the summer of 2011 for his coverage of government attacks on Planned Parenthood. *You are wonderful. No, you are wonderful.*

## Obamacare Versus Catholic Religious Freedom? Yawn

The code words were "access" to "health care." Many medical providers shrink from the idea that elective abortions for convenience, or even to eliminate children with disabilities like Down syndrome, could be defined under the Hippocratic oath as "health care." Abortionists don't "cure" women of a fatal disease. They stop them from being "punished with a baby," as Barack Obama so aptly defined it for the left.

"Access" to abortion is one issue. Federal subsidies—taxpayers' funds—to pay for it were something else entirely. Federal funding of abortion was banned by the Hyde Amendment in 1976. But liberals agitating for taxpayer-subsidized abortions have blurred the distinction between access and funding, purposely. In 2012, liberals brought the same confusion to contraceptives. Absolutely no one in this "sex-positive" America of the twenty-first century has proposed a ban on contraceptives. But liberals wanted someone else other than the sex partners to pay for the "protection," whether it was the government or private insurers. To oppose this was to oppose "access" to birth control. That was their game.

Senator Kirsten Gillibrand (D-NY) exemplified the liberal blur that suffused the media narrative, pretending that this new feminist offensive was some kind of lurch backward in time: "I'm dumbfounded that in the year 2012, we still are fighting about birth control." [5]

The Obama administration announced on January 20 that it was giving religious institutions one year to comply with a mandate for insurance coverage of sterilization, abortion-inducing drugs, and contraception in their health plans without a copay. "The government should not force Americans to act as if pregnancy is a disease to be prevented at all costs," insisted then-archbishop (now cardinal)

Timothy Dolan of New York, head of the U.S. Council of Catholic Bishops. "Historically, this represents a challenge and a compromise of our religious liberty."[6]

The same networks that were outraged and scandalized by Komen's temporary cutoff of Planned Parenthood now couldn't find any newsworthy angle.

No member of Congress had voted for this policy—in fact, pro-life Democrats like Representative Bart Stupak of Michigan voted for Obamacare only after they were assured by the White House there would be no taxpayer funding of abortion as written into the Hyde Amendment in 1976. Amazingly, the major media found nothing newsworthy, never mind historic about this. ABC, CBS, CNN, and NBC all ignored it when the story broke. NPR covered it—ready for this?—with a positive tone. The headline on their website: "Administration Stands Firm on Birth Control Coverage."[7]

CBS waited ten days to *mention* it on *This Morning* and provided no subsequent coverage. CNN briefly mentioned the rule when it was announced on January 20, then didn't bother to mention it again for ten days. ABC and NBC waited sixteen days to cover the anti-Catholic ruling, finally citing the new rule on *This Week* and *Meet the Press* on February 5. Only conservative outcry for some media fairness after their Komen feeding frenzy forced the subject to the surface.

After Komen knuckled under to fierce media pressure, the networks mustered a few stories on how the mandate was causing Obama some political heartburn, even including liberal Catholics like Mark Shields panning the president's mandate. Only CBS offered Cardinal Dolan (or any Catholic clergyman or spokesman) an interview to make an argument for the Catholic Church position.[8]

But when the White House announced a "compromise"—never agreed to by the Catholic Church—on February 10, the networks fell back in line. CBS anchor Scott Pelley declared Obama's decision was "one part Solomon, one part semantics." ABC assured viewers that "both the Catholic Health Association and abortion rights groups approved" of the new rules—without noting the CHA was a liberal group not in line with the Catholic Church on abortion that supported Obamacare and wanted to stay on Obama's good side. When the Catholic bishops that night declared the "compromise" was unacceptable, ABC and CBS at least briefly noticed the change. NBC, under bright-eyed Obama fan Brian Williams, never did.

Intolerance when practiced by liberals isn't "news." Across the country, Democrats were pushing Catholic social workers out of helping government social services. In Massachusetts, Illinois, and the District of Columbia, Democrats have insisted on forcing Catholic Charities to quit its longtime assistance in providing adoption and foster-care services because they refused to place children with homosexual couples. The Conference of Catholic Bishops lost a federal contract to aid survivors of sex trafficking because Obama's bureaucrats at the Department of Health and Human Services (HHS) objected that contraceptive and abortion referrals would not be provided.[9]

Do you recall any news coverage of this assault on religious liberty? The colluding media never wanted to concede that Obama was hostile to Catholics. Far better to print the Catholic Church in the kind of negative light that would make opposition a positive exercise. So journalists routinely implied the bishops were sexless old fuddy-duddies who didn't really know their flock or represent their cultural views. The priests only have some of these people's attention for an hour on Sunday, and then Catholics can safely return to the twenty-first century, while the priests return to their pedophiliac ways.

The attacks have been vicious, and effective in demonizing the Catholic Church. But they have not succeeded in squashing opposition to this administration's assault on religious liberty.

Reaffirming the fact that the president's statement was more a PR stunt than an actual compromise, Nebraska and six other states filed suit on February 23, saying that the HHS regulations violated the First Amendment and were an "interference with religious liberty." Incredibly, the networks again ignored this action.

On May 21, forty-three Catholic dioceses and organizations sued the Obama administration over its very narrow idea of how a "religious institution" can be defined under the Obamacare law. This registers as the largest legal action in American history in defense of religious liberty, and against a sitting president. As a news story, it doesn't get more major than this. It was truly jaw-dropping that ABC and NBC completely ignored this action on their evening newscasts, while CBS devoted just nineteen seconds that night to this historic event.[10]

Which isn't to say that the media were uninterested in the Catholic Church. On May 23, *CBS Evening News* anchor Scott Pelley began his newscast by going back to the story of clerical sexual abuse: "Tonight, the Monsignor takes the stand. The highest ranking Catholic Church official ever charged in the child abuse scandal blames a higher power, the former cardinal of Philadelphia."[11]

This is how the media wanted to define the church hierarchy: archaic, tone-deaf, and corrupt.

Then, on May 25, the networks all jumped on a story that the pope's butler was hiding confidential Vatican documents at his house. They offered thirteen stories in five days proclaiming "another black eye for the Vatican" and alleged "corruption at some of the highest levels."

All three networks used highly charged language to portray the church as some sort of criminal enterprise.

NBC's Jim Maceda was happy to wonder out loud about whether "the man closest to the pope may have lifted another veil on the secretive and perhaps illegal activity inside the Vatican itself."[12] The networks had no suspicion that the Obama people had done anything "secretive and perhaps illegal" in rewriting Obamacare. By their measurement, one can conclude that Obama is less ethically suspicious than the pope.

## All Women Are Flukes

Barack Obama was portrayed as the knight in shining armor for the damsel in distress named Sandra Fluke. Democrats intended her to be their star witness at a House Oversight and Government Reform Committee hearing on February 16. They wanted her on the first panel of a religious-liberty hearing along with a Catholic bishop, a Jewish rabbi, the president of the Lutheran Church–Missouri Synod, and an evangelical professor.[13]

Representative Darrell Issa explained that he accepted Democrats' late application for Barry Lynn, head of the leftist Americans United for Separation of Church and State, but dismissed Fluke as an expert. She was merely a student at Georgetown Law School. It didn't matter. The Democrats wanted this painted as a Clueless White Guy panel and knew the media would swallow it whole. Representative Carolyn Maloney (D-NY) asked: "Where were the women?"[14] That question echoed throughout the media—without an obvious rebuttal. Two women spoke on the committee's second panel of the day, but the media found that an inconvenient truth.

With the liberal spin established, a week later, the Democratic Steering Committee invited Fluke to be the star witness at a staged press event. If the Republicans had tried something this partisan—and fabricated—the networks would not have sent a camera, not in a thousand years. But the Democrats could always manufacture "news" when the partisan event favored their allies in the press.

Fluke was celebrated by the liberal media as a perfect representative of All Women: a law school student protesting that the oppressive, intolerant Catholic administrators of Georgetown University must look beyond their ancient and patriarchal views and fund contraceptives for their employees through their insurance plan, as Obamacare intended.

The suggestions was that this poor student spending thousands of dollars annually on her schooling somehow couldn't muster the fifteen or twenty dollars at CVS for her monthly birth control, and someone else should come to the rescue, except somehow the Catholic Church was preventing it. The villain in this tale was Rush Limbaugh, who reacted to Fluke's demand for subsidized contraception by laughing at this nonsense, but then mocked her as a "slut" and a "prostitute." Limbaugh admitted later this was an inappropriate use of words and apologized. This naturally did nothing to assuage a furious press that said absolutely nothing when these words were wielded against conservative women, like when Bill Maher called Sarah Palin a "dumb twat,"[15] or MSNBC's Ed Schultz called Laura Ingraham a "talk slut."[16]

They all failed to report—or even consider—that while many taxpayers would oppose subsidizing birth-control pills on religious grounds, many others would also find that subsidizing contraceptives for people engaging in casual sex makes as much sense as subsidizing their X-rated movies or negligees.

Sensing the opportunity created by the press, President Obama called to offer public support to Fluke, which became another celebrated media event. Fluke went on Andrea Mitchell's afternoon show on MSNBC to thank the president: "He encouraged me and supported me and thanked me for speaking out about the concerns of American women, and what was really personal for me was that he said to tell my parents that they should be proud."[17] The networks replayed that and added that Democrats were gleefully exploiting their outrage in fundraising appeals. *Thank you, Sandra, Thank you, Mr. President!* [All caught on tape, lovingly.]

Conservative Georgetown women were shut out. Andrea Morabito wrote, "Funny how the same side that cries 'Get your rosaries off my ovaries' is the same side saying, 'on second thought . . . please pay for me to have all the sex I want!' The people who espouse 'pro-choice values' are the same people who say religious institutions have no right to choose.

"It costs over $23,000 for a year at Georgetown Law. Sandra, are you telling us that you can afford that but cannot afford your own contraception?" [18]

CNSNews.com reported that despite Fluke's claim that pills cost $3,000 a year, "a Target store only three miles from the law school currently sells a month's supply of birth control pills for only $9 to people who do not have insurance plans covering contraceptives." Even Planned Parenthood's website tells women, "Birth control pills may be purchased with a prescription at a drugstore or clinic. They cost about $15–$50 a month." [19]

Fluke was never portrayed as a radical. Indeed, that's why she was a victim: she was just your normal, everyday student holding normal views. Really? Conservative blogger Stephen Gutowski found that Sandra Fluke advocated that insurance policies shouldn't pay just for contraceptives, but also for sex change operations as well. In a journal article, she complained: "A prime example of direct discrimination is denying insurance coverage for medical needs of transgender persons physically transitioning to the other gender. . . . Transgender persons wishing to undergo the gender reassignment process frequently face heterosexist employer health insurance policies that label the surgery as cosmetic or medically unnecessary and therefore uncovered." [20] Liberal media coverage? Zero.

The Democrats even brought Fluke to their convention in Charlotte, North Carolina, where as a pure partisan hack, she should have lost any claim on victimhood. Sounding like Ted Kennedy's scabrous "Robert Bork's America" speech in 1987, Fluke claimed that in Mitt

Romney and Paul Ryan's America, "It would be an America in which you have a new vice president who co-sponsored a bill that would allow pregnant women to die preventable deaths in our emergency rooms."[21]

As usual, Fluke and her feminist allies were taking a rhetorical flamethrower to the simple notion that taxpayers shouldn't have to fund abortions, a position Ryan supported in the Protect Life Act of 2011. Do you recall a single news report pointing that out?

## Keep Your Probe out of My Virginia

The so-called War on Women reared its ugly head again when the state of Virginia considered requiring women to see an ultrasound image of their unborn child before an abortion. For early pregnancies, this would require a transvaginal probe, not the traditional abdominal ultrasound. Faced with a storm of liberal media outrage, Virginia governor Bob McDonnell said he would support only an abdominal ultrasound.

The leftist assault compared a vaginal ultrasound to rape, and media outlets obediently repeated that. On February 21, *New York Times* editorial page editor Andrew Rosenthal argued that "since most abortions take place in the first 12 weeks of pregnancy, most women will be forced to submit to trans-vaginal ultrasounds, a coerced penetration that in other circumstances would constitute rape under Virginia state law."[22]

Unsurprisingly, the women on ABC's *The View* came unglued on February 16. Whoopi Goldberg complained, "Women will be required to undergo sonograms, ultrasound when they are about to have an abortion and the other one is that if a heartbeat isn't detected, then they will get a trans-vaginal ultrasound which is basically going into the vagina and very intrusive." To ABC's daytime hosts, a transvaginal sonogram before an abortion is intrusive . . . but a transvaginal abortion is not.

Joy Behar then screeched: "It's like, what are we?! What is this, the Taliban now?! What are we, in Afghanistan?! Where are we exactly in this country?" When the panel's Republican-leaning Elisabeth Hasselbeck said the government should never intrude on a woman's body, Goldberg insisted there is no Republican or Democrat stance on this bill, only the "human stance."[23]

The people who wanted a woman *not* to see her unborn baby before killing it were somehow advocating the "human stance."

On MSNBC on February 23, anchor Luke Russert—whose Catholic father, Tim Russert, used to regale audiences about his meetings with and great reverence for Pope John Paul II—allowed pro-lifers to be trashed as rapists. Even the traditional abdominal ultrasound was somehow still a "sex crime" in the war-on-women frenzy at MSNBC. Russert asked liberal Virginia delegate Charniele Herring: "You said the original procedure was akin to rape. Uh, where is this new procedure, do you feel? Is the new procedure still, do you feel, a sex crime, in the sense that it's so invasive?"

Then he asked another War on Women softball. "Was this policy really done backdoors by mainly all males on the Republican side? That seems to be what some reports out of Virginia suggest." Herring replied, "I believe it was. I don't know if a woman was at the table."[24]

In prime time on February 24, MSNBC host Rachel Maddow mocked Governor McDonnell in an interview with Karen Finney: "I know as the Democrats' communications director you'd never call anybody Gov. Vaginal Probe." Finney replied, "I never would, honestly Rachel, I never would have thought that we would be in a position to actually call someone Gov. Vaginal Pro—, Transvaginal Probe. I mean, did you ever think you would be having this conversation on your show?" Maddow replied, "Never. Never in my life. Never, not just in my show, never in my world!"[25]

So at MSNBC, if you stand in the way of government-funded abortions, you hate women. Like Fluke, Finney cast Republicans as literal lady-killers: "I think they're also not paying attention to the fact that women have very much been awakened over the last several months. Again, look at these Republican legislatures and these sort of anti-women bills, you know, having to prove that you were raped in order to, you know, use Medicare, Medicaid, to have an abortion. I mean, some of the, you know, redefining rape, letting women die."

## What Shooting at the Family Research Council?

The liberal media were so unsympathetic to social conservatives in 2012 that they didn't even find it newsworthy when they were shot. Floyd Corkins, a volunteer in the first half of 2012 at the D.C. Center for the LGBT Community, marched into the Family Research Center on August 15 with a 9mm SIG Sauer pistol, denounced FRC's policy positions, and shot a security guard in the arm before being subdued. In his bag, police found fifty rounds of ammunition and fifteen sandwiches from the Chick-fil-A restaurant, which had been treated as notorious by secular leftists for donating to "anti-gay" Christian groups like the FRC and the Fellowship for Christian Athletes.[26]

A "hate crime" to be covered, anyone? Not when the crime was launched against perhaps the preeminent pro-family organization in America. ABC led *World News* with the story on the FRC shooting and saluted the heroic security guard for saving the FRC from a mass shooting in their offices. They were the exception.

CBS gave the story twenty seconds. NBC spent seventeen seconds.[27]

As usual, what helped Obama was news, and what made Obama's side look bad was deemphasized. On both CBS and NBC, the tiny FRC brief was followed by a full story promoting President Obama's new deferral program for illegal alien "Dream Act" students. NBC gave that two minutes, CBS two minutes and fifty seconds.

The newspapers had the story, but some found it equally boring. *USA Today* gave it ninety-eight words on page 3A, beneath other brief items such as "Dallas Gets Tough on West Nile Virus."

Our taxpayer-funded media were silent. *PBS NewsHour* offered nothing. It did have time to announce, "About four million Bumbo baby seats are being recalled because infants can fall out of them." NPR offered no story on *All Things Considered* that night but did find time to report on cheating at a national Scrabble tournament. NPR also skipped it on the next morning's *Morning Edition*, but covered the riveting story of "inter-tribal cattle violence" in South Sudan.

MSNBC's prime-time lineup, starting with Chris Matthews, said nothing about the shooting at FRC—except for Rachel Maddow, who offered a slightly longer brief than Brian Williams. This is the same network that went over the top and around the bend over the fact that someone at a Tea Party rally was peacefully carrying a weapon. So why couldn't they produce one full story on an actual shooting at a conservative office, with the intent to commit mass murder?

CNN covered it, but within twenty hours of the shooting, CNN morning anchor Zoraida Sambolin was unsympathetic enough to argue with a conservative guest, Brian Brown of the National Organization for Marriage, insisting that the left-wing lobby the Southern Poverty Law Center (SPLC) had somehow accurately categorized the FRC as a "hate group." The CNN anchor read from an old pamphlet and insisted the FRC was guilty of "spewing hate" about gay activists, but Brown replied, "By no means can you say just because of a statement like that this is the same as the KKK or the Aryan Brotherhood. That's totally unacceptable." [28]

On the morning after the shooting, the network pattern continued: ABC offered another full story (adding the LGBT-center volunteer connection). By contrast, NBC offered a tiny anchor-read update.

CBS aired nothing, but did find the time for a story on the fortieth anniversary of the movie *Deliverance*. Burt Reynolds in make-believe is somehow more newsworthy than a left-winger aiming to massacre an office of conservative Christians.

Imagine this situation in reverse: a volunteer for the Family Research Council marching into some gay group's headquarters with a gun, and after shouting his opposition to the homosexual agenda, opening fire and wounding a guard before being subdued. Never mind the evening news. This would be "Breaking News!" and for days there would be endless coverage of ongoing conservative hatred and violence.

Instead, this became grounds for liberal humor. On the FX comedy show *Totally Biased with W. Kamau Bell*, the host joked, "Yesterday the Family Research Council, a conservative think tank, was shot up by Floyd Corkins, a liberal protester. Don't worry, nobody was killed. Why? Because it was shot up by a liberal protester. [Laughter] That's not our thing. Our thing is more blogging."

Once the initial shock wore off, new details in the Corkins case still didn't cause one ripple of disturbance in the liberal media. In October, Corkins was indicted on terrorism charges, with no liberal media notice (save a few paragraphs for the locals in *The Washington Post*).

But the story took a deeply disturbing turn on February 6, 2013, when Corkins pled guilty to three charges, including the terrorism charge. Corkins declared in a statement that he "intended to enter the FRC that day to kill as many people as possible and smother Chick-fil-A sandwiches in their faces." How was that not inflammatory enough for news coverage?

Then add this. Corkins explained he used a "hate map" by the SPLC to find his targets, a map showing the locations of groups SPLC designated as "hate groups" that were somehow comparable to the Ku Klux Klan because they were "nationally recognized advocacy groups that openly identify themselves as having socially conservative agendas," especially opposition to gay marriage. It wasn't just the FRC, but also the Traditional Values Coalition and Public Advocate of the United States.

In 2011, the liberal media insisted that Sarah Palin somehow played a role in the shooting of Representative Gabby Giffords by putting a target on her district. But no one would touch the Corkins story and dare to connect the SPLC to the FRC shooting in the very same way they had slammed Palin. CNN, whose anchor protested that the SPLC was right to smear the FRC as a "hate group," only announced beforehand (in a fifty-eight-word news brief) that Corkins would appear in court. There was no report after the outrageous new information that Corkins took the SPLC's map as he planned a killing spree of conservatives.[29]

Unsurprisingly, a Nexis survey found there was no Corkins report on ABC, CBS, NBC, MSNBC, NPR, or PBS. *The New York Times* disposed of it with a 145-word Reuters dispatch on page 17. *USA Today* and the *Los Angeles Times* couldn't find an inch of space for it.

*Washington Post* reporter Ann Marimow relayed late in her story: "At the time of the shooting, conservative commentators also accused media outlets of giving the shooting less coverage than other gun crimes because the perpetrator was a liberal. Those accusations resurfaced Wednesday."[30] Those weren't accusations. They were the unavoidable facts.

Hate has always been a conservative quality. It could never be located inside Obama's liberal base. They aren't haters, just bloggers.

# CHAPTER 7

# The Gaffe Patrol

Only Republican misstatements are a media target.

One of the most obvious tricks of the media is how they declare themselves to be entirely objective when deciding which statements by politicians and their campaign aides qualify as "gaffes" and which do not. Gaffes, as everyone knows, can be dangerous, sometimes extremely so, when they can easily be used to cause a candidate to lose an election. *Gaffes* strengthen media caricatures in the public mind, creating character sketches in twenty-five words or less, whether it's Dan Quayle's misspelling of *potato* or Sarah Palin's alleged remark that she could see Russia from her house (something uttered not by Palin, but by her *Saturday Night Live* impersonator, Tina Fey).

The best gaffes are those that entertain, which makes them easy to spread. They are also a handy pretext for the howls of liberal outrage (and laughter) that resound throughout the media echo chamber. The manufacture and promotion of alleged gaffes by conservative candidates is therefore one of the main tricks liberal journalists use to shape and influence public opinion, and ultimately, tilt elections.

The shamelessness of the media's decision-making process was displayed after the 2008 election, when *The New York Times* ran a story on the Obama campaign unironically headlined "Near-Flawless Run Is Credited in Victory."[1] Reporters uniformly thought the Democrat campaign was superbly managed, but check out this sentence below the headline: "And they played it safe when they could, as in the selection of Senator Joseph R. Biden Jr. of Delaware as his running mate."

Biden? As everyone knows, Joe Biden was the Senate's leading gaffe machine, with a long history of embarrassing statements to his credit. In June 2006, he asserted: "You can't go to a 7-Eleven or a Dunkin' Donuts unless you have a slight Indian accent." During the campaign itself, Biden delighted conservative radio hosts by praising Obama as "bright, clean, and articulate." He was a caricature, a massive liability. Then again, Democrats know they can count on their friends in the press to ignore or excuse any embarrassing misstatements by their candidates. They could turn a gaffe machine into something bright, clean, and articulate. All it takes is an airbrush with whitewash.

Liberal journalists have a repetitive tendency to praise their favorite candidates as incredibly skilled campaigners. Ultimately, they are congratulating themselves for keeping the Democratic campaign humming. Exhibit A is Bill Clinton's national career, from Gennifer Flowers forward. Journalists have continuously oohed and aahed that Clinton is a masterful politician, even as they were crushing information about the latest bimbo or intern, or campaign donors from China and Indonesia. Would they really give Bill Clinton a pass with his sexual affairs if he had an *R* on his résumé?

But to read *The New York Times*, you would think the media had nothing to do with Obama looking like a champion and McCain or Romney being shrouded in gloom. For example, in that same 2008 *Times* story, the "paper of record" expressed amazement that John

McCain would bungle so badly in declaring, right as the economic crisis began on September 15, 2008, "the fundamentals of the economy are strong." How could a credible candidate say such a thing? Was he completely clueless? Out of touch? What planet was he living on? The Obama machine quickly turned this supposed howler into a barrage of free advertising, and the colluding media turned it into "news."

What the *Times* story papered over were McCain's contextualizing remarks: "People are frightened by these events. Our economy, I think still, the fundamentals of our economy are strong. But these are very, very difficult times. And I promise you we will never put America in this position again. We will clean up Wall Street. We will reform government. And this is a failure."

But never mind the nuance. Chris Matthews began his *Hardball* broadcast: "Why is John McCain talking like Herbert Hoover? Depression or just depressing?"[2] NBC anchor Brian Williams relayed that "a Democratic politico said to me this week, if the Democrats do their job, they'll make this 'fundamentals of the economy' quote to McCain what 'mission accomplished' was to President Bush."[3]

After the media pounding was done, the *Times* wrote that this episode proved, self-fulfillingly, "the McCain campaign team often seemed to make missteps and lurch from moment to moment in search of a consistent strategy and message, while the disciplined and nimble Obama team marched through a presidential contest of historic intensity learning to exploit opponents' weaknesses and making remarkably few stumbles. The story of Mr. Obama's journey to the pinnacle of American politics is the story of a campaign that was, even in the view of many rivals, almost flawless."

This kind of thing would never happen to Obama. Consider how the press handled his statement in a press conference on June 8, 2012, in the midst of a heated reelection campaign, that "the private sector is doing fine." There was no kinder context. It was a whopper of a gaffe. This came at a time when there was still 8.2 percent unemployment and a falling median household income, housing was still in the tank, and monster deficits looked like a wrecking ball on the national economy. Conservative media had a field day. Rush Limbaugh said Obama couldn't possibly believe that, unless his idea of "doing fine" was building up government programs like food stamps.[4]

In response, the Obama media closed ranks around their candidate. NBC morning anchor Ann Curry played defense with her guest, MSNBC leftist Chris Hayes: "He [Obama] is right in saying that the private sector is doing better than the public sector, is he not? And so that was his point, that this comment was taken out of context."[5]

Felicia Sonmez of *The Washington Post* asked, "Should out-of-context statements be out-of-bounds in campaigns?"[6] *New York Times* reporter Jackie Calmes also felt the need to explain what President Obama meant, and specifically ruled out comparisons to McCain's similar gaffe four years before: "McCain . . . spoke in September 2008 as the financial system was already imploding, and his comment underscored his well-known and self-acknowledged unfamiliarity with economic policy." Yet Calmes complained, "for the day at least, the damage was done, as Republicans hijacked the news cycle with their barrage against Mr. Obama's six words in a professorial 29-minute exchange."[7]

So there you have it: When Obama loses his natural media advantage, it's not because he erred or misspoke; it's Republicans "hijacking the news cycle."

## Romney Lives Up to "Predatory Capitalist" Stereotype

On January 9, 2012, Mitt Romney told an audience that his health-care plan would allow them to choose and dismiss insurers and health-care providers. "I want individuals to have their own insurance. That means the insurance company will have an incentive to keep you healthy. It also means if you don't like what they do, you can fire them," he said. "I like being able to fire people who provide services to me."

It fit their stereotype. Liberal reporters leaped at the chance to play up the cartoon of Romney as a greed-head venture capitalist. All the networks reported the story, and many of them publicly donned caps as informal campaign advisers. *Washington Post* columnist Dana Milbank had an idea: "one of President Obama's first reelection ads." ABC's David Muir reported "Mitt Romney is getting grilled over his own words in the last 24 hours. At one point telling an audience he understands what it feels like to worry about losing your job. At another rally today, he said he likes being able to fire people." Muir added, "The Obama campaign's senior strategist quickly calling Romney's words a 'rare moment of candor.'"[8] David Axelrod's Twitter account set the narrative: the words "Rare moment of candor" appeared onscreen.

*Face the Nation* host Bob Schieffer eviscerated Romney on *CBS This Morning*. Apparently the incompetent Romney was "looking for every way he can try to lose and drive down his percentage of victory. . . . I guess the only thing worse you could say, in a time like this, when people are out of work is that Herbert Hoover is my hero or something like that. It just boggles the mind."[9] This is one of those dirty tricks, building a sense of hangman's gloom under the guise of "objective" psychoanalysis and commentary on campaign strategy.

On NPR's *Morning Edition*, reporter Ari Shapiro insisted that putting the statement in context wouldn't help: "Never mind that he was talking about insurance companies. The quote played right into the stereotype of Romney as a predatory capitalist, who made his fortune ruining people's lives."[10] As we'll soon see, NPR's Snidely Whiplash spin here was the polar opposite of the way the taxpayer-subsidized reporters handled gaffes that played into what could be called "the stereotype of Obama as an arrogant socialist elitist, who built his political career on trashing job-creating business executives as predatory capitalists."

But the context was plain: Romney was simply saying if someone fails to provide a satisfactory service, it's nice to have the freedom to fire them, instead of being stuck with a badly performing provider—especially with your health care. Liberals who expect people to put up with government bureaucrats no matter how badly they perform were never going to grant a point on this one.

The same maneuver was repeated on February 1 when Romney said on CNN, "I'm in this race because I care about Americans. I'm not concerned about the very poor. We have a safety net there. If it needs repair, I'll fix it." CNN morning anchor Soledad O'Brien, a very aggressive Obama supporter on-air, used a quote from columnist Kathleen Parker to double-bash Republicans, asserting that Romney couldn't connect with people while the "far less perfect Newt Gingrich can attract support against all reason."

ABC's David Muir used the clip to do a "greatest gaffes" package of recent vintage. "He again said, if the safety net for the poor has holes in it, he would work to repair them. But it comes after a string of moments, critics say, [that] make Romney seem un-relatable. 'Corporations are people, my friend.' Betting Rick Perry '10,000 bucks.'" Add the "I like being able to fire people" rerun.

Muir even added a radio clip of Rush Limbaugh on the air: "He makes himself a target with this stuff. He comes across as the prototypical rich Republican. It's gonna make it harder and harder and harder to go after Obama." Limbaugh was right—making our point, not theirs.

On CBS, Jan Crawford recycled three Romney gaffes: the "very poor," the "10,000 bucks" bet, and the "fire people." On NBC, Peter Alexander noted "[a]ll this dragging Romney off message on a day he intended to enjoy as a victory lap." It's typical for liberals to pro-claim Republicans are being dragged off message at the very mo-ment they're doing the dragging. Alexander then added a clip of his MSNBC colleague Chris Matthews: "It is not a good life to be poor. And anybody who thinks so is oblivious."

Alexander saved his greatest-gaffes reminders for the next morn-ing on NBC: "And as for those gaffes it's not the first time for Mitt Romney. Remember that he said corporations are people, or there was the $10,000 bet during the debate, and that's part of the prob-lem. Just one more item that could go onto the president's re-election campaign team's Greatest Hits reel against Romney."

The networks were always eager and willing to put Obama's fa-vorite clips into heavy rotation.

## "You Didn't Build That"

On July 14 in Roanoke, Virginia, President Obama told overheated people in the crowd to make way for "paralegals," not paramedics. Then he made a statement that shocked anyone who has built a busi-ness, large or small. He arrogantly proclaimed that no one is really responsible for growing their own companies. The credit should go elsewhere, especially to government:

"If you were successful, somebody along the line gave you some help. There was a great teacher somewhere in your life. Somebody helped to create this unbelievable American system that we have that allowed you to thrive. Somebody invested in roads and bridges. If you've got a business, you didn't build that. Somebody else made that happen."

How was this not a gaffe of monstrous proportions? Fox News and conservative talk radio aggressively reported the damaging re-

mark, yet ABC, CBS, and NBC failed to mention it for four days—
and then only after Romney made it the centerpiece of a campaign
speech.[11]

Romney responded sharply: "The idea to say that Steve Jobs didn't
build Apple, that Henry Ford didn't build Ford Motor, that Papa John
didn't build Papa John Pizza, that Ray Kroc didn't build McDonald's,
that Bill Gates didn't build Microsoft, you go on the list, that Joe and
his colleagues didn't build this enterprise, to say something like that
is not just foolishness, it is insulting to every entrepreneur, every in-
novator in America, and it's wrong."[12]

ABC, CBS, and PBS all avoided this eloquent and devastating re-
joinder, and NBC ran only a few words of it before interrupting. On
the July 18 *Today*, NBC viewers heard, "To say that Steve Jobs didn't
build Apple, that Henry Ford didn't build Ford Motor, that Papa John
didn't build Papa John Pizza," and then reporter Peter Alexander
stopped in mid-sentence like he had a bad case of attention-deficit
disorder. He switched to a soundbite of Romney spokesman John
Sununu saying Obama needed to "learn how to be an American,"
followed by an outraged Obama campaign attacking Sununu for attacking the president's patriotism. Romney couldn't be allowed to go
on offense for more than ten seconds before being slapped right back
into a defensive crouch.

Then consider the print press. *The Washington Post, USA Today*,
and *Los Angeles Times* couldn't locate Romney's best attack. *The New
York Times* must have inspired NBC by running the Romney quote
alongside Sununu. Reporters Trip Gabriel and Peter Baker even insisted Team Romney lost the day: "The off-message moments blew
a bit of fog over what the Romney campaign had intended to be a
coordinated series of sharp attacks on Mr. Obama over free enterprise."[13]

On the July 26 *CBS This Morning*, cohost Charlie Rose was in full
damage-control mode, claiming the president was misunderstood.

"But the President was saying, if you look at the full context of that, he was talking about building roads to these businesses, and they didn't build the roads; where the Romney campaign seems to try to indicate that he was saying, they didn't build the businesses." CBS political analyst John Dickerson replied, "Exactly, and what the President was saying, is it takes a village."[14] This is a little like claiming Obama could have never been elected president without the highway system. They'd laugh at that in a liberal newsroom.

But it was NPR that took the prize. On the July 25 *All Things Considered*, they revisited the controversy by offering listeners a whopping seventy-second soundbite of Obama in Roanoke. But first, anchor Audie Cornish turned to NPR White House correspondent Scott Horsley, who spent ninety seconds explaining that the businesses the Romney campaign was using to rebut Obama's remark were all beneficiaries of government largesse. This claim was especially egregious: "There's Applegate Insulation in Michigan. They note on their website that customers may be eligible for tax incentives if they install their product." That, to liberals, is a government grant to business.

This was exactly the attack Democrats at the Center for American Progress were promoting on their blog, Think Progress. Horsley never told his listeners where he received these talking points.[15]

When Obama said, "Look, if you've been successful, you didn't get there on your own," he knew whereof he spoke. Everything he's gained in politics has been granted to him by an adoring news media.

## "Mitt the Twit" Gets Heckled (by Media) Abroad

On May 28, President Obama infuriated the leaders of Poland while honoring the late Jan Karski with the Medal of Freedom. He said that Karski had smuggled himself into a "Polish death camp" in order to witness the Holocaust. (It was a German Nazi death camp *located* in Poland.) The Polish government demanded an apology and this stirred in the European papers and on the Agence France-Presse wire. Despite the international incident, ABC, CBS, and NBC aired nothing on the gaffe. Instead, ABC's *Good Morning America* and NBC's *Today* both found "news" in the microscopic scoop that the Romney campaign had misspelled "America" in an iPhone app.[16] Omissions like these helped Obama preserve his reputation as (a) intelligent about history and (b) not a jerk who sticks it to our allies.

Nor was it a story in the fall of 2011 that after endless reports about George Bush's low standing in the Arab world, the Arab American Institute found that Barack Obama, who allegedly was taking the globe by storm, was now viewed even more unfavorably than Bush was at the end of his tenure.

But when Mitt Romney traveled to Europe and Israel in late July, the long knives were out. NBC anchor Brian Williams sat down with him in London on July 25 and they talked about the Summer Olympics there. Noting Romney's role in bringing the Winter Olympics to Salt Lake City in 2002, Williams asked, "And in the short time you've been here in London, do they look ready to your experienced eye?" Romney calmly replied that it was hard to know. "There are a few things that were disconcerting, the stories about the private security firm not having enough people, the supposed strike of the immigration and customs officials, that obviously is not something which is encouraging."

This was the NBC anchor's gentlest question in a hostile interview, and it matched what Williams reported the week before: "Today, the man whose company was hired to provide security at all the Olympic venues admitted his company screwed up." A member of Parliament told NBC it was a "humiliating shambles for the company." The word "fiasco" also came up in reports on ABC and CBS.

But Romney's remarks—a mild-mannered echo of the network's

own reporting—still became an international scandal. On July 27, NBC's Peter Alexander was holding up *The Sun* of London, owned by Rupert Murdoch: "Here is a headline from one London tabloid. It reads 'Mitt the Twit.'"[17] Alexander deemed the comments a "political firestorm" and played a clip of an unidentified British reporter snidely noting, "If he's here to make friends, he has got a funny way of showing it."

Over on CBS, Jan Crawford eagerly held up the same tabloid and asked, "Can you see it? 'Mitt the Twit.' That's not the type of headline you want." Crawford labeled Romney's remarks "a storm in the tea cup [that] started a trans-Atlantic war of words."

On *Good Morning America*, George Stephanopoulos played up Romney's "stumble out of the gate." ABC's David Muir insisted that the "Brits are boiling." CNN reporter Jim Acosta's online piece was headlined "Romney Trip Begins in Shambles." Acosta did a roundup: "He's the 'Party Pooper' in the *Daily Mail*, 'Nowhere Man' in the *Times* of London and 'Mitt the Twit' in *The Sun*."

*The Washington Post* was especially harsh. "Someone should have told Mitt Romney that they still speak English in England," lectured *Post* political reporter Chris Cillizza as he awarded Romney the "Worst Week in Washington" award that Sunday.[18] "Romney's 'performance' could well be forgotten by the time his European trip concludes with visits to Poland and Israel. But a headline that reads 'Mitt the Twit' (as *The Sun*'s did) probably isn't a good thing for a presidential candidate." Which is precisely why it received so much play in the liberal press.

As Romney's trip continued, so did the negative spin from the evening newscasts. Despite pressing economic and foreign policy problems, both ABC and CBS on July 27 highlighted trivial details such as Romney's motorcade in London getting stuck in traffic—which underlined the candidate's warning about the Olympics.

On July 29, *CBS Evening News* correspondent Jeff Glor piled on:

"After a rough first stop on his seven-day overseas trip, Mitt Romney was hoping Israel would go better than Britain. The day was not error-free," for Romney "had to back off an aide's suggestion he supports an Israeli strike against Iran's nuclear program."

The same abuse erupted in Poland. Romney tried to avoid the press, so they yelled at him . . . about their gaffe story line. The questions could have passed for heckling, like "What about your gaffes?" and "Do you feel that your gaffes have overshadowed your foreign trip?" A Romney aide then admonished reporters to "show some respect" for the "holy site for the Polish people" and cursed at them. CNN reporter Jim Acosta lectured the aide in his report. "[P]eople get tired, people get testy, but you also have to keep your cool at the same time." [19] Reporters can heckle and scream at Romney, but the candidate's team had to "keep cool."

Media Research Center analysts examined all twenty-one ABC, CBS, and NBC evening news stories about Romney's trip to London, Israel, and Poland between July 25 and July 31. Virtually all of these stories (eighteen, or 86 percent) emphasized Romney's "diplomatic blunders," from his "golden gaffe" at the Olympic games to "missteps" that offended the Palestinians.

Over seven days, Romney netted fifty-three minutes' worth of stories from the three networks. In comparison, Obama's 2008 tour through the Middle East and Europe resulted in ninety-two minutes over eight days. In July 2008, Barack Obama's international tour took him to Israel, where, in an attempt to show toughness over Iran, the then-senator incorrectly told reporters that he was a member of the Senate Banking Committee. But no one at the networks noticed any "gaffes" or "missteps" there.

In fact, NBC's Brian Williams could hardly contain himself in Berlin. On the July 24, 2008, *Nightly News*, he trumpeted, "the man from Chicago, Illinois, the first ever African-American running as presumptive nominee of the Democratic Party, brought throngs of people into the center of Berlin, streaming into this city, surging to get close to him, to hear his message."

On the same program, Andrea Mitchell was beside herself, marveling at the large crowds: "It's hard to figure out what the comparison is. What do you compare this with?"

Then–*CBS Evening News* anchor Katie Couric couched the visit in the most favorable terms, hyping, "Barack Obama extends the hand of friendship to Europe." Mark Phillips insisted, "They've been calling this the Obama show in Berlin, his appeal here part exotic politician, part rock star. And a rock-festival-sized crowd of more than 200,000 gathered to see him."

At the end of Romney's tour, Brian Williams summed up the week as concluding "with controversy, some hurt feelings, and some raw tempers." Obama was always a "rock star," and Romney's visit was always "marred by missteps." Conservative columnist Charles Krauthammer blasted the news coverage, calling the trip "a major substantive success" that was wrapped "in a media narrative of surpassing triviality." [20]

## No Chains for Joe Biden

Joe Biden can put Dan Quayle to shame in making mindless statements. He is a walking embarrassment to Barack Obama, to the point where there was open speculation about replacing him on the ticket. But the press corps continually covered for him, hailing Biden for his "candor" and "authenticity," which are positive spin for "a ticking talk bomb."

On August 14, 2012, Biden implied to a mostly black audience in Virginia that by pushing deregulation and spending reductions, the Republicans somehow favored reinstituting slavery for blacks: "Look at what they [Republicans] value, and look at their budget. And look what they're proposing. [Romney] said in the first 100 days, he's going to let the big banks write their own rules—unchain Wall Street. They're going to put y'all back in chains."

This was more than a gaffe. It was an insult of the highest order, a crass attempt to fuel the flames of racial animosity against the GOP.

There were only three full stories on ABC, CBS, and NBC, and nine other mentions in passing.[21] *The New York Times* buried the fuss on page A14 in a five-paragraph story under the soporific headline "A Metaphor Draws Notice."[22]

While pundits on MSNBC argued Biden was "almost gaffe-proof" because everyone expected him to bumble, CNN's Soledad O'Brien pushed Representative Emanuel Cleaver (D-MO) to admit the obvious: "You cannot tell me that if in fact we were talking about Mitt Romney saying a line like that . . . that people would not be going crazy and crying about race-baiting and talking about tone and tenor and coded language. I think we would, wouldn't we?"[23] In fact, many reporters were furious and charged racism when Newt Gingrich insisted (accurately enough) that Obama was the "food stamp president."

Biden was so gaffe-prone reporters might be excused for missing some of them. In the same speech, Biden urged the Danville, Virginia, crowd, "With you, we can win North Carolina again!" Only ABC noticed this . . . in one brief mention. Meanwhile the networks all ignored Biden's claim to still be living in the last century: "Folks, where's it written we cannot lead the world in the 20th century in making automobiles?"

On NBC's *Meet the Press*, former GOP speechwriter Peggy Noonan complained, "If it had been a Republican vice presidential candidate who had made those gaffes . . . the subject today of the panel would be: 'How stupid is this person, can this person possibly govern?'"

But reporters had a pattern of either ignoring Biden's gaffes or declaring them lovable burps. In 2008, Biden turned to wheelchair-bound Missouri state senator Chuck Graham and told him to "stand up, Chuck, let 'em see ya." [24] This should have been heavily played by any TV show that wanted an entertaining gaffe clip. Unquestionably, it would have, had it come from Paul Ryan. But it was never aired. In October of that year, Biden said: "The No. 1 job facing the middle class . . . is a three-letter word: Jobs. J-O-B-S, jobs." Again, zero coverage. As vice president, that skip-or-excuse tendency remained:

- On March 17, 2010, Biden mistakenly told Irish prime minister Brian Cowen that his mother had passed away. "His mom lived in Long Island for ten years or so. God rest her soul. And—although, she's—wait—your mom's still—your mom's still alive." [25] (In 2012, Biden mocked Paul Ryan for quoting his father, without really noticing that Ryan's father had died when he was a teenager.) Network coverage? Zero.

- Later in 2010, Biden turned to President Obama as he prepared to sign the Affordable Care Act (Obamacare) and on live national television whispered, "This is a big fucking deal." Had he ever noticed a big live microphone before? But the Democratic National Committee made T-shirts, and the media papered it over. It received just four network stories and came with excuse-making spin. ABC's Bill Weir smiled and said, "Joe Biden gives us another gem." Since the official story line was that Biden was a gaffe machine, none of his individual misstatements were held against him. ABC's Juju Chang confirmed this view: "I think a lot of people are giving Joe Biden some slack on this." Her colleague Robin Roberts added: "He's been known to kind of let things fly a little bit."

- In October 2011, Biden told *Human Events* editor Jason Mattera that if Republicans didn't pass the White House jobs plan, "Murder will continue to rise, rape will continue to rise, all crimes will continue to rise." Broadcast network coverage? Zero, except one brief mention by Jonathan Karl on ABC's *This Week*. CNN's Kate Bolduan showed the exchange and called it a "fiery, unscripted moment." [26]

• In October 2012 at a rally in La Crosse, Wisconsin, Biden claimed Planned Parenthood "under law cannot perform any abortions." [27] In reality, the organization is the largest abortion conglomerate in the country, performing more than 333,000 "terminations" a year in 2011, about one every ninety-four seconds. Network coverage? Zero. But just two days earlier, these programs devoted a combined five minutes to Mitt Romney's statement to *The Des Moines Register* that "there's no legislation with regard to abortion that I'm familiar with that would become part of my agenda."

Despite all this, reporters poured sugary prose on Biden. On August 17, *Politico*'s Jonathan Martin mourned "a media culture that implores politicians to seem authentic but is ready to punish them when they really are—but the challenge is especially exquisite in Biden's case."

Martin wasn't kidding about being in awe. "He is an irrepressible, garrulous and emotive politician, who's flourished and fumbled through 40 years in national office by practicing politics the old-fashioned way—from the gut and without much script. He's as fine a one-on-one politician of any officeholder of his generation, a talent especially prized because it is not a particular gift of Obama's." [28]

On October 8, former *Newsweek* reporter Howard Fineman oozed at the *Huffington Post* that "what Biden lacks in academic chops he more than makes up for in street smarts; genetic political talent (his Secret Service code name is Celtic, enough said); an eye for and an ability to earn the loyalty of brilliant, dedicated staffers; an instinct for the jugular; and a thirst for political combat." [29]

After the election, *New York Times* reporter Mark Leibovich—the one that marveled "You ate your tweeties" to Obama strategist David Axelrod—wrote an article headlined "How This Got to Be a Biden Moment—In a few short months, the vice president has become a star."

Leibovich wrote: "In a few short months, the motor-tongued, muscle-car-loving heartbeat-away hell raiser has been transformed from gaffe-prone amusement to someone whose star shines as brightly as his teeth." [30]

Who was responsible for this transformation? Reporters not only protected him, they argued that Biden was a tremendous asset to the White House, not a "gaffe-prone amusement"—just as the White House would want it.

## Akin to Hurt Republicans on Abortion

On August 19, 2012, Representative Todd Akin, Missouri's GOP nominee for the U.S. Senate, appeared on the Fox station in St. Louis with Charles Jaco, a leftist and former national reporter for CNN and NBC. (This is a man who had attacked conservative bloggers as lacking "opposable thumbs." [31]) Jaco asked a series of pointed questions about what he felt were Akin's extremist conservative stands, including on abortion. When Jaco asked Akin if he supported abortion after a rape, Akin replied, "First of all, from what I understand from doctors, that's really rare. If it's a legitimate rape, the female body has ways to try to shut that whole thing down." [32]

The answer was plain stupid. The phrase "legitimate rape" is politically insensitive, if not monstrous, and the notion that the female body can prevent pregnancy from a rape is just medically wrong. But notice what started a national media feeding frenzy: a former national reporter pushing Akin on the toughest abortion decisions. Did Jaco ever try this with the incumbent, Senator Claire McCaskill?

Here's your answer. After boasting that his Akin interview had "created worldwide headlines," Jaco asked McCaskill two weeks later, "Would it be unfair to describe you as pro-choice?" No, she said. "So when you heard Congressman Akin's comments, were you taken aback, or how did it strike you?" [33]

Jaco also described McCaskill on air as a "centrist Democrat." In reality, McCaskill failed to cast a single pro-life vote in her first term in the Senate, earning a perfect 100 score from NARAL Pro-Choice America and a perfect zero from the National Right to Life Committee. She voted for everything the left wanted, from embryo-destroying stem-cell research to UN funding for communist China's forced one-child policy.

But the national media leaped all over Akin's medical gaffe. The ABC, CBS, and NBC evening newscasts and morning shows offered a massive ninety-six minutes (and forty-five segments) of coverage over three and a half days. [34] The disparity between Akin and gaffe-prone Vice President Biden's "chains" controversy from the week before was 5 to 1. Biden was excused. Akin was savaged.

For an illustration of liberal-media hypocrisy over the rape issue, consider this. When Juanita Broaddrick appeared on *Dateline NBC* in 1999 and accused President Clinton of raping her in a Little Rock hotel room, providing a friend who shared her hotel room who confirmed her badly swollen mouth and ripped panty hose after her encounter with the then-attorney general of Arkansas. The three networks produced a paltry few minutes of coverage: two news reports, two briefs, and parts of three interviews. They had no ardor for the idea that our president was a rapist.

But they had ninety-six outraged minutes for Akin's inappropriate *comments* on rape.

"Todd Akin sparked a firestorm," reported Natalie Morales on NBC.[35] CBS reporter Nancy Cordes said Akin's comments "caused a firestorm" and added, "National Democrats are already seizing on his comments as they try to push the notion that Republicans are out of touch when it comes to women's health."

National Democrats define national "news." It's all right there in the transcript.

*NBC Nightly News* anchor Brian Williams piled on with the echo chamber: "Firestorm. A congressman's words about rape rocket across the country . . . women's issues are front and center again." Introducing the lead story moments later, Williams announced that Akin's comments "exploded well beyond the borders of Missouri."[36]

Correspondent Andrea Mitchell predicted—promoted?—political disaster: "Republicans fear their hopes for the White House and control of the Senate could turn on what happened at a St. Louis TV station. . . . In a race where the President had a 15-point advantage with women voters in the last NBC News/*Wall Street Journal* poll, Republicans were reeling."

Days later, Mitchell was still shoveling, as Akin was described as "inflicting unforeseen and great damage on the national party. . . . [O]nly days before their convention, Republicans remain trapped in a national debate about abortion and rape."

On MSNBC, Chris Matthews began, "Let me start tonight with this right-wing assault on women, this caveman view of the sexes that has now shown its ugly head. . . . Finally, we meet the missing link, the evidence that the party of Lincoln cannot get in bed with the most freakish elements of the right."[37]

But no one in the media noticed "freakish elements of the left" that defend abortion at any time, for any reason. Instead, consider the hard line of *New York Times* columnist (and longtime reporter) Thomas Friedman, as proclaimed on the September 2 *Meet the Press.*

"I'm a Planned Parenthood Democrat on the issue of choice. And I think that that is where the country should be. That is where many, many women in this country are. And I'm glad there are people running for the presidency who will defend that position. Period. Paragraph. End it." [38]

Somehow, it was not a gaffe in Media Land when Joy Behar, a panelist on ABC's *The View*, implied in a *Boston Herald* interview that the Republicans wanted to kill and destroy the female half of the human race: "People like Akin that think the vagina is some sort of Magical Mystery Tour and men like that are running this country. This is why I took this job. I have a job already at *The View*. But I feel this country is going downhill because of people like Akin and Ryan and Romney. They're trying to kill us and destroy us." [39]

No one should fail to notice that Akin was favored in this race before this imbroglio. *The Rothenberg Political Report* considered the race a toss-up that "tilts Republican" and called McCaskill "the Senate's most endangered incumbent." Akin led McCaskill in eight of nine polls in the year leading up to the gaffe. This answers the question why "national Democrats" would pounce and define it as "news." If McCaskill had been ahead by 15 points, this would never have been covered, even noticed.

## Mauling Mourdock, Omitting Obama Abortion Extremism

The same dynamics were in play in Indiana, with conservative candidate Richard Mourdock locked in a tight race with Representative Joe Donnelly. Once again, the local media pounced on the rape exception on Mourdock in an October 23 debate.

"I believe that life begins at conception. The only exception I have for—to have an abortion is in that case for the life of the mother. I just—I struggle with it myself for a long time but I came to realize that life is that gift from God, and I think even when life begins in that horrible situation of rape that it is something that God intended to happen."

A defensible moral argument? Assuredly, and we will defend it as such. A smart political statement? Absolutely not. It was a gaffe. Unlike Akin, Mourdock wasn't asked directly about a rape exception. A consultant might have winced that he would bring it up unprompted or that he would discuss God's will—always a "fruitcake alert" for secular liberal journalists—but it's appalling that Mourdock was punished for sticking up for the humanity of a baby conceived in rape.

Like clockwork, all three networks leaped on the story. On *CBS This Morning*, reporter Jeff Glor spread the Obama spin: "Senior Obama campaign adviser David Axelrod tweeted, 'Mitt's man Mourdock apes Akin in Indiana debate reflecting a GOP that is way out of mainstream.'"[40] Glor made sure to play a soundbite of Akin, to underline Axelrod's tweet.

None of them were going to consider for even two seconds a debate between religious authorities on rape and abortion, or inviting a pro-life speaker who was conceived in rape, like Ryan Bomberger or Rebecca Kiessling.

This is how insular it was. On the October 26 *Morning Edition*, NPR reporter Scott Horsley explained, "The Obama campaign has been reminding women this week about Governor Romney's support for Indiana Senate candidate Richard Mourdock, who sparked controversy when he said that abortion is wrong even in the case of rape, because if a rape victim becomes pregnant, it's what God intended."[41] Obama's campaign then took that audio (starting with "Indiana") and placed it right into a campaign radio advertisement, followed by a man and woman discussing how nutty Mourdock was.[42]

A few days later, reporters were still hounding Romney to distance himself from the apparent slime of Mourdock. On the Bill Press radio show, producer Peter Ogburn reported, "Our friend Sam Youngman from Reuters—who we have on the show as often as we can, because he's on the road. But he was on the road yesterday. He said at a breakfast stop, me and Steve Peoples from Associated Press and Lisa Lerer from Bloomberg asked Romney repeatedly about Mourdock."[43]

Clay Waters at TimesWatch reported a Nexis search found seven *New York Times* stories that allowed Mourdock's Democratic opponents to paint him as "extreme" or "extremist." The photo caption accompanying Mourdock's picture continued that DNC-friendly pattern: "Richard Mourdock's opposition to abortion in cases of rape has given Democrats an opening to paint Republicans as extremist."[44]

On the October 28 CNN show *State of the Union*, anchor Candy Crowley wouldn't ask about Benghazi damage for Democrats, but she pounded Republican National Committee (RNC) Chairman Reince Priebus about damage to those anti-woman Republicans: "Does it hurt the party image to have these issues out there in a way that makes the party or that is portrayed as making the party look unbending and, you know, anti-woman, as is described in the Obama ad?"[45]

Priebus stated the obvious—no party has a monopoly on gaffes— but the network news squashers specialize in ignoring the obvious. Obama and Biden can say the most foolish or obnoxious things, and the networks skip them. None of them, not even Crowley, found it "anti-woman" when Arizona's Democratic Senate candidate Richard Carmona joked during a debate that his male moderator was "prettier" than Crowley.[46]

This is where media bias on deciding what is a gaffe (and what is not) matters. It was never a gaffe when Senate candidate Barack Obama ran in 2004 (and 2008, and 2012) after having voted four times in the Illinois Senate to allow abortions after the "fetus" became a baby outside the womb. Or forbidding medical professionals from saving the life of an aborted baby who survived. More than one nurse has recounted the heartbreaking account of rocking a baby, even hiding in a closet . . . while the little one died. Absolutely nobody with a press pass found that idea ideologically extreme or scientifically bizarre.

The Media Research Center found that from the launch of his candidacy in January 2007 through the end of the primaries in June 2008, just six out of 1,289 network evening news stories about Obama (0.46 percent) mentioned his position on abortion, and none discussed it in any detail. They never devoted one TV story to examining Obama's abortion record.[47] The same thing happened in 2012. Obama and liberal reporters are in complete agreement, so there's nothing objectionable to report.

To any reporter who cared enough to investigate, Obama's record was self-evidently extreme. In one debate in 2002, in a great spasm of ideological ardor, he argued it was unnecessary to add a doctor (other than the abortionist) to evaluate the medical condition of a baby who survived the abortionist's attempt to "terminate the pregnancy." Obama said that was political, not medical: "adding an additional doctor, who then has to be called in an emergency situation to come in and make these assessments, is really designed simply to burden the original decision of the woman and the physician to induce labor and perform an abortion."[48] *The Weekly Standard* found audio of this debate in August 2012. The network coverage was zero.

CBS briefly covered Obama's remarks to a right-to-life question at Rick Warren's church yet completely ignored his infamous declaration that deciding when life begins is "above my pay grade." They just ran the quote "I am pro-choice. I believe in *Roe vs. Wade*. And I come to that conclusion not because I'm pro-abortion, but because ultimately I don't think women make these decisions casually."

This is the same Senator Obama who declared in April 2008 that he wouldn't want his daughters to be "punished with a baby" for having premarital sex without contraceptives. CBS ignored that, too, as did ABC. (NBC skipped it except for a clip on *Meet the Press.*) There is apparently nothing harsh Obama can say about babies that will be considered newsworthy by Barack's disciplined message providers in the media.

# CHAPTER 8

## The Fluff-My-Pillow Interview Tour

*One servile interviewer is much better
than a rowdy press conference.*

One extended dirty trick in the presidential campaign extended far beyond the news media. Time and again, Obama was welcomed (and beloved) on so many soft-soap shows, interviews Mitt Romney wouldn't do. Romney thought it wouldn't be presidential to appear on *Saturday Night Live*, although Obama and McCain both tried that in 2008. A sore-loser Romney fan might suggest that perhaps you should be president before worrying about being presidential.

It is natural for any politician to seek out the media venues that make him look the best, the most personable and appealing and articulate. It's also natural that when Republicans do that, the "objective" media will be slamming the Fox News Channel.

When Vice President Dick Cheney accidentally shot a hunting partner in the face in Texas in 2006, CBS reporter Jim Axelrod announced, "The Vice President chose to make his first public comments on Fox News Channel's *Special Report*, a broadcast Mr. Cheney sees as friendly and has turned to before." That was polite compared to CNN's Jack Cafferty, who lamented, "It didn't exactly represent a profile in courage for the Vice President to wander over there to the F-word network for a sit-down with Brit Hume. I mean, that's a little like Bonnie interviewing Clyde, ain't it?"[1]

This tsk-tsk routine happened in 2012, too. On September 19, 2012, NPR reporter Brian Naylor announced that in the wake of the 47 percent tape, "Mitt Romney went to the friendly confines of the Fox News Channel yesterday afternoon in another round of damage control." But then Naylor turned to Obama: "Last night, at a taping of *Late Night with David Letterman* on CBS, Mr. Obama acknowledged, in his words, 'We all make mistakes.'"[2] The Letterman show wasn't the "friendly confines," even when the host was oozing about the president's weight: "180 sure looks good on you."

Despite the news media's "slobbering love affair" with Barack Obama, he has rarely reciprocated. In August, *The New York Times* hailed Obama as "Avid Reader, and Critic, of the News." Reporter Amy Chozick touted how Obama, a "voracious consumer of news," told columnists in private meetings about the concept of "false balance"—that reporters "should not give equal weight to both sides of an argument when one side is factually incorrect. He frequently cites the coverage of health care and the stimulus package as examples," the sources said.[3]

He actually wanted his most massive government interventions to be chronicled without any "false balance" from the other side.

Chozick cited just one example, a *USA Today* story from 2009 headlined "Traffic Set to Slow as Stimulus Gears Up." How could it be factually incorrect that the "stimulus" meant a boom in road and bridge work in Obama's first summer as president? This wasn't about facts, it was about spin.

As Mitt Romney emerged as his Republican opponent, the thin-skinned president signaled he was interested in coasting to reelection by largely ignoring the "accountability press," the serious, probing, policy-wonkish, pin-down-the-fact kind of reporters. He preferred sappy interviews with late-night comedians and infotainment hosts—and network "news" anchors who achieved the perky, unchallenging wavelength of *Entertainment Tonight* questioners.

On May 4, veteran White House reporter Keith Koffler penned an insightful blog post titled "Obama Abolishes the Press Conference." He noted, "President Obama has held just one full length, multitopic, solo press conference in the last six months, effectively abolishing the most accessible venue for American citizens to observe the thinking and learn the views of their leader."[4]

As the Republican candidates were pounded by Brian Williams or George Stephanopoulos in debates in late 2011 and early 2012, Obama stuck to a few obligatory pressers with foreign leaders—which are often drab affairs for White House reporters. Only four or five questions are allotted, they're usually dragged out by the necessity of translators, and they're split between the two heads of state, and usually focus on the foreign policy matters between the two countries.

And then the stall. Slowly, ponderously, in as boring a fashion as can be mustered, the president takes forever to answer—or not answer—the question.

On May 21, President Obama took questions for 44 minutes in Chicago, and then all that came after that were two tiny opportunities: 25 minutes in Mexico on June 20, and a quick 22-minute briefing room drop-by on August 20.[5]

Three months after the election, *Washington Post* media reporter Paul Farhi underlined that Obama hadn't granted an interview to the *Post* since early in his first year, with the same snub for *The Wall Street Journal* news reporters. The president hadn't spoken with *The New*

*York Times* since the fall of 2010. *The Boston Globe* and the *Los Angeles Times* never had an interview with Obama as president—and neither did his (supportive) hometown papers in Chicago.

Obama-loving *Post* editor Kevin Merida—whose term as national editor coincided almost exactly with Obama's—pooh-poohed this lack of access. Who needs access to the president when you run a newspaper in the nation's capital? Interviewing the president "isn't essential to what we do day to day. We've demonstrated we can produce great White House coverage . . . without ever getting an interview with the president."[6] After the election, the *Post* promoted Merida again, to managing editor, the number-two slot.

This supine posture was a sharp contrast to the Bush era, when the media subjected itself to a frenzy of self-loathing after the last press conference before the Iraq War on March 6, 2003. They had access to Bush but were far too easy on him, they thought. ABC White House reporter Terry Moran made waves by telling the *New York Observer* that Bush left his journalism colleagues "looking like zombies."[7] *New York Press* columnist Matt Taibbi suggested reporters were routed, like Texans at the Alamo: "The entire White House press corps should be herded into a cargo plane, flown to an altitude of 30,000 feet, and pushed out, kicking and screaming, over the North Atlantic." By October 2003, PBS omnipresence Bill Moyers mentioned Taibbi's gibe to the left-wing website Buzzflash.com and added, "I'd say it was more a collective Jonestown-like suicide. At least the defenders of the Alamo put up a fight."[8]

This was not the way the left described the press and Obama. In fact, Moran marked Obama's arrival in office by gushing to an interviewer that he was "the first President since George Washington to be taking a step down into the Oval Office."[9] When Obama finally held a real press conference after his reelection on November 14, *Nightline* anchor Moran didn't focus on the questioners. He just praised the swagger of the answerer. "But the real takeaway from the White

— 144 —

House today? There's nothing like a re-election to give the President a jolt of confidence. . . . Today, an Obama smackdown." [10]

Moran was the zombie he had warned against.


## "Obama the Puppet Master"

On February 18, 2013, the insider newspaper and website *Politico*—another liberal media organ Obama had denied an interview—published a big story by Mike Allen and Jim VandeHei headlined "Obama the Puppet Master." The article began: "President Barack Obama is a master at limiting, shaping, and manipulating media coverage of himself and his White House."

Even when journalists are willingly manipulated, they have to praise the man pulling the strings?

It quickly grew silly when the duo denied the reality that "a liberal press willingly and eagerly allows itself to be manipulated." They argued, "Conservatives assume a cozy relationship between this White House and the reporters who cover it. Wrong. Many reporters find Obama strangely fearful of talking with them and often aloof and cocky when he does. They find his staff needlessly stingy with information and thin-skinned about any tough coverage." [11]

The words to focus on here are "strangely fearful" and "needlessly stingy." Liberal reporters were telling *Politico* that Obama has no reason to fear them and no need to scrimp on information as if they will harm him in the polls. Memo to Obama: *We all voted for you, we're your allies*. But even if reporters were asking serious questions in the briefing room and complaining to the press officers, none of that emerged in what viewers were watching at home.

Some sounded angry. ABC Radio reporter Ann Compton, who has covered every president since Gerald Ford, told *Politico*, "The way the president's availability has shrunk to the press in the last two years is a disgrace." Aides don't explain how big meetings developed policy in secret, and many of them never appeared on his official schedule. "This is different from every president I covered. This White House goes to extreme lengths to keep the press away."

In response to *Politico*, former White House reporter Matthew Cooper penned an online piece for *The Atlantic* titled "Is Obama Too Mean to the Media, or Are Reporters Just Whiny? It's mostly the latter." He claimed every White House grew more protective of its president, and told reporters to "just grow up." [12] Cooper admitted that he worked at *Time* for seven years with Jay Carney, now Obama's press secretary. He got married in 1997 to Mandy Grunwald, one of the original Bill Clinton bimbo-crushers, so Democratic press manipulation wasn't frowned upon when he worked with Carney.

Cooper was not alone. Todd Purdum of *Vanity Fair*, a former *New York Times* reporter who married Clinton press secretary Dee Dee Myers, hit the same note, smacking the "silly season" for the White House press corps. "They contend that White House beat reporters for the major newspapers and networks are most likely to know the issues, ask tough and unpredictable questions, and hold the president to account. Most of these reporters are fine, hardworking journalists, and many are wonderful people; a good number are my friends. But, as a *class,* they are the world's biggest whiners. I know because I was once one of them, and a first-class whiner myself. I don't think their argument holds water."

Purdum noted that Towson University professor Martha Joynt Kumar, who studies the president and the press, counted that Obama consented to 674 one-on-one interviews in his first term, compared to only 217 by George W. Bush. [13] But this misleads. Those Obama interviews routinely went around the briefing-room crowd to supine top anchors and dazzled local-TV hosts. Obama would rather have an interview with Robin Roberts or Diane Sawyer or Barbara Walters, and leave Compton and Jake Tapper on the sideline.

At the end of 2011, with the reelection year approaching, Barbara Walters hosted the president for an hour in prime time. Oh, how the tough questions flew. Like, she asked, "I know that you answer people's letters all the time. And what we thought that we might do, we asked middle school and high school students to throw a few questions. I'd like to read their questions: 'If you were a superhero, and you could have one superpower, what would it be?'"

Obama answered, "You know, I've talked to Malia about this. We both agree that flying seems like it would be a pretty good thing to be able to do."

Walters posed a self-lampooning question about reincarnation to the First Lady: "If you were to die and come back as a person or a thing, what would you want it to be?" This appeared to be too much for Mrs. Obama, as she interrupted mid-question, "Oh, God, Barbara." Then Walters observed, "I'm looking at you. You're holding hands. That's very sweet. How many years married?" The president said "twenty next year." Walters cooed: "And still hold hands?"

Then out came the Babwa Wawa dagger as she told the audience: "The Obamas' marriage has always been a political asset, not so for every politician, like Republican candidate Newt Gingrich, who has had to address questions of whether infidelity is fair game during a presidential campaign."[14]

Not that Walters wasn't capable of hardball interviews. Ask Sarah Palin, who witnessed Walters in a year-end "Most Fascinating People of 2010" interview telling Palin that people find her "scary" and blaming her for Republican Senate losses and repeating Katie Couric's insulting question about whether she was reading anything.[15]

Michelle Obama appeared on ABC's *The View* on May 29, and Walters began by asking her, "There have been rumors—if the president is not reelected [hands raised to mouth, eyes wide as saucers, dramatic 'God forbid!' face]—or that in the future, that you might consider running for political office." Michelle Obama said the rumors weren't hers. Walters insisted, "Would you ever? . . . You would be a very popular candidate." [16]

On September 25, the president and First Lady appeared again on *The View* as Obama avoided Benghazi questions from real journalists, and cohost Sherri Shepherd put them through this gauntlet of inquiries.

1. "President Obama, are you a romantic kind of husband?"

2. "I heard that there's a plaque in Chicago. It marks the site of your first kiss. Tell us about that first kiss."

3. "You guys have a ritual where, now, First Lady, you go to bed at ten in the evening. Your husband comes to bed at one in the morning. But you have a ritual where he tucks you in at night. What is that?"

Here was the toughest question from Barbara Walters: "Would it be so terrible if Mitt Romney were elected? He was governor. He will probably be a little more moderate. . . . My point is would it be disastrous for the country if Mitt Romney were elected?" Obama said no, but he didn't just want the economy to "survive" under Romney, he wanted it to "thrive" under Obama. [17]

Three weeks and a day later, Ann Romney appeared without her husband—no doubt because in September 2008, cohost Whoopi Goldberg asked John McCain about his view of upholding the Constitution: "Do I have to worry about becoming a slave again?" To which Joy Behar joked, "she's picturing herself on the plantation."

Mitt stayed away, and still the difference in aggression was stunning. Barbara Walters asked Mrs. Romney about her husband flip-flopping on abortion. Behar asked, "Do you think that access to contraception and abortion is an economic issue?" Goldberg argued

Mrs. Romney would be "talking to the mothers whose children are coming home in bags, you know, from wars . . . so how will you explain to them that your sons haven't gone?" Whoopi wrongly asserted that Mormons were pacifists who didn't serve in the military. No one asked Obama why he didn't serve in the military. They were too busy asking about plaques honoring the Obamas' first kiss.

Walters even stooped to pushing a Romney son, Josh, sitting in the front row of the audience, if he agreed with his brother Tagg that there are times he feels he'd like to "take a swing" at President Obama.[18]

This underlines the bizarre game of the allegedly softer interview venues. The Obamas could land the safest of softball interviews in TV environments that the Romneys would have to consider potentially devastating booby traps. One couple knew and expected a valentine. The other couple could only imagine the serious potential for hardballs, gaffes, and controversies.

So in the closing days of the fall campaign, Obama would go on Nickelodeon to be interviewed by liberal former TV news reporter Linda Ellerbee, and children. Romney bailed out. Obama would go on MTV to be interviewed by veejay Sway Calloway and college-age voters. Romney would not. Obama was fawned over by David Letterman. *Time* magazine described it as "pretty much like a stump speech with prompts from Letterman and commercial breaks." Romney knew he could not—just remember Letterman expressing his desire for Romney to be jailed for the Seamus-cartop-carrier story.

There was no concept of fair play or equal time in formats where low-information voters were being addressed by Obama. It was a slam dunk for Obama's media advisers as they "microtargeted" their voting blocs, ultraconfident that Obama could use these shows to seem cool, funny, relatable—and Romney could not.

## Making Gay "History" with Robin Roberts

ABC went soft on the president when he selected them to make news, an announcement that would thrill Hollywood and many of Obama's most enthusiastic campaign fundraisers: "I think same-sex couples should be able to get married."

The White House handpicked *Good Morning America* cohost Robin Roberts, and cohost George Stephanopoulos led into the interview by praising her: "Boy, do you know how to make a splash. A little news from the President yesterday. And, Robin, what a watershed moment. You know, whatever people think about this issue, and we know it's controversial, there's no denying when a president speaks out for the first time like that, it is history."

Roberts replied: "And let me tell you, George—I'm getting chills again—because when you sit in that room and you hear him say those historic words, it was not lost on anyone that was in the room like that." Would those chills have been there if he had embraced traditional marriage? Reporters get chills when he speaks Liberal.

During the ABC interview, Roberts offered several softball questions, including one about Mother's Day. The closest Roberts came to a conservative viewpoint was mentioning that as Team Obama has criticized Romney for changing positions on social issues, "Do you see where some people might consider that the same thing, being politics?"

Obama stopped short on imposing gay marriage on all fifty states, and Roberts did tone down the goo briefly by insisting, "But Mr. President, it's not been being worked out on the state level. We saw that Tuesday in North Carolina, the 30th state, in essence, to announce its ban on gay marriage."[19] Obama gave very long, "thoughtful" answers uninterrupted by the network.

Media reports were explicit that the Obama White House chose

Roberts because of her reputation for warm and fuzzy news, not to mention her race and even her age. "The White House went with Robin because of her personal rapport, their friendship, the past interviews—but also her race [black], even her age," one producer at ABC said to *Politico* media reporter Dylan Byers. "There is a very strong, very basic connection there." Think Oprah.

Byers added: "By giving the interview to an African-American and Christian—two groups whose opposition to same-sex marriage has been significant—the White House may have been aiming to make Obama's announcement more palatable to groups that differ with his support for gay marriage."[20]

At ABC, Roberts rarely if ever handles political interviews in the morning—George Stephanopoulos hogs them. Roberts offered a "warmer, gauzier" and less combative presence, former CNN White House correspondent Frank Sesno told Paul Farhi at *The Washington Post*. The White House wanted a "conversation across the back of the fence," not a newsmaker interview: "If you're the White House and you have to deal with something this white-hot, do you want to engage this as a news story or as conversation across the back of the fence?"

Gay activists agreed. Fred Sainz, a publicist for the gay-left Human Rights Campaign, also praised the selection to Farhi. "I thought the selection of Roberts was genius," he said. "She comes across as the neighbor you'd be happy to have a cup of coffee with. That's the way to frame this issue, as an ongoing conversation with the American public."

ABC News spokesman Jeffrey Schneider said Roberts had a reputation as "direct but fair." But do the Republicans get to have a "conversation" on ABC when they take on a very controversial social issue?

In the fall of 2007, the Bush White House offered an interview to Juan Williams to mark the fiftieth anniversary of school desegregation in Little Rock, but NPR refused to let the White House pick an interviewer. NPR insisted it would select the reporter—so Williams conducted the Bush interview for Fox News.[21] (This was an early sign that NPR was going to end up firing Williams for being too Fox-friendly.) ABC didn't play by those rules.

It's not surprising that when Roberts interviewed Ann Romney on July 19, she was tougher on the challenger's wife than she was with the president. She toed the Democrat line by expressing dissatisfaction with the Romneys putting out only two years of tax returns: "Both Bushes gave multiple years, ten and 12 years. President Obama gave seven years of tax returns. Your husband has been adamant about only the two years that will be released. Why will he not follow the example of others on both sides of the aisle?"

After Mrs. Romney reiterated that her husband wouldn't release more than two years and that they had nothing to hide, Roberts hectored, "Why not show that then? Why not release the—because then it's a moot point and people move on."[22]

## Charlie Rose Calmly Babbles like a Brook

In July, Barack and Michelle Obama sat down with *CBS This Morning* cohost Charlie Rose for an interview on *Sunday Morning*, the placid little magazine show that ends with video of moments in nature like a babbling brook.

One might have expected that CBS would focus on the plight of every family struggling with unemployment or a house that's underwater financially, or facing its loss of religious liberties with a federal government drunk with power. Instead the interview started with "questions" like these from Charlie Rose:

- "It's not a bad place to live. [The White House.] . . . Well, you got a basketball court; you got a tennis court. You have a fountain. You can see the Washington Monument."

- "How are you going to spend your summer? . . . What is summer vacation?"

- "You didn't have all of these important things to do, and you could travel to anyplace in the world, where would you want to go? What would you want to see and experience?"

- "Does this place change you?"

It seemed obvious to the audience that Charlie Rose was channeling his inner Barbara Walters. The "What kind of tree would you like to be?" question was on the tip of his tongue.

Then there was the marriage question to the president. "I read you, though—this, that I found fascinating. You said, 'I trust her [Michelle] completely, but at the same time, she's also a complete mystery to me in some ways. It is that tension between familiarity and mystery that makes for something strong.' Is that even more so now, and in this place?"

Rose said the original quote came from 1996, but its American debut was a *New Yorker* puff piece that coincided with the Obama inauguration in 2009. CBS was sitting down with the Obamas in 2012 and asking a repeat of a stale question used to promote the Obamas at their highest political summit.[23] You can tell where CBS is happiest. It is forever January 2009.

In fact, Rose showed Obama a *Newsweek* cover from the first inauguration: "Take a look at this. That's four years ago. . . . This was also a time of 'Yes, We Can,' 'Hope and Change.' What happened to that, because that's not the narrative today?" Obama lamented, "I haven't been able to change the atmosphere here in Washington, to reflect the decency and common sense of ordinary people—Democrats, Republicans and independents—who I think just want to see their leadership solve problems. And, you know, there's enough blame to go around for that."

Rose followed up: "And do you blame yourself, in part, because, I mean, you had this confidence—that you had the skills that would allow you to bridge the gap." Obama replied: "I think there's no doubt that I underestimated the degree to which in this town, politics trumps problem solving." [24]

That's the sentence CBS plucked out to lead the whole program: Obama, sad that "politics trumps problem solving," as if that kind of behavior never happened among the Democrats. Reread Obama's answers. He blamed everyone for his failures—everyone but himself. That wasn't a takeaway?

In January, Rose's cohost Gayle King had interviewed Michelle Obama on the occasion of a new book simply called *The Obamas*, by *New York Times* reporter Jodi Kantor. Michelle Obama insisted that she got along wonderfully with every staffer in the White House and complained that she was tagged as nosing around in the West Wing policy decisions. "That's been an image that people have tried to paint of me since, you know, the day Barack announced, that I'm some angry black woman," she sniffed.

After the interview aired, Rose noted that "there seems to be a nice chemistry there. I mean, you've known this person for a long time." King acknowledged that, "I think we should say it's no secret here at the table that we're friends."

No one told viewers that on page 42 of Kantor's book, she placed King right in the inner circle on the night of the first inauguration: "At 1:00 am, the Obamas returned to the White House for the real celebration, a private party for their family and closest friends and allies—downstairs, in the entertaining spaces, not upstairs in the home that they still had not really seen that day. Celebrities including Oprah Winfrey and Gayle King mingled with new cabinet officials, the First Lady's relatives from the South Side, and the president's best friends from Chicago." [25] Obviously CBS hired King in part because she was friends with the Obamas. It's what makes that industry and the Obama administration indistinguishable.

## NBC Slow-Jams Its News for Obama

When Obama came through the curtain of *The Jimmy Fallon Show* on April 24, the crowd unleashed a screaming standing ovation reminiscent of the Beatles on *The Ed Sullivan Show*. Then they "slow-jammed the news," which was really just Obama making a campaign speech as Fallon's band played bedroom-eyes soul music in the background.

Obama pandered to the young audience by opposing any increase in interest rates on federally supported student loans. "I've called on Congress to prevent this from happening. What we've said is simple: now is not the time to make school more expensive for our young people." Yeah!

Fallon followed up by uttering embarrassing lines in a bumbling Barry White basso profundo like "Awww yeah. You should listen to the president. Or as I like to call him, the Preezy of the United Steezy." Move over, Bill Clinton. Obama is the coolest person in the room.

After Obama attacked Republicans, blaming them for raising interest rates on college students to keep taxes low for billionaires, Fallon added: "Mmm, mmm, mmm. The Barack Ness monster ain't buying it. . . . And the President knows his stuff, y'all. That's why they call him POTUS, which means person on top—what is it?" Obama replied, "Jimmy, POTUS stands for President of the United States." Singer Tariq Trotter then sang in tribute: "He's the POTUS with the mostest!" [26]

Fallon ended this spectacle later by saying, "We don't take sides politically on this show." Few would remember that six months earlier, Congresswoman Michele Bachmann was greeted with the Fallon house band performing an instrumental version of an obscure 1980s tune titled "Lyin' Ass Bitch." [27]

Obama was performing in the place of Fallon's usual slow-jammer, *NBC Nightly News* anchor Brian Williams, who desperately wants people to think he's hip and funny. Williams provided a series of soft-touch interviews with Obama as he prepared for a re-election campaign. The first came on September 11, 2011, the tenth anniversary of the al-Qaeda terrorist attacks. Williams asked how he and Mrs. Obama feel when they walk through Arlington National Cemetery, and he followed up by typically observing, "We caught the president yesterday in an emotional and reflective time." Williams routinely touted Obama as "reflective" maybe because he routinely asked gaseous please-reflect-for-me questions.

When they ran more interview footage on the morning of September 12, the toughest question Williams asked was if Obama remembered he had told NBC's Matt Lauer in 2009 that if the economy didn't turn around he'd be a "one-term proposition." Obama replied that "you know, what we've done is we've been able to stabilize the economy. And, you know, that is an enormous accomplishment." Unemployment stood at 9.1 percent in the August 2011 report, and Obama was bragging. Williams and NBC aired no fact-check or follow-up to that whopper of a lie.

On the September 12 *Nightly News*, Williams suggested Obama's economic poll numbers weren't great—but he also obediently slammed the Republicans. He informed Obama, "Members of your base are asking when are you going to get your Harry Truman on?" That would seem to include his journalistic supporters, like Williams. Then Williams disparaged those Tea Party hard-liners for poisoning the political well:

"All of this, of course, is if you get what you want in a highly toxic atmosphere, and it sure looked to me from the outside like you went

into the debt-ceiling fight thinking, 'Surely they will do the states-
manlike thing. Surely they won't go there.' And it seemed to me as if
Speaker Boehner was coming to you, saying, 'Look, if it were up to
me we would do this, but I've got this membership problem.' And
they went there, and now that marks our politics." [28]

Once again, Obama was painted by the networks as the least partisan player in Washington and Republicans as the worst kind of self-
interested obstructionists. Just days before, on September 7, 2011,
Williams moderated a Republican debate at the Reagan Library in
California. He infuriated Republicans with withering questions, such
as telling Texas governor Rick Perry, "Your state has executed 234
death row inmates, more than any other governor in modern times.
Have you struggled to sleep at night with the idea that any one of
those might have been innocent?" [29]

It doesn't matter that Williams works for NBC, which was owned
by General Electric, which has donated millions to the Reagan Library. The Republicans had only themselves to blame for selecting
him as their moderator.

Team Obama also selected Williams for an interview with the
president in May to celebrate the first anniversary of the president's
order to kill Osama bin Laden. Williams played up the drama to
celebrate the president's bold risk-taking, as if Obama would have
been impeached if the mission were unsuccessful: "If this had failed
in spectacular fashion, it would have blown up your presidency, I
think, by all estimates. It would have been your Waterloo, and, perhaps, your Watergate, consumed with hearings and inquiries. How
thick did the specter of Jimmy Carter, Desert One hang in the air
here?" Williams had worked briefly in the Carter White House, so he
could relate.

The NBC star attempted to feel Obama's pain, that he had to keep
the operation quiet: "Keeping this secret also meant going on about
the business of the presidency. Touring that awful storm damage in

Alabama while knowing at that very moment U.S. Navy SEALs were already on the move halfway around the world. You had to go to Tuscaloosa. You had to go have fun at the Correspondents' Dinner. Seth Meyers makes a joke about Osama Bin Laden . . . How do you keep an even keel? Even when we look back on the videotape of that night, there's no real depiction that there's something afoot." [30] Williams even labored to confirm on this prime-time program that the White House sacrificially lowered itself to ordering food from Costco to avoid this big mission from being detected.

While the capture or killing of bin Laden was a major objective of American policy for ten years, this Williams interview wasn't a nonpartisan national moment. It was a reelection special, touting Obama's "even keel" and masterful decision-making. In mid-August on *Rock Center*, reporter Natalie Morales interviewed Ann Romney, and both that show and the *Today* show featured Morales grilling her with four argumentative questions on the family tax returns: "A lot of people still are asking why not be transparent and release more than the 2010 and the estimates for 2011." Mrs. Romney responded forcefully: "Have you seen how we're attacked? Have you seen what's happened?"

Morales implied the Romneys resented any questions: "It's been in the press quite a bit. Now are you angry that it's been in the press? I mean, should you not be questioned about your finances?" Romney pushed back: "We have been very transparent to what's legally required of us. But, the more we release, the more we get attacked. The more we get questioned, the more we get pushed."

Morales completely ignored Senate Majority Leader Harry Reid's completely unsubstantiated and false accusation on the Senate floor that Mitt Romney didn't pay any taxes at all. Morales also urged Mrs. Romney to compliment the Obama family: "Clearly the campaign has gotten to be so negative on both sides. Is there a positive that you see in President Obama and the First Lady?" Romney described how she admired Michelle Obama for taking on the obesity issue and the First Family being a "role model" for others.

Apparently that wasn't enough Obama praise for Morales, who demanded more: "What about President Obama? What can you say, a positive that we don't often hear?" Mrs. Romney said, "I think all of us are so proud that America backed him and I think that piece of it is never going to go away that, that America is a place where anything is possible and anyone can dream whatever they want and anyone can accomplish anything they want. And he is the embodiment of that and I think it's a thrill for all of us to have him as a President." [31]

For the media, the thrill of electing Obama was intense and never-ending. Even the Republicans were being pressured to agree.

# CHAPTER 9

# The Convention Curse

Intolerant, fundamentalist racist conservatives
versus inspirational centrists.

The national party conventions used to be an enormous four-day roadblock across prime-time television, a major undertaking for network news operations, with squads of reporters spreading across the convention floors. Over the last twenty-five years, the parties have been losing their grip. Increasingly, pompous anchors have openly complained of being manipulated—the most famous being ABC's Ted Koppel leaving the 1996 Republican convention in San Diego halfway through, huffily declaring, "This convention is more of an infomercial than a news event."[1]

The more that party organizers have made conventions staged and milquetoast affairs, the more audience interest has waned. The networks went from granting the parties three hours of prime time, then two, and then one. By 2012, the networks granted only an hour for the nomination on the last hour on Tuesday, Wednesday, and the big acceptance speech on Thursday night.[2] Before the prospect of

Hurricane Isaac ruined the GOP's plans for a Monday night starring the nominee's wife, Ann Romney, the networks all plotted to skip over her speech for reruns of *Castle*, *Grimm*, and *Hawaii Five-O*.[3]

There's an upside—the decline of air time left a lot less room for Republican-bashing. To put that one in its proper perspective, we counted 125 questions on the networks in four nights about Dan Quayle's draft status or possible adultery at the 1988 RNC convention.[4] But the network tactics and dirty tricks have stayed remarkably consistent.

In every Republican convention we've been studying at the Media Research Center since 1988, no matter whether the candidate was a Reagan conservative or a McCain moderate, the anchors and pundits have scorned the Republicans as ultraconservative, too exclusionary and hostile to women and minorities, too mired in scandal, and too negative in their attacks on Democrats. In short, they were painted as an all-around turn-off to independent voters.[5]

By contrast, at every Democratic confab we've taped and studied, whether the candidate was liberal like Michael Dukakis or more moderate in tone like Bill Clinton, the networks painted the Democrats as almost disturbingly centrist, free of ethical problems, and stuffed full of "inspirational" addresses as speakers slashed the Republicans as—well, ultraconservative and hostile to women and minorities.[6] Their tone was promotional, aiming to help the Democrats build a "bounce" in the polls, and it was usually successful.

The same tactics emerged in 2012. *New York Times* political writer Adam Nagourney performed the quadrennial newspaper ritual with a spin line that media liberals have been using since liberalism consolidated its grip on the Democrats: "Some leaders expressed worry that the turn to contentious social issues in the days leading up to the Republican National Convention, where the party platform is likely to embrace a tough anti-abortion stance and strict curbs on immigration, could undercut the party's need to broaden its appeal.

Many of them said they feared it was hastening a march to becoming a smaller, older, whiter and more male party." [7]

This was also the *Times* spin going into the 2010 midterms. The Tea Party was going to shrink the GOP and make it older, whiter, and more male. Facts never get in the way of a good liberal-media story line. Nagourney merely echoed what then-NBC anchor Katie Couric was pushing on Quayle almost 20 years earlier, in 1992, and which countless journalists have asked countless times since: "Do you think the Republican Party has grown, or become, too exclusionary, too intolerant, and that this kind of rhetoric is divisive and counterproductive?"

Both parties have factions, but Nagourney argued that the divisions in the Republican Party were the worst in (faulty) recent memory. The *Times* headline: "A Party in Principle Fears Danger in Factions." When it ran in the other Times Company–owned paper, *The International Herald Tribune*, the headline was "Republicans Vow Unity; Reality Is Less Tidy." [8]

This is how the *Times* defines "reality." Try putting the words "Democratic Party" within twenty-five words of "factions" in a Nexis search. The results will stun you. Over the last two years, the *Times* has exclusively used these terms only in stories on foreign countries. One editorial briefly referred to "factions" among Democrats . . . referring to the election of 1860. [9]

For the TV stars, CBS's Norah O'Donnell predicted that she and her colleagues would harass Republicans on social issues: "Everybody is going to be asking about Akin, abortion rights, women's rights, et cetera, during the Republican convention." [10] Shortly before the convention opened on Tuesday, Chris Matthews told *Hardball* viewers to "be on the alert for the tribal messages, the war drums of racial division." [11]

No speaker at the Republican convention in Tampa would match the war-drum nastiness of one journalist, David Chalian, a former

ABC and PBS man working for Yahoo! News. The convention was delayed by a day as Hurricane Isaac passed over Tampa, prompting nasty references to Hurricane Katrina. NewsBusters posted video of Chalian cracking into an open microphone about the Romneys: "They are happy to have a party with black people drowning." [12]

Guess how many networks (other than Fox News) covered this gaffe, even after Yahoo quickly fired Chalian, despite his apologies? CNN mentioned it days later on its media-in-review show *Reliable Sources*. The rest of the networks stayed silent, even MSNBC, the ones who were listening intently for conservative "war drums of racial division." Chalian even drew support on Twitter from PBS anchor Gwen Ifill: "One mistake does not change this. David Chalian is God's gift to political journalism." [13]

By contrast, NBC anchor Brian Williams exemplified the network "news" template in a September 6 interview with top Obama aide Valerie Jarrett. He worried out loud that Team Obama was "in for a good savaging" in a forthcoming book by Bob Woodward: "You, I guess, have to play mistake-free ball now for 60 days, hope for nothing but positive coverage. That's a tall order." [14]

It sounded like a tall order that Williams would lunge to fulfill. There was no mention of Woodward's book on the *NBC Nightly News* before the election, and Woodward made no book-promoting appearance on *Today*.

## Reading from the DNC Instructions

The network stars were shameless enough to quote Democrats at the Republicans.

In an interview with former Florida governor Jeb Bush, NBC *Today* cohost Matt Lauer repeated shrill attack lines from deputy Obama campaign manager Stephanie Cutter to question the honesty of Paul Ryan's vice presidential nomination acceptance speech: "'Forty minutes of vitriol and half a dozen previously debunked attacks.' Was it an honest speech? Or was it just a campaign convention speech?" [15]

ABC's instant analysis of Paul Ryan's RNC address included former Democratic operative George Stephanopoulos noting "we saw how much this crowd loved it" . . . before immediately adding, "I got an e-mail from a top Democrat saying the speech was audacious in its dishonesty." Stephanopoulos added in his own words that the speech was "brazen in some of these claims." [16]

When *CBS This Morning* interviewed Paul Ryan on the first morning of the Democrats' convention, cohost Charlie Rose quoted Obama: "Here is what the President said in asking the question about fixing the economy. He said what grade he would give himself. He said, 'I would say an incomplete, but what I would say is that steps that we have taken to saving the auto industry, and making sure that college is more affordable, and invest in the clean energy and science and technology and research. Those are all the things that we're going to need to grow over the long term.' That's from the President." (Ryan replied that an "incomplete" was a terrible answer from the president after four years on the job.)[17]

Republicans were constantly on the defensive. When Lauer interviewed New Jersey governor Chris Christie, he asked three consecutive questions about Romney failing to release more than two years of tax returns, and then closed by slamming an offhand Romney joke about not needing to see his birth certificate. Lauer lamented: "Governor Romney made a comment at a rally, I think it was on Friday and he said no one has ever asked to see my birth certificate, an obvious reference to the birther debate. Is it funny—he says it was a joke. Is it funny to, to kind of pay attention to a fringe group and question the very legitimacy of the President of the United States' citizenship?" [18]

Lauer didn't note, and obviously didn't care, that the Obama campaign actually raised money off the birth-certificate issue, selling mugs and T-shirts mocking the conspiracy theory.[19]

But a week later, when Lauer's cohost Savannah Guthrie interviewed liberal Harvard professor Elizabeth Warren, a candidate for the U.S. Senate, there was no tender regard for Romney's biography. Guthrie asked: "Is it your job here, as you understand it, to argue that Mitt Romney is the personification of that Wall Street greed and excess?" Then Guthrie again urged her to bash Romney: "Do you think Romney's Wall Street background disqualifies him from caring about the middle class or knowing what to do about the middle class?"[20]

When *CBS Evening News* anchor Scott Pelley interviewed Romney on the Monday night of the Republican convention, Pelley lectured the nominee about how his moderate-Republican father would be dismayed. "This Republican Party that you're leading is not your father's Republican Party. He opposed Barry Goldwater in 1964, when this car was built. He was for—a passionate advocate for government support for housing for poor people. I wonder how you would explain this Republican Party to your father?"[21] Can anyone imagine Pelley asking President Obama about his late parents without the mandatory handkerchief and dewy eyes?

A week after the Democratic convention closed, Pelley touted his latest Obama interview. "There was a remarkable moment of candor when he told us the sacrifices he makes being President wouldn't be worth it except for one thing. Listen for it!"

Obama boasted that all the lost freedom, of being unable to drive or walk around like a normal citizen, was worth the sacrifice. "What makes it worth it is when you meet some couple that says, 'You know what? Our kid was able to stay on our health insurance plan and it turns out they were just diagnosed with a curable cancer, but if they hadn't stayed on our plan we would haven't caught it.' That's what makes it worth it."[22]

Apparently, it's an outburst of "remarkable candor" to tout yourself as the magnanimous savior of cancer-stricken children. Some might expect that a journalist of Pelley's stature wouldn't be so excitedly gullible. But that's how collusion works.

One CBS report most effectively demonstrates the old "Tiffany Network" ardor to polish the Democratic diamonds. As Team Obama withdrew the grand notion of the president giving his acceptance speech in 74,000-seat Bank of America stadium, claiming inclement weather that never emerged, CBS made no mention of empty seats or Obama's ego, and Pelley even skipped the stadium's bank name, calling it merely "the massive stadium that is home to the Carolina Panthers." Reporter Byron Pitts relayed that "according to the DNC, 65,000 people would have filled this stadium. Another 19,000 on the waiting list." Pitts could only find delighted Obama devotees who weren't the slightest bit critical of the decision:

BYRON PITTS: For Stacey Tillman of Harrisburg, North Carolina, a suburb of Charlotte, these tickets meant the chance of a lifetime. Like thousands of others, two weeks ago she waited in long lines for nearly four hours in 90-degree heat for a chance at a ticket to hear the president speak in person. What was your reaction when you heard the news?

STACEY TILLMAN: Disappointing, but at the same time, the weather's been a concern all week. We've been watching it, and I think that it was probably a good decision.

PITTS: David Miller of West Virginia says he'll keep his ticket as a souvenir, and do as the campaign recommended and go to a viewing party tomorrow night.

DAVID MILLER: Whether we get to see him live or we get together as a community and get to watch him in our homes together, the volunteers really support the president no matter what.[23]

## More Ugly Talk of Racist Republicans

When the Republican convention was over, liberal radio host Bill Press laughed at it as "pale, male, and stale."[24] Before it began, *Newsweek* special correspondent Michael Tomasky claimed that the convention would be a "toxic waste dump of hate and lies and race-baiting. . . . [T]his Romney-Ryan campaign is becoming among the most racist we've ever seen."[25]

But the allegedly racist Tea Party had supported a plethora of minority candidates, often against the establishment. In 2010, they backed Marco Rubio in Florida, against moderate Charlie Crist (who later changed parties). They backed Nimrata "Nikki" Haley, an Indian-American with a Sikh background. They loved another Indian-American, Louisiana governor Bobby Jindal, as a policy wonk. They helped elect new Latino governors in 2010 like Brian Sandoval in Nevada and Susana Martinez in New Mexico and black congressmen like Tim Scott and Allen West.

There were so many talented conservative minorities that it made reporters peer into a virtual kaleidoscope of Clarence Thomases. How the national media hated this narrative! It had to be crushed. *The Washington Post* publicized this narrative under the headline, "Incidents on the floor mar GOP's message of diversity." The *Post* reported the Republicans gave "prime speaking slots to Latinos and blacks who have emphasized their party's economic appeal to all Americans. But they have delivered those speeches to a convention hall filled overwhelmingly with white faces, an awkward contrast that has been made more uncomfortable this week by a series of racial headaches that have intruded on the party's efforts to project a new level of inclusiveness."[26]

There is no greater headache, or acid reflux, than the blatantly slanted media narrative on "diversity." In one incident the *Post* was spreading, two apparent GOP convention attendees reportedly threw peanuts at a black CNN camerawoman and told her this was "how we feed the animals."[27] That's the theme the liberal media wanted to keep propagating, twenty-four hours a day.

The *Post* and the networks didn't notice that black female congressional Republican candidate Mia Love had her Wikipedia biography on the Internet defaced as she spoke on August 29, with disgusting slurs like "House Nigger" and "dirty, worthless whore who sold out her soul."[28] The media liberals didn't mention the sale of racial buttons at the Democrat convention like "Once you vote black you never go back. Obama 2012." Former *Newsweek* reporter David Graham showed that button off at *The Atlantic* website as among "[t]he best of the official and unofficial campaign gear on display."[29]

Being a rising minority star in the Republican Party makes you a media target, not a darling like Obama. Take Senator Marco Rubio. On Tuesday night, NBC anchor Brian Williams hammered away at Rubio on rape: "I want to ask you about your party. You, I've watched you on television for days, talking about this gathering and, and being a proud Floridian. Are you happy with the tone and tenor of the conversation, right now? The rape debate got out of control, went several days. Is this where you want it in the big tent business?"[30] (Williams had another version of this hardball pitch to Paul Ryan, asking if he would "own the fact that the platform of this party allows a woman, who has been raped, no exception but to carry that child to term.")[31]

On Wednesday morning, the Rubio pounding continued. On ABC's *Good Morning America,* cohost George Stephanopoulos again quoted from Democrats: "Look at what the chairman of the Democratic convention, the mayor of Los Angeles, Antonio Villaraigosa, said last night. He said you can't just trot out a brown face or a Spanish surname and expect people to vote for your candidate. He was referring to you tomorrow night."[32]

*CBS This Morning* cohost Charlie Rose expressed grave pessimism at GOP outreach to minorities: "You are a rising star in this party," he said to Rubio. "How is it changing? Because many people worry that people who are Hispanic, African-American and other minorities don't have a place in this party. You're becoming something that is more narrow rather than outreaching."[33]

On Wednesday night's *PBS NewsHour*, anchor Gwen Ifill sympathized with Rubio on illegal immigration but hammered at "hot-button" conservatives opposed to "comprehensive" amnesty: "You have said this. Jeb Bush has said this. John McCain has said this. Yet the party platform uses kind of hot-button trigger terms like 'illegal aliens' and it calls for self-deportation. And that seems to be a gateway issue for a lot of Latino voters."[34]

Later on Wednesday night, as another new GOP star, New Mexico governor Susana Martinez—Hispanic and female—was speaking at the podium, ABC ignored her speech, preferring to interview liberal Univision anchor Jorge Ramos instead, as he shoveled dirt into the GOP's political grave:

"I think Republicans have a real, real challenge trying to get Latinos. Because just a few words in Spanish from Susana Martinez over principle is not enough," warned Ramos while ABC showed video of Martinez speaking. "If they insist on talking about immigration, they're going to lose even more of the Hispanic vote. The last poll that I saw, they don't even get 30 percent of the Hispanic vote. If they can't get 33 percent, 35 or 40 percent, they're going to lose the election."[35]

The others also skipped over Governor Martinez to make room for liberal blather. On CBS, anchor Scott Pelley pounded John McCain: "Mitt Romney has limited experience in foreign policy and, like several recent presidents, he has no experience in the military. Why should he be the next commander in chief?" McCain didn't make the obvious point that Obama had zero military service, and no blow-dried anchorman cared in 2008. He didn't even ask Pelley if he ever served (he didn't). The senator merely said Romney "has the right instincts the way Ronald Reagan did." [36]

NBC had a four-Caucasian conversation during the Martinez speech. Former anchorman Tom Brokaw took a shot at Obama-bashing conservatives in reviewing Condoleezza Rice's speech. "What was so striking to me was one other line that she had: 'It does not matter where you come from. It matters where you are going.' Well to a lot of delegates, on this floor, it does matter where President Obama came from. Because they've been very critical of his Kenyan father, who had a different faith than many of them would embrace, and they've raised lots of questions about where his ultimate loyalty is." [37]

How Brokaw deduced a majority of delegates were birthers is any-one's guess. But it underlines the contempt that media liberals have for the GOP rank and file.

The next morning on NPR's *Morning Edition*, reporter Ted Rob-bins concluded a story: "For a Republican Party struggling to connect with Hispanic voters, Governor Susana Martinez may be the perfect symbol." [38] *National Journal* reporter Major Garrett declared on CBS: "Another big star last night was Susana Martinez. The reaction on the floor was absolutely sensational. Not too many people have seen her before, heard her before. . . . I think she was a breakout star last night." [39]

The Republicans had a "breakout star" and "perfect symbol" that ABC, CBS, and NBC ignored or avoided.

## The Good Wife and the Housewife

Another obvious and routine double standard emerges in the net-work interviews with the spouses of the candidates. The feminist lawyer spouse gets the softballs, while the traditional "housewife" gets prosecuted.

In 1992, PBS anchor Judy Woodruff famously drew the ire of First Lady Barbara Bush for her double standard. At the Democratic convention, Woodruff repeatedly asked Hillary Clinton unchallenging questions, admitting out loud she was welcoming Democrat talking points: "The Clinton campaign has been saying this is a week that they were trying to tell the American people more about who Bill Clinton really is. What is it that you think the American people should know about your husband that they might not know or might not understand?"

Weeks later, when Woodruff sat down with First Lady Bush on PBS, she hammered her about the GOP convention being too nasty: they questioned the Democrats' patriotism, they weren't welcoming to gays, a speaker "joked that Gov. Clinton is a skirt chaser . . . does that have a place in this campaign?"

Mrs. Bush took Woodruff to task, deliciously: "Look, you're saying nothing nice . . . where were you during the Democrat convention defending us?" Woodruff just kept on hammering about the skirt-chasing jokes, but Mrs. Bush let loose: "You didn't listen to the Democrat Convention I think. . . . Now c'mon, be fair." [40]

There is no greater demonstration of misplaced idealism than a Republican expecting the national media to be fair in a presidential campaign. Two nights later, Woodruff administered the same beating about GOP negativism to the vice president's wife, Marilyn Quayle. [41]

Since the Republican convention came first, Ann Romney wasn't able to critique the double standard. But NBC anchor Brian Williams was strangely offended that Mrs. Romney hailed her husband's presidential potential in her convention address. "Last night, as you wrapped up, you said 'this man will lift up America.' In an interview you did with Natalie Morales for my other broadcast, *Rock Center*, you used different language: 'I believe in my heart that Mitt is going to save America.' And that jumped off the screen to me. Someone who knows you conceded that if Mrs. Obama used words like that—

'Barack was going to save America'—there'd be all kinds of hubbub. What do you mean? Those are powerful words." [42]

This is how shameless (or just clueless) Williams was. In her 2008 convention speech, Mrs. Obama said the same thing, if not stronger. She described her husband's impending ascension to the presidency as the juncture "where the current of history meets this new tide of hope." [43]

So when Williams interviewed her shortly after her convention speech in 2008, the NBC star must have complained about the tone, right? Mrs. Obama repeated her puffery to Williams: "I come here as a wife who loves my husband and believes he will be an extraordinary president."

Instead of expressing umbrage, Williams jumped right back to placing the "hubbub" in its proper perspective: those evil Republicans. "What of the attacks has busted through to you? What makes you angriest at John McCain, the Republicans? What's being said about your husband that you want to shout from the mountaintops as not true?" [44]

This question is so predictable from NBC. It's almost exactly how Jane Pauley interviewed Mrs. Clinton in 1992: "What was the worst thing you've heard said about you? . . . All right, what was the grossest distortion of your record?" [45]

But Williams wanted to break new grounds in servility. For Mrs. Obama in 2008, he asked people to imagine a "bigger picture" of a country that would finally let the descendants of slaves live in the White House that slaves built: "How do you begin to wrap your head around the bigger picture of, if you're successful, you'll move into a house where, when the Adams [family] moved in, slaves were finishing the plaster over the fireplace. How does that work?" [46]

When Williams interviewed Mrs. Obama at the Democrat convention in 2012, he was still aglow. "In your job you get to listen to all of the psychiatrists analyze your husband. Peter Baker, this morning's

— 173 —

*New York Times*: He's 'a proud yet humbled President, a confident yet scarred President, a dreamer mugged by reality.' Does that resemble the man you know?" [47]

That's not a softball question. That's a spoonful of baby food. He went on to another syrupy question, trying to kiss up to her about how rapidly the First Daughters were growing up.

To be fair, other anchors were also aggressively slanted, pushing around Mrs. Romney and saving their goo for Mrs. Obama. CBS anchorman Scott Pelley reminded Mrs. Obama how "in your speech on the first night of the convention, you said that the presidency 'does not change a person, it reveals the person.'" He added: "And I wonder, has this experience revealed anything to you about your husband that you did not know?" [48]

Then he asked the First Lady "What do you get tired and frustrated about?" She tried to demur, suggesting she was impressed with her husband's focus on moving America forward. Then Pelley ludicrously suggested, "You could have said that persistent questioning by reporters gets under your skin. That's a possibility." She couldn't answer that, either.

She should have burst out laughing. During the Republican convention, Pelley attempted to embarrass Ann Romney with a gotcha question: "The president is starting a tour called the Romney-Ryan Wrong for Women tour. . . . A lot of women look at the Republican platform on abortion, contraception, a number of issues, and ask the question whether Republicans have women's best interests at heart?" [49]

## Inclusive Democrats Didn't Include God

Conservative Christians have been scorned as the death of the Republicans at every convention since Ronald Reagan was nominated, but the increasingly secularizing, God-deleting base of the Democratic Party is routinely ignored.

One controversy briefly erupted at the Democratic convention. Republicans discovered the word "God" was nowhere in the official document for the party, the Democratic platform. The 2008 Democratic platform made one reference to God: the "God-given potential" of working people.[50] In 2012, even that paltry phrase was scrapped. GOP vice presidential nominee Paul Ryan launched the Republican critique on *Fox & Friends*: "I guess I would just put the onus and the burden on them to explain why they did all this, these purges of God."[51] Ryan also attacked the platform's failure to affirm Jerusalem as the capital of Israel, which was upsetting to Jewish and Christian voters.

Melanie Roussell, national press secretary for the Democratic National Committee, called the issue a "faux controversy," since the Democrat platform did express support for "faith," just without the G-word.[52] The media largely followed the DNC script, as usual. In the middle of Wednesday, Los Angeles mayor Antonio Villaraigosa quickly held a delegate vote to add those missing words to the platform. The voice vote was obviously, and audibly, split down the middle, if not a little bit against the inclusion of God. The fanaticism of this party was there for all to hear it and Villaraigosa had to know it. So the mayor proclaimed that two-thirds of the assembly had voted yes, which was nonsense and caused booing. Even the pundits on NPR's *Talk of the Nation* agreed the voice vote was split.[53]

"You don't want to put delegates in a position where they're booing God and Jerusalem, especially on videotape. It has to be included in all the coverage of the convention," proclaimed Steve Hayes on Fox's *Special Report*.[54] But Hayes, like Mrs. Bush, was too idealistic.

*CBS Evening News* was the "toughest" network covering this scandal by giving this controversy fifty-one seconds (with no video), as anchor Scott Pelley announced: "One of the things that these conventions do is write the party platform—a symbolic document that is immediately forgotten." Reporter Nancy Cordes relayed, "the convention chairman came out here and announced that they were adding those two items to the platform despite some pretty loud boos from some of the delegates in this room." There was no reference to a voice vote. This was damage control, not reporting.

*NBC Nightly News* gave the platform mess a few seconds, but Chuck Todd quickly pivoted to how delegates spent "most of the day basking in the afterglow of last night's rousing convention kickoff."

But ABC's *World News* shamelessly just skipped it. Instead, they devoted twelve minutes—more than half the newscast—to sappy spin on the convention, including three minutes to fill-in anchor David Muir talking to Caroline Kennedy about the tribute to her late uncle Ted Kennedy. Muir asked her, "You wrote that 'I have never had a President who inspired me the way people tell me my father inspired them. But for the first time, I believe, I have found the man who could be that President.' Do you still feel just as inspired by President Obama?"[55]

On the *PBS NewsHour*, they didn't report on the vote, other than a vague mention tossed in by pseudo-conservative analyst David Brooks: "Some of the platform fights, if you have got a problem with people who go to church, don't leave God out of your platform. If you have got a problem with some Jewish voters because they don't think the president is standing with Israel, don't leave Jerusalem out of your platform."[56]

Even the alleged newspapers of record were also treating it like a "faux controversy." *The New York Times* ran a 1,143-word piece on the platforms on Wednesday and never mentioned the lack of the word "God." On Thursday, a story on page 14 was headlined "Pushed by Obama, Democrats Alter Platform Over Jerusalem," with the God controversy popping up very briefly in the fifth paragraph.[57] That was all.

*The Washington Post* published a 3,594-word front-page story on Wednesday on the history of recent party platforms, but it never mentioned the missing G-word, or Jerusalem.[58] Thursday's paper briefly mentioned the voice vote in the eighth paragraph of a story on page A-8.

On *Fox News Watch*, conservative panelist James Pinkerton guessed just how this would have been reported very differently if the shoe was on the other party's foot: "If it had been a Republican convention, the media would have hauled out acoustical engineers, and sound decibel checks, and they would have proved which was bigger and so on. Those two [protesting] people in the white T-shirts would be household names by now. *The New York Times* would have them on the front page, on the *Today* show, telling their story about how atrocious the Republicans are."[59]

Perhaps the media's double standard on religion was most effectively embodied by Brian Williams and NBC. While he could only spare a few seconds for the "God" gaffe for Democrats, the prime-time NBC magazine show *Rock Center* devoted an hour-long special to the Mormon church.

"Most Americans say they know next to nothing about the Mormon Church. Tonight, a rare look inside the lives of modern Mormon families. . . . A church still dealing with the issue of polygamy. . . . And other issues of inequality."

Williams touted pop culture mocking the faith on Broadway and on TV, starting with a clip of Fox's sleazy cartoon *Family Guy* in which lead character Peter Griffin declares: "I'm going to be a Mormon. . . . Come on, nailing a different wife every night. That's a no-brainer."

After briefly describing the founding of the religion, Williams quickly focused on negative perceptions of Mormonism: "Part of the history of the Church that they can't shake is polygamy.... [E]ven though polygamy was officially banned a century ago, it's something the Church still has to deal with.... Critics in other religions have openly called them a cult."[60]

The networks could not see how much they looked like an Obama-worshipping cult.

# CHAPTER 10

# Secret Tapes and the 47 Percent

Only hidden cameras we like make "news."

When it comes to dirty tricks and secret tapes, Americans will harken back to President Nixon and Watergate. It was considered grotesquely paranoid for a Republican president to record conversations with his unwitting aides in the White House. His defenders insisted he was not the first.

They were correct, but it didn't matter. There were secret White House tapes of John F. Kennedy and Lyndon Johnson. But with them, it was different. The surreptitious habits of these liberal Democrats weren't considered sleazy or unethical. They were considered a gift to history.

It's just another day at the Office of Dirty Media Tricks.

On September 17, 2012, Mitt Romney was victimized by a political enemy at a Boca Raton, Florida, fundraiser who recorded his remarks without his consent. What followed was what many liberal journalists insisted was the death blow to the Romney campaign.

Bloomberg's Josh Barro wrote a piece headlined "Today, Mitt Romney Lost the Election."[1]

He was right. The liberals' joy was palpable after the hard-left magazine *Mother Jones* posted a three-month-old secret tape of Mitt Romney talking to donors at the private residence. The headline emphasized: "When he doesn't know a camera's rolling, the GOP candidate shows his disdain for half of America."[2] Romney said he would never convince 47 percent of the electorate to vote for him, since they were dependent on government.

Remember that David Axelrod's case for reelecting Obama relied heavily on convincing voters that while the economic recovery barely had a pulse, they couldn't trust Mitt Romney. After the election, he said at the University of Chicago that he wanted voters to think Romney "was out of touch with their economic experience, and that his fundamental view of the economy was one which didn't incorporate them. And frankly, when that 47 percent tape came out, it was a pretty strong ratification of our view."[3]

Axelrod was more emphatic with *Politico*: "I think that the greatest gift we got may have been that 47 percent tape, which was him [Romney]."[4]

The partisan provenance of the tape didn't matter. It was acquired through James Carter IV, an unemployed grandson of ex-president Jimmy Carter. Later, Jimmy told Piers Morgan at CNN that, "[w]hen James went to meet President Obama, President Obama ran across the room, embraced him, and thanked him profusely for his time."

He should have hugged the networks, too. Over three full days of coverage, on the Big Three evening and morning shows, they devoted almost an hour and a half (1 hour, 28 minutes, 23 seconds) to the Romney tape, which made up all or part of forty-two campaign stories.[5] Team Romney felt this was not a story that deserved eighty-eight minutes of news time, but the Obama administration clearly felt it was as good as eighty-eight minutes of free campaign advertising.

The network carnival barkers erupted with the chants of "bombshell" and "earthquake" on a "seismic day" for the Republican campaign. A viewer might imagine the earth would open up and swallow Romney whole. NBC's Brian Williams proclaimed, "These are tough days for the Romney campaign. Inside 50 days to go now until the election, and they are dealing with something of a public relations disaster." [6]

The networks were right. There was an earthquake—of their own making. *CBS Evening News* anchor Scott Pelley used the usual lingo when the "news" was designed to eviscerate Republicans: "With 49 days to Election Day, a candidate for president doesn't want a distraction from his message, but it's happened in a big way to Mitt Romney." [7]

On CBS, Bob Schieffer was handing out the shovels to dig a grave for Romney. "I just can't think of anything that he could have said that could have hurt his cause more," and "He's got a lot of work to do to dig out of this hole." [8] NBC brought on ersatz-conservative Joe Scarborough to proclaim, "This is one of the worst weeks for any presidential candidate in a general election that any of us can remember." [9]

Among Romney's remarks caught on tape was his accurate observation about the liberal tilt of ABC's *The View*. The show "is high-risk because of the five women on it. Only one is conservative and four are sharp-tongued and not conservative." The conservative on this list had to be Elisabeth Hasselbeck, who came to Romney's defense on the 47 percent remarks. "I think there's a general feeling that, with more and more people becoming dependent on the government, that by next July we could perhaps be celebrating Dependence Day, not Independence Day," she said.

"Oh, Elisabeth," Barbara Walters scoffed off-camera, like an embarrassed mother. "This is not something that I'm just feeling alone," Hasselbeck insisted. "Yes it is," Walters said, to laughter from the audience.[10] Hasselbeck was certainly alone at that table.

Romney told his donors that Obama could count on 47 percent of the voters who will vote for him no matter what, "who are dependent upon government, who believe that they are victims, who believe that government has a responsibility to care for them, who believe that they are entitled to health care, to food, to housing, to you name it." He added: "My job is not to worry about those people. I'll never convince them that they should take personal responsibility and care for their lives."

It was a monumentally stupid remark. That 47 percent of the electorate dependent on the government includes deadbeats—yes. It also includes the United States military. And retired citizens on (their) Social Security. And folks who don't want government largesse, but are struggling. Romney wasn't intending to insult these constituencies—but he did. He rushed to the (public) microphones to correct the record. It did no good.

Reporters knew that this is not the way any candidate would talk in public. A politician should appeal for any and every voter he can attract. This reminded many political junkies of 2008, when a *Huffington Post* journalist, Mayhill Fowler, had a recording of Obama telling donors in San Francisco about working-class Democrats, "It's not surprising, then, they get bitter, they cling to guns or religion or antipathy to people who aren't like them, or anti-immigrant sentiment, or anti-trade sentiment as a way to explain their frustrations."[11]

That bitter-clingers gaffe was reported at the time because 1) Hillary Clinton made it a central thrust of her improbable campaign to be the lunchpail candidate; 2) liberal reporters are more amenable to (mildly) damaging stories in the primaries, with the strategic thought that the Democrat nominee will be forever "inoculated" from the charges in the general election and beyond; and 3) the *Huffington Post* is a liberal website, not a "far right" blog they could reject for baldly ideological reasons.

The liberal media displayed zero interest in revealing anything Obama said and did behind closed doors as he ran for reelection. As sexy as hidden cameras are to journalists, there were no liberal Mayhill Fowlers to expose Obama in 2012, and conservative hidden-camera journalism has been dismissed as too ideological to be trustworthy.

When conservative activists exposed the leftist pro-Obama group ACORN with hidden cameras in 2009, the networks waited for days to touch it and then aired just one solitary story (ABC, CBS) or three (NBC) as Congress defunded them.[12] When the pro-life activists of Live Action exposed Planned Parenthood clinics advising a "pimp" on how to evade the law with underage prostitutes, these three networks simply put their heads in the sand and pretended it didn't exist, even as CNN and Fox aired the video.[13]

But somehow, *Mother Jones* was the gold standard for quality, nonideological reporting . . . or liberals are just brazen enough to think the only criterion that matters is political usefulness.

## No Time for Romney Points on Obama's Economy

Something Romney said actually caused a thrill up the leg of Chris Matthews. On MSNBC, he took to bad singing: " 'If I were a rich man, Yubby dibby dibby dibby dibby dibby dibby dum.' Dumb. It's one thing to be rich and have the majority of voters convinced you're out to help the rich. Is there anything dumber, though, to be caught pandering to your fellow rich?"[14]

Speaking of dumb, the media seemed deaf and dumb to Obama's flaws on the economy. The media elite's incessant hammering on the

"47 percent" tape underlined just how eager they were to avoid conservative arguments that would put a dent in Obama's image as an economically competent president. Consider the network suppression of these matters:

**The So-Called Stimulus.** A January 2009 report from Obama's economic team suggested that massive new "stimulus" spending would stem the rising unemployment rate at about 8 percent.[15] Signing the $787 billion package on February 17, 2009, Obama proclaimed this marked "the beginning of the end" of America's unemployment woes.[16] At that time, unemployment was at 8.3 percent. It rose above 9 percent by May, and peaked at 10 percent in October. The official rate stayed above 9 percent through October 2011, and then above 8 percent until September 2012.[17]

This was the worst bout of high unemployment since the Great Depression, but during the entire 2012 campaign, ABC, CBS, and NBC never mentioned that Obama's economists predicted that passing the "stimulus" would keep unemployment below 8 percent. On May 25, 2012, the Congressional Budget Office estimated the cost of the "stimulus" was higher ($831 billion) and estimated the "increased number of people employed by between 0.2 million and 1.5 million."[18] That computes to between $540,000 and $4.1 million per job. Network coverage? Zero.

**The Deficit.** Would the average voter remember that Obama promised in early 2009 he would "improve" on the Bush fiscal record? He could not have been more public and unequivocal. The president held a nationally televised "Fiscal Responsibility Summit" at the White House on February 23, 2009, and boldly promised, "Today, I'm pledging to cut the deficit we inherited by half by the end of our first term in office."[19] He repeated that pledge before a joint session of Congress.[20]

It was a powerful statement. Maybe that's why ABC, CBS, and NBC all reported on this. ABC's Jake Tapper stated, "The president says he plans to cut the $1.3 trillion in half by the end of his first term. He says first term, knowing that whether or not he gets a second term depends on how he delivers on all of these big ambitious promises."[21]

Notice that Tapper (as did NBC's Savannah Guthrie) accepted Obama's goal of cutting in half the deficit estimate for fiscal year 2009, which was not yet half elapsed. The deficit for the last full fiscal year of President Bush, fiscal year 2008, ending on September 30, was only $438 billion, which itself broke the historic record. It may be polite to say Obama "inherited" the spending of his first year in office, even if he was president for the last seven months of it. But Obama voted in the Senate for the massive increase in spending— the Troubled Assets Relief Program—in 2008, and he was planning a dramatic multi-year increase in spending through the "stimulus," so his intentions of expanding the deficit were quite clear to journalists.

Under Obama, the deficits stayed Empire State Building high, from $1.4 trillion in fiscal 2009, to $1.3 trillion in fiscal 2010 and fiscal 2011, to $1.1 trillion in fiscal 2012. Three years after his pledge, Obama told an Atlanta TV station, "Well, we're not there because this recession turned out to be a lot deeper than any of us realized."[22]

So was the president held accountable for his own pledge? This old promise was either ignored or barely noticed by the network evening news shows. Only ABC's Tapper—a man with a tendency to be an outlier and break from the pack occasionally—returned to a video clip of the original 2009 promise and explained—once, on February 13, 2012—that this was a "broken promise for President Obama."[23] On October 19, CBS reporter Jan Crawford reran a soundbite from Mitt Romney from the first debate: "He said that he'd cut in half the deficit. He hasn't done that, either. In fact, he doubled it."[24]

Brian Williams and the *NBC Nightly News* never located any troublesome deficit-promise soundbites.

On November 13, 2011, very early in the election cycle, NBC's

*Meet the Press* did—sort of. They played a 2008 clip of candidate Obama: "The problem is, is that the way Bush has done it over the last eight years is to take out a credit card from the bank of China in the name of our children, driving up our national debt from $5 trillion for the first 42 presidents, number 43 added $4 trillion by his lonesome. That's irresponsible. It's unpatriotic."

If Bush's deficits made him irresponsible and unpatriotic, what did Obama's make *him*?

Without underlining that Obama had added more than $5 trillion to the debt in only one term, David Gregory pressed Democratic Party chair Debbie Wasserman Schultz: "That's his rhetoric. Should it not be turned on him now?" Schultz dodged the question and changed the subject: "What we should be turning on is that Mitt Romney, for example, who purports to be the alternative to President Obama, would've allowed Detroit to go bankrupt, would've allowed more than a million jobs in the pipeline to just, just evaporate. We wouldn't have had an American automobile industry." Gregory allowed her to filibuster and get away with ignoring the issue: "We're going to leave it there." [25]

None of the network evening shows replayed that "unpatriotic" charge back at Obama. There's another standard dirty-trick double standard: Democrats are allowed to call Republicans pretty much anything.

**Poverty.** In September 2011, the Census Bureau reported there were 46.2 million Americans defined as living in poverty—the highest number in the fifty-two years the bureau has been publishing figures. The census report the next year found the same number. [26] That's 6.4 million more people than at the end of the Bush era, in 2008, for an increase of 16 percent. [27]

The U.S. Department of Agriculture reported that the number of Americans using food stamps rose to almost 47 million before Election Day. That's a dramatic increase from 31 million in November 2008, when Obama was first elected president.[28]

Of the evening newscasts, the *CBS Evening News* was the leader mentioning the data on poverty and/or food stamps. On the 310 evenings from January 1 up to Election Day, they filed five stories. *NBC Nightly News* aired two.

ABC's *World News* never cited this data, although they aired two Romney soundbites mentioning high rates of Americans in poverty, once about single mothers, once about Hispanics. On September 17, as David Muir talked up "withering criticism" of the GOP nominee from inside his own party, Romney told the Hispanic Chamber of Commerce, "Over two million more Hispanics are living in poverty today than the day President Obama took office."[29]

After several stories on the Benghazi attack on September 12, NBC anchor Brian Williams turned to the home front: "The Census Bureau, the folks who count us all, are tonight out with a look at who we are these days. And their numbers on the economy and poverty in America are both stunning and sad, especially what they say about the once-great American middle class." Williams and his correspondent, Chris Jansing, never uttered the name "Obama" or made any kind of political connection.[30] It was somehow just a sociological accident, and Obama's economic policies were somehow utterly unconnected to it.

**Obamacare.** Despite Republican fury against Obamacare during the primaries, where every candidate pledged to repeal it, the network evening news shows contracted a severe case of apathy as bad numbers started arriving and Obama's plan cratered. Before he won the White House in 2008, Obama had promised to sign a "universal health care bill into law by the end of my first term as president that will cover every American and cut the cost of a typical family's premium by up to $2,500 a year."[31]

They called their bill "The Affordable Care Act," because they believed nationalizing the system would lower consumer costs. When he signed the bill in 2010, Obama repeated: "This legislation will also lower costs for families and for businesses."[32]

But in September 2012, the annual health benefits survey of the Kaiser Family Foundation—a longtime backer of socialized medicine—showed average premiums rising again. From 2009 through 2012, they rose by an average of $2,370 per family.[33] Costs were going in the exact opposite direction of what had been promised. It was now clearly the Unaffordable Care Act. Network coverage of the Kaiser survey? Zero.

That wasn't the only problem. Liberals always insist that the number of Americans without health insurance is a national scandal, and push government schemes with the ideal of leaving no one uninsured. That was the driving justification for nationalizing one-seventh of the economy. But a March 2012 analysis by the Congressional Budget Office estimated that even with all the new taxes, subsidies, and regulations implemented by 2016, about 26–27 million Americans would remain uninsured.

The news only got worse. Despite Obama's promise that if you like your health-care plan, you can keep it, the same CBO report determined that 3–5 million fewer people would have coverage through an employer "compared with the number under prior law."[34] In March, there was heavy TV coverage of Obamacare as its constitutionality was argued before the Supreme Court—but there was not a single word about the millions who would lose their employer-based insurance, or the tens of millions who would remain uninsured despite the passage of Obamacare.

The wheels had come off this colossus but the American people were being kept in the dark.

There was a mention of the CBO report on ABC's *World News* on March 26, the day the Supreme Court heard oral arguments, but it was used in Obama's favor, not against him. If the court struck down the individual mandate, correspondent Terry Moran insisted, "the Congressional Budget Office estimates that 16 million fewer Americans would have health insurance. So the stakes are very high." [35] ABC left the impression that Obamacare was fairly close to providing insurance for all, so it should be untouched by the Court. It just wasn't true.

In July, about a month after the Supreme Court decision, the CBO revised its estimates upward, predicting 30 million would remain uninsured and 4–6 million would lose their employer-based health care. [36] Network coverage of that increasingly dour scenario? Again, still zero. Zippo.

What about the Republican argument that small businesses would resist expanding beyond fifty employees, the level at which they would be forced to provide expensive health-care coverage or be fined under Obamacare? The negative effect on small businesses and job creation were all but omitted in 2012. There were just two pieces of stories focusing on the small-business impact on the evening newscasts on June 28, the day the Supreme Court upheld Obama's scheme.

ABC's David Muir offered fifteen seconds to pessimistic small businessman Jorge Lozano, and NBC's Anne Thompson devoted forty-six seconds to a small businessman, Joe Olivo, who would delay hiring new employees or instead find part-time workers to avoid Obamacare, a "potential unintended consequence of a law aimed at expanding health care." [37]

CBS never focused on the potentially damaging effects on small business and their hiring patterns. Total network coverage? Sixty-one seconds.

**Keystone Pipeline.** A Gallup poll in March 2012 found that 57 percent of Americans favored the Keystone XL pipeline, which would run from Canada to the Gulf of Mexico. Only 29 percent were opposed. [38] On January 18, 2012, President Obama pleased the radical environmentalists on the left by denying a permit to the pipeline proposal. Republicans were disgusted. On NBC, Newt Gingrich declared, "This is a stunningly stupid thing to do. And there's no better word for it. These people are so out of touch with reality it's as though they were governing Mars." [39]

But the media weren't exactly in touch with the majority on this proposal, either. All three networks aired full stories on the Obama decision that night. CBS anchor Scott Pelley said "election-year politics is far from over," and NBC anchor Brian Williams predicted "you can be sure, as the campaign season enters the home stretch, we'll be hearing a lot more about this long stretch of pipe." [40]

Not really. After that one night of coverage, the networks virtually buried the story and tried to make people forget one of Obama's more unpopular decisions. There were only seven mentions on the three networks through the rest of the campaign, and a grand total of *one* additional full story—a March 22 *CBS Evening News* piece about an Obama photo op underlining his support for the southern leg of the pipeline, from Oklahoma City to the Gulf of Mexico, a part of the project that didn't require Obama's approval.

"It was a day when both parties played a bit loose with the facts," insisted CBS correspondent Norah O'Donnell. She pointed out Obama didn't note that only the northern part of the project required his approval. Speaker John Boehner then said, "So the president can take credit for having nothing to do with the bottom half of this pipeline, and the fact is, there's only one permit that requires his approval because it crosses our national boundaries."

O'Donnell suggested Boehner somehow played loose with the facts because Obama blocked it after "the Republican governor of Nebraska, Dave Heineman, asked the president to reject it because of environmental concerns." [41] Two days after Obama's second inauguration, Heineman approved the pipeline with an altered route. [42] The networks skipped over that, too.

It didn't matter to the networks that many Democrats and labor unions favored the pipeline project. What mattered was the president making an important concession to radical environmentalists to keep them energized and not protesting in the streets before the election.

## What Outrageous Obama Clips?

The media were very skilled at diagnosing Romney's problems over hours of "news" coverage, but they could easily swerve to change the subject away from Obama problems or gaffes—if they had to acknowledge them at all. So Republican operatives went looking for Obama video snippets to fire back at the *Mother Jones* salvo.

Through the Drudge Report, the Romney camp tried to shift the campaign conversation away from the "47 percent" hype by directing the networks to a 1998 tape of Obama at Loyola University, where he professed his love for redistributing other people's money, solidifying the socialist worldview Obama has so zealously denied. "I think the trick is figuring out how do we structure government systems that pool resources and hence facilitate some redistribution because I actually believe in redistribution, at least at a certain level to make sure that everybody's got a shot."[43] The networks gave this real bombshell six and a half minutes of attention. That's "fairness" to these TV people, a 13-to-1 advantage for Obama.

NBC and MSNBC waited to "verify" the old Obama video before airing it and dispatched someone to the university for the full videotape. On her MSNBC daytime show, reporter Andrea Mitchell insisted that "because we have not independently at NBC News and MSNBC authenticated it, we're not airing it. But the basic issue is, they're accusing President Obama, as John Sununu said to me yesterday, of class warfare, that is trying to change the subject."[44] NBC really wanted to keep the negative focus on Romney.

Mitchell did not explain why there was no NBC delay in airing the *Mother Jones* video while they verified it. They began replaying it within twelve hours. There was no delay to see if Romney's tape was out of context, although Romney complained that the tape was only "snippets" of his remarks. The magazine then posted the "complete" video in two parts, except it wasn't. Conservative bloggers discovered the tape had a Nixon-like two minutes edited out of it in the middle. By then the networks had already hammered the anti-Romney message home.

Two weeks later, on October 2, the Drudge Report featured another video as a forthcoming Fox News scoop—a June 5, 2007, Obama speech before black ministers at Hampton University, touted as "Obama's other race speech." The networks quickly disposed of the story on the next morning. NBC's Chuck Todd barely mentioned it. ABC's Jake Tapper reported: "Conservatives are calling it explosive. The Obama campaign is calling it a desperate attempt by Romney's allies to change the subject." At least he threw in a clip from that speech with Obama extolling his "friend and great leader" Rev. Wright.[45]

On CBS, reporter Jan Crawford threw it in briefly at the end of her story, and then CBS demonstrated Team Romney wanted nothing to do with these clips. Cohosts Charlie Rose and Norah O'Donnell asked Romney aide Kevin Madden three times for his opinion on this story, and he avoided the subject like he was being asked to swallow poison.

Then O'Donnell turned to Obama spokesman Robert Gibbs: "I want to give you an opportunity to respond to that tape that was aired by Fox, the President talking about what happened in New Orleans. Does the President believe the Bush administration did not help the victims of Hurricane Katrina because of their race?" CBS had just aired a clip from the tape of Obama slamming the Bush response as "colorblind in its incompetence," so Gibbs repeated that sentiment. Then he shamed CBS for echoing Sean Hannity: "I have to say I'm a little amazed that, as you mentioned, a widely-covered speech, likely by people at your network, has somehow caused a kerfuffle five years later because somebody like Sean Hannity decided to re-air what was covered extensively." Cohost Charlie Rose obediently replied, "Let me move on." [46]

It was a trick perfected by Bill Clinton: confront an allegation by declaring it Asked and Answered, an old story already covered, when in fact it had barely been touched. Many liberal journalists dismissed the Hampton speech tape as old news in 2012, something that was already covered as news in 2007. In reality, at that time, the coverage of the speech to black ministers was sparse. It drew an anchor brief on ABC and NBC, and nothing on the newscasts of CBS, PBS, and NPR. *The Washington Post* barely managed a paragraph on it.

But journalists will be bored by anything Obama said in public, no matter how odd. Obama began the speech by saying he attended a service in Los Angeles to "commemorate the anniversary" of the Los Angeles riots of 1992, as if the rioters had been engaged in a noble cause. Obama's language of "quiet riots" caused by American neglect of poverty isn't seen as controversial language by liberals, just as the word "redistribution" makes them smile, not gag.

On the other hand, Romney saying that a large chunk of Obama's voters are dependent on government was treated as a disastrous outburst.

There's another reason the networks could have ignored the old June 2007 speech. It was almost exactly the same as an Obama speech on May 5, 2007, to the National Conference of Black Mayors.[47] Asked and Answered. Time to move on. Once they've decided a speech isn't newsworthy, into the shredder it goes.

## Rev. Wright Hush Money?

What was new in the Hampton speech was Senator Obama's tribute to "my friend and great leader" Rev. Jeremiah Wright, and the notion that "[o]ur God is big enough" for liberal programs like "affordable health care for every American." Rev. Wright's noxious sermons became the most threatening scandal of Obama's first campaign for president—but too late in the primaries to really stop him. The networks fervently came to his defense and were thoroughly enraptured by the "race speech" designed to end the scandal. Videotapes showed that Wright screamed "God damn America!" from the pulpit and suggested America deserved 9/11, that the attacks on New York and Washington, D.C., were America's chickens "coming home to roost."

In May, author Ed Klein revealed that for his new anti-Obama book, *The Amateur*, he taped an interview with Rev. Wright, who had told him, "After the media went ballistic on me, I received an e-mail offering me money not to preach at all until after the November presidential election. . . . It was from one of Barack's closest friends." [48] The liberal media never "went ballistic" on Wright, unlike the conservative media. They defended him while Obama defended him, and dropped him when Obama dropped him.

On Fox News on May 17, Klein told Sean Hannity that the friend Wright implicated was Eric Whitaker, a personal friend of Obama's from Harvard days who had replaced Michelle Obama in running the Urban Health Initiative at the University of Chicago Hospital. He routinely vacationed with the Obamas and golfed with the president in the first term.

Hannity asked, "Do you think it's possible that Whitaker could have made that offer just independently on his own?" Klein said no, "Because I don't think Whitaker would have done something as important as that without—first of all, he was a confidante of Barack

Obama's. I mean, they were as close as brothers could be. And I don't think he would have done something as dramatic as offering a $150,000 bribe without checking with his pal, Barack, and saying, 'maybe we should do something about silencing this minister.'"[49] Network coverage? Zero.

Eric Whitaker was and continues to be a complete nobody as far as the media is concerned. NBC never mentioned the name before Obama's reelection. CBS mentioned him once, and ABC's Diane Sawyer called him "one of Obama's closest friends from Chicago" on Inauguration Day in 2009. On his "Political Punch" blog at ABCNews.com, Jake Tapper reported Whitaker's brief denial: "I have received your message asking whether I'd offered any sort of a bribe during the 2008 campaign. The answer is no." Wright declined to comment to Tapper.[50]

In her book on the Obamas, *New York Times* reporter Jodi Kantor asserted that Whitaker and Marty Nesbitt were assigned by Obama to "keep him normal while in office. . . . Nesbitt and Whitaker were so close with the president that they did not wait for invitations to visit the White House; they just sent him a message they were coming."[51]

The two Obama buddies "had shared too many basketball games with him to count, so close to the president they earned inauguration seats right near Jill Biden, the vice president's wife." They also served this function during the campaign, Kantor added. "It wasn't the first time they had served a protective function: during the painful fracas over provocative statements made by their pastor, the Rev. Jeremiah Wright Jr., during the campaign, they had rotated, along with Valerie Jarrett, traveling with the candidate, so he would never be without a friend close by."[52]

For her part, Kantor had a different tale about who hushed Wright: a man who would later be honored with a show on MSNBC, Rev. Al Sharpton. "It was Sharpton who finally convinced him to quiet down."[53]

Perhaps this hush-money story is too inflammatory to accept from such a disgruntled source. After all, Rev. Wright also repeatedly charged that AIDS was concocted by the U.S. government. But these same networks have been eager to welcome authors with all kinds of harsh allegations about Republican presidents.

For example, in 2004, NBC's Matt Lauer welcomed Kitty Kelley for three days of interviews to unload personal allegations against George W. and Laura Bush.[54,55] In 2000, CBS put an anti-Bush author on *60 Minutes* claiming Bush had been arrested for cocaine possession in 1972.[56] That anti-Bush author, J. H. Hatfield, had been convicted in 1988 of paying a hit man five thousand dollars to murder his former boss with a car bomb.[57] The Bushes denounced the book as untrue, and St. Martin's Press recalled 70,000 books. CBS put his claims on the air anyway.

The networks wouldn't touch allegations of a Wright hush-money offer. But CBS and NBC each briefly sprung into action on Wright at the whisper of a chance—exposed by *The New York Times*—that a Republican Super PAC might run an ad against Obama using Rev. Wright.

On the May 22 *CBS This Morning*, Bob Schieffer expressed happiness that this plot was foiled: "You know, we saw this week, Charlie, we saw Republicans roundly denounce a plan that some Republicans had to launch this race-baiting campaign tied—trying to tie the president once again to Jeremiah Wright. Now we're seeing people on the Democratic side denouncing this, saying, wait a minute, this has gone too far."[58]

Republican "race-baiting" is deplored, even, as in the case of the *New York Times* story, it has yet to display itself. By contrast, Obama's racial appeals about rioters aren't "news."

# CHAPTER 11

## The Fractured Fall Debates

When will the Republicans stop accepting a quadruple thumping?

There are few things that Republican presidential contenders control more than the choice of debate venues and debate moderators. It's also apparently a memo they've never read. Every election cycle, they choose liberal media moderators who then act like media liberals and Republicans are . . . astonished. The 2012 cycle demonstrated once again the perils of primary debates with "objective" media anchors like Brian Williams and George Stephanopoulos whacking away at GOP candidates. The price of admission to their networks is too high and the potential for damage is too great, but Republicans don't get it.

Republicans did finally make some movement in the right direction, having debates hosted by conservative organizations, allowing networks to come along and cosponsor events if they wished. These debates let the actual Republican primary voters set the agenda, as opposed to debates allowing Stephanopoulos to ask six questions implying Republicans wanted the government to limit access to condoms and birth control pills.[1]

Unfortunately, the Republican Party establishment once again made no serious attempt to balance the slate of moderators for the presidential debates in the fall, with enormous audiences of around 60 million people. In every tedious cycle at the Commission on Presidential Debates, it looks like it begins by Republicans waving a white flag and welcoming another potential quadruple thumping by liberal media-elite moderators.

They never insist that one of the four questioners come from Fox News, precisely because the Democrats feel about Fox the same way that conservatives have always felt about every other TV news network.

As Bill O'Reilly complained on *CBS This Morning* to cohost Charlie Rose: "CNN gets in; Fox—nobody would touch with a ten-foot pole. That's what gets disturbing, because there are serious journalists at Fox News that can moderate these debates, starting with Bret Baier." Baier even delighted media liberals during the primaries by asking if Republicans would raise their hands if they would accept a deal of ten dollars in spending cuts for a dollar in tax hikes, and the hands didn't go up.

O'Reilly said he prefers a tough-as-nails moderator, who would "come in with a *60 Minutes* mentality and ask questions and get answers." This, of course, ignores how *60 Minutes* has bowed deeply to Obama at every opportunity, as well as the fact that moderators are not the debaters. They are called moderators for a reason. Their job is to ask good questions, and get out of the way.

It is what made the late Tim Russert the gold standard in his field.

Charlie Rose insisted to O'Reilly, "you sound like you want the presidential debate to be a cable news program."[2] But maybe that could be fun, too. Two moderators who would each purposely, by design, debate one of the candidates, like CNN's *Crossfire* in its heyday. O'Reilly or Sean Hannity could interview the Democrat from the right, and they could recruit Bob Beckel or Hannity's old partner

Alan Colmes to interview the Republican from the left. Why not? Presidential candidates in both parties have been far too risk-averse to bite on the kind of format that risks a balance of hardballs.

The most fraudulent debate format is the phony "town hall" Potemkin villages that are routinely slanted against the Republicans. Either the "undecided voters" should be selected without the moderator knowing precisely what they're going to ask, or they should load the "town hall" audience instead with committed partisan voters and let them question the opposing candidates, like Question Time in the British Parliament. At least in this format both sides would take hardball questions.

Then there's the question of the media bias surrounding the debates. Over and over, liberal journalists will crown the Democrat the winner unless it cannot plausibly be declared, and even then, someone will try. For example, before the 2012 debates, the Media Research Center documented how, in eight out of the last nine general election presidential debates, George Stephanopoulos proclaimed a win for the Democratic candidate. (That's every debate since he joined ABC News right out of the Clinton White House in 1997.)[3]

While Team Obama tried to lower expectations before the first debate—standard political posturing—journalists weren't as shy. Carole Simpson, a longtime ABC reporter who moderated the town-hall debate in 1992, told CNN this would be no charisma contest. "Romney is practicing zingers. He's not very funny," Simpson said, saying she saw him bomb before voters in Iowa. But Obama? "He's been on Letterman. He's been on Leno. He's been on *The View*. They're doing all of these shows and I think he's much more comfortable in his skin."[4]

That's not the way it turned out, and the media were furious.

## First Debate: Obama Clobbered in Colorado

Nothing seemed to cause as much media angst about Obama's re-election as the first fall debate. At age seventy-eight, retired *PBS NewsHour* anchor Jim Lehrer was talked into his eleventh appearance as a moderator by the Commission on Presidential Debates. (He moderated all three presidential debates in 2000.) To his credit, Lehrer played it straight down the middle, taking his title seriously. He rejected the "gotcha" brand of journalism.

Lehrer asked the blandest of questions, merely seeking the differences between the candidates, as in "What are the major differences between the two of you about how you would go about creating new jobs?" and "What are the differences between the two of you as to how you would go about tackling the deficit problem in this country?"[5]

Obama performed badly enough that Bill Maher was mocking him on Twitter by mid-debate,[6] and Chris Matthews came out angry. "I don't know what he was doing out there," he raged. "I don't know how he let Romney get away with the crap he threw out tonight."[7]

As even former NBC anchor Tom Brokaw acknowledged the next day, liberal journalists were loaded and ready to pronounce this election over and Romney's campaign dead after the first debate: "If it had been Romney performing like the president last night, it would have been over."[8] But the thumping Obama received was so complete that virtually no one denied it.

But how did they report Obama lost? Therein lies the rub: journalists as well as Democratic operatives attempted the spin that this was all about style and presentation. Obama was "flat," "lackluster," "not himself," and "not firing on all cylinders." In other words, Obama wasn't Glorious Obama. Many went further, pushing the Matthews narrative that Romney was somehow mean-spirited and even deceptive in his presentation.[9]

Lehrer was also blamed. Former *Newsweek* reporter Howard Fineman complained on MSNBC that "Jim Lehrer was practically useless as the moderator. It was criminal negligence not to follow up on the question—Mr. Romney specifically what tax loopholes or deductions do you want to get rid of—he didn't ask it." [10]

Fineman thought Lehrer should have taken Obama's argument and repeated it. The president strangely suggested that his New Math said Romney wanted "a $5 trillion tax cut, on top of $2 trillion of additional spending for our military, and he is saying that he is going to pay for it by closing loopholes and deductions. The problem is that he's been asked over 100 times how you would close those deductions and loopholes, and he hasn't been able to identify them." [11]

Liberal journalists think their fellow journalists are supposed to underline Obama's "best" lines, repeat them, and help them sink into the minds of the voters.

On Current TV, leftist talk-show host Stephanie Miller spoke for many in comparing PBS star Jim Lehrer to Lance Ito, the feckless judge in the O. J. Simpson murder trial. Apparently, that makes Romney the wife-killer in this metaphor: "Almost everything Mitt Romney said was a lie which the fact-checkers had talked about today already, and Jim Lehrer was like the Judge Ito in my opinion, he just let Romney, I mean, it's just like, it's filibuster, right? He just kept talking." [12]

Strangely, Team Obama and the media then jumped on Romney for his talk of cutting off PBS funding. "I'm sorry, Jim, I'm going to stop the subsidy to PBS," he said, during the debate. " I'm going to stop other things. I like PBS, I love Big Bird. Actually I like you, too. But I'm not going to—I'm not going to keep on spending money on things to borrow money from China to pay for." [13]

The point was obvious: PBS isn't a pressing need worth throwing on the mountain of national debt. But the networks pounced anyway. The next day, *CBS This Morning* cohost Norah O'Donnell lectured: "This may have been the first time in a presidential debate that Big Bird was mentioned. It seems kind of like a silly thing to bring up." [14] When CNN asked about it, Representative Mario Diaz-Balart (R-FL) grew angry: "I think focusing on a light moment, which was clearly what it was, is doing a disservice to the people of America who are struggling," he bellyached. "That's the best you can come up with from this debate?" [15] CNN also brought on PBS president Paula Kerger to boast about what a great value PBS is for the taxpayers. [16]

On Friday morning, CNN's Soledad O'Brien also turned to PBS *Reading Rainbow* host LeVar Burton, who laid into Mitt Romney for attacking . . . children? "I was outraged. I couldn't believe the man actually fixed his mouth to say that. I interpreted it as an attack on children, Soledad." CNN's headlines onscreen were "Save Big Bird!" and "Romney Takes Aim at Big Bird." [17]

By Friday night, NBC's Brian Williams filed an entire pro-PBS story—with the exception of that one Romney soundbite, now repackaged as a self-inflicted wound. It starred Obama joking, "He'll get rid of regulations on Wall Street, but he's going to crack down on *Sesame Street*. Thank goodness somebody's finally cracking down on Big Bird." [18] NBC was doing Obama's nightly messaging and passing it off as journalism, again.

## The Vice Presidential Debate: Raddatz Singles Out Ryan

The moderator of the vice presidential debate, ABC correspondent Martha Raddatz, was a fresh face, but any Republican trying to pick moderators would have known she displayed the typical pro-Obama tilt in her reporting with the slightest research. The president's sending General David Petraeus to oversee the war in Afghanistan was a "great save." It was "truly historic" when Obama's Joint Chiefs chairman backed gays in the military. Obama accomplished "another huge victory in the War on Terror" when a drone attack killed radical jihadist/American citizen Anwar al-Awlaki. She described the secretary of state like this: "Let's face it. Hillary Clinton is cool, and trending."[19] But in 2009, when thirteen Americans lost their lives in a mass shooting at Fort Hood in Texas, it wasn't a loss for Team Obama. Raddatz notably lamented that she wished the killer didn't have a Muslim name, perhaps because Americans were so hopelessly Islamophobic: "As for the suspect, Nidal Hasan, as one officer's wife told me, 'I wish his name was Smith.'" Diane Sawyer quoted Raddatz again the next morning.[20]

Raddatz had several too-close associations with the Democrats. One was old: Barack Obama was a guest at her marriage in 1991 to Julius Genachowski. This came right after Obama graduated from Harvard Law School, where he was classmates with Genachowski, who would later became Obama's chairman of the Federal Communications Commission. (He and Raddatz divorced in 1997.)

One was much newer. Raddatz attended a Women's History Month reception in March 2012 at the vice presidential mansion. About 110 guests mingled in the foyer of the veep's residence with Biden and his wife, Jill, including not only Raddatz but CBS's Erica Hill and CNN's Gloria Borger, as well as Democratic luminaries like top Obama aide Valerie Jarrett and former secretary of state Madeleine Albright.[21]

Do you think Ann Coulter was invited?

When the debate began in Danville, Kentucky, Raddatz started by asking about the September 11 attack that killed four Americans (including the U.S. ambassador) at our consulate in Benghazi, Libya. Between the attack and this debate, Team Obama strangely attempted to characterize the attacks as not a terrorist attack, but a spontaneous response to a "very offensive video" on YouTube mocking the prophet Muhammad.

That spin had completely collapsed as unfactual. The day before the debate, the State Department disowned this spin line: In a conference call to reporters, senior officials argued, "That was not our conclusion. . . . That is the question you'd have to ask others."

So Raddatz began: "The State Department has now made clear, there were no protesters there. It was a pre-planned assault by heavily armed men." But this didn't acknowledge that Susan Rice's Sunday-show talking points said the exact opposite. Instead, she asked: "Wasn't this a massive intelligence failure, Vice President Biden?"

Biden declared it a "tragedy" and risibly added, "we will get to the bottom of it, and whatever—wherever the facts lead us." Ryan strongly attacked when the question turned to him, questioning Rice's truthfulness and Obama's continued blame on the YouTube video.

Then Raddatz repeated the liberal media spin that Romney and Ryan were uncivil for this critique based on what had become the established facts: "Right in the middle of the crisis, Governor Romney—and you're talking about this again tonight—talked about the weakness, talked about apologies from the Obama administration. Was that really appropriate right in the middle of the crisis?"

This amounted to a softball for Biden when it was his turn to reply. Raddatz did ask a follow-up: "Why were people talking about protests? When people in the consulate first saw armed men attacking with guns, there were no protesters." Biden blamed the "intelligence community." [22] There was no ownership of the fiasco. Saying "the intelligence community" was like saying "someone from the Congo." The White House knew it was a terrorist attack within twenty-four hours—yet continued, for days, blaming a silly video no one had ever seen. And they got away with it.

It's amazing that liberals insisted during the Bush years that the president was the dimmest of dimwits yet was also responsible for every foreign policy mistake. Now the geniuses Obama and Biden could claim complete ignorance when our diplomats die. In the Bush years, bad intelligence was pinned squarely on Bush as commander in chief. In the Obama years, claims of faulty intelligence somehow absolve everyone on his team.

Overall, the Media Research Center scorecard was mixed. Raddatz balanced her questions in the foreign policy section—eight pro-Romney, seven pro-Obama (not counting neutral questions). But on domestic policy, especially on Ryan's area of greatest expertise, that of taxes and spending, she practically joined Biden in trying to damage Ryan, with a dozen questions that incorporated liberal campaign themes, compared to just four from the Romney viewpoint, a 3-to-1 tilt.[23]

It was beyond annoying watching her interrupt Ryan just when he was going to land a punch. Take green jobs. Ryan charged: "The vice president was in charge of overseeing this. Ninety billion dollars in green pork to campaign contributors and special interest groups. There are just at the Department of Energy over 100 criminal investigations that have been launched into just how stimulus—"[24] Biden interrupted, and Raddatz gave Biden the floor.

*Washington Post* writer Dan Zak penned a TV review of the debates that bragged "only Vice President Biden acted as though he could sit at the desk in the Oval Office and have his feet touch the ground." In the paper, he began with "A pro debated a novice," but on Twitter, Zak previewed he would write: "A man debated a boy Thursday night."

But Zak acknowledged the truth about Raddatz: "Fairly or not, she reserved most of her skepticism for Ryan." Even Zak found it obvious: "'No specifics then?' she asked about his ticket's tax plan. 'Can you guarantee this math will add up? . . . How do you do that? . . . I wanna know how you do the math.'"[25]

ABC showered their own colleague with praise. They exclaimed "Martha Raddatz for President!"[26] This only underlined why the moderator shouldn't be the star of the show.

## The Town-Hall Debate Tilts Left—Again

CNN's Candy Crowley seemed like the most promising of the moderators to press both sides for answers, but that's not how it turned out at all. Crowley ended up being the worst of the four in tilting the debate toward the president. Even Frank Fahrenkopf, the cochair of the Commission on Presidential Debates, admitted error three months after the election: "We made one mistake this time: Her name is Candy."[27]

The viewing public might think a "town hall" debate is the most freewheeling populist forum of all the debates. That has never been the case. In reality, the citizen questioners are selected from a Gallup survey of self-declared "undecided voters," but that often strains credulity. The questioners are more carefully selected for the questions they're bringing to the table.[28] Usually that means that the moderators tilt the "real people" to match their liberal bias.

In advance of the debate, Media Research Center analysts reviewed every town-hall debate from 1992 to 2008 and discovered that the citizen questions selected by media moderators slanted by a margin of 2-to-1, with 28 liberal questions and just 14 conservative questions.[29]

The same tilt happened again in 2012. Crowley organized six pro-Obama/liberal-themed questions, versus three pro-Romney questions, and two others scored as neutral. After the debate, she suggested she had wanted to throw in more liberal questions, like "climate change—I had that question, for all you climate change people."[30]

To many conservatives, the most jaw-droppingly partisan question came from Susan Katz, who lectured Romney: "I attribute much of America's economic and international problems to the failings and missteps of the Bush administration. Since both you and President

Bush are Republicans, I fear a return to the policies of those years should you win this election. What is the biggest difference between you and George W. Bush?"[31]

The idea that Katz brought no bias to this debate was obliterated the next morning, when she appeared on CNN. Anchor Carol Costello asked if she was now decided. Katz replied to Costello that she voted for Obama in 2008 and planned to do so again because "I saw in President Obama someone who has ripened with time who deserves another four years to see his vision through."[32]

Katz wasn't alone in showing a bias. On feminism, Katherine Fenton stood and asked Obama: "In what new ways do you intend to rectify the inequalities in the workplace, specifically regarding females making only 72 percent of what their male counterparts earn?"[33] Later, Fenton told the liberal website Salon that she was passionate about "women's equality in the workforce" and "I'm very protective of my reproductive rights." Her "gut" told her Obama would be better for women.[34] No kidding.

On immigration, Lorraine Osorio asked: "Mr. Romney, what do you plan on doing with immigrants without their green cards that are currently living here as productive members of society?"[35] Osorio, the daughter of Salvadorans, told ABCNews.com that "actions speak louder than words," and that Obama's policy deferring deportations demonstrated his commitment to young immigrants.[36] Did that sound undecided?

On gun control, Nina Gonzalez asked Obama: "During the Democratic National Convention in 2008, you stated you wanted to keep AK-47s out of the hands of criminals. What has your administration done or planned to do to limit the availability of assault weapons?"[37]

*The New York Times* editorial page was delighted: "It took an ordinary citizen, Nina Gonzalez, to stand up at the presidential debate on Tuesday to raise what has been a phantom issue on the campaign trail: the lack of effective gun controls."[38]

NBC correspondent Chuck Todd summed up Wednesday morning: "The President also benefitted from many questions posed by the *so-called undecided voters*, covering issues near and dear to his liberal base." Even NBC was acknowledging the dishonesty of the town hall–style debate.[39]

## Candy Crowley Backs a Lie

Of the three questions that could be considered as coming from the Republican perspective, the toughest question for Obama was the one about his administration's obvious failure to provide necessary security for the Libyan consulate, which was attacked on September 11. A man named Kerry Ladka asked: "The State Department refused extra security for our embassy in Benghazi, Libya, prior to the attacks that killed four Americans. Who was it that denied enhanced security, and why?"

After the president and Romney each answered the question, Crowley then recalled that Secretary of State Hillary Clinton took responsibility for the deaths in Benghazi, and asked the president, "Does the buck stop with the Secretary of State?" Obama said the buck stopped with him, but he laid into Romney, whose suggestion, Obama said, that "anybody on my team would play politics or mislead when we've lost four of our own, Governor, is offensive." That came right after he claimed "the day after the attack, I stood in the Rose Garden and told the American people and the world that we are going to find out exactly what happened, that this was an act of terror. . . ."

Barack Obama had lied. He hadn't labeled the Libya attack an act of terrorism. The look on Romney's face said it all: Mr. President, here comes checkmate.

Romney wanted Obama to clarify: "You said in the Rose Garden the day after the attack, it was an act of terror? It was not a spontaneous demonstration, is that what you're saying? . . . [Speaking to Crowley:] I want to make sure we get that for the record because it took the president 14 days before he called the attack in Benghazi an act of terror." [40]

What came next was the most stunning and disgraceful single example of moderator malpractice in the history of televised presidential debates. Crowley allowed Obama to lie to the American people about his administration's Libya cover-up. Even worse, she then validated this lie of extraordinary magnitude by certifying it as honest, and by attacking Mitt Romney when he pressed the president on his administration's cover-up. Crowley robbed tens of millions of Americans of the truth on national prime-time television. Real journalists—especially those who were fed the Obama administration's Libya lies for more than two weeks—should have been furious.

Crowley jumped in to assert to Romney: "He did, in fact, sir . . . call it an act of terror." Obama crowed triumphantly: "Can you say that a little louder, Candy?" Crowley repeated: "He did call it an act of terror." [41]

No, he did not. Not according to the transcript from the White House, which has Obama only speaking generically about how "no acts of terror will ever shake the resolve of this nation," not assigning that label to the violence in Benghazi. [42] Among many others, the official *Washington Post* fact-checker, Glenn Kessler, pointed out the obvious: "He [Obama] did not say 'terrorism'—and it took the administration days to concede that it [was] an 'act of terrorism' that appears unrelated to initial reports of anger at a video that defamed the prophet Muhammad." [43]

Here's where Crowley's fractured "fact check" makes no sense. Back on September 30, on her CNN Sunday program *State of the Union*, she hit Obama strategist David Axelrod on exactly this point: "Why did it take them [the White House] until Friday [September 28], after a September 11 attack in Libya, to come to the conclusion that it was premeditated and that there was terrorists involved? John McCain said it doesn't pass the smell test, or it's willful ignorance to think that they didn't know before this what was going on." [44]

Of course, Axelrod shot back that Obama in the Rose Garden called it an "act of terror." By her very question to Axelrod, she knew this answer wasn't truthful. It was actually a ridiculously dishonest answer. If he meant to blame the terrorists for their attack on the consulate, why not just say so? Instead of the nebulous "no acts of terror will ever shake the resolve of this nation," he would have said, "This act of terror will never shake the resolve of this nation."

And his secretary of state would not have made pious public statements apologizing for a video that never caused anything. And his representative to the United Nations would not have traveled to five major network shows in one day to blame that video.

Axelrod was lying. Crowley knew the Obama administration initially tried to deny the Libya attack was terrorism. But all that disappeared when it truly mattered, on a debate stage with more than 60 million Americans watching. She now defended his lie as the truth.

How does Crowley square her October 16 performance with her September 30 performance? Try this theory: after liberals savaged Jim Lehrer as "useless" for somehow allowing Obama's first-debate fiasco, they'd successfully worked the refs, both Crowley and Raddatz, to push back at the "lies" of the Republicans. Crowley was "useful"—in denying the facts. And a hit with her peers. Quite possibly she saved the Obama campaign.

That night on PBS, John Heilemann of *New York* magazine thought Crowley's tilt to Obama was decisive: "The worst hand that the administration and President Obama have to play in this debate was on Benghazi, and because particularly of Candy Crowley's follow-up on that question, it allowed Barack Obama to win an exchange that I didn't necessarily think it was possible for him to win." [45]

The next morning, even Current TV host Eliot Spitzer acknowledged the truth, telling fellow host Bill Press that Crowley caused the "emotional highlight of the night" by declaring Romney was wrong. "I think that really deflated what otherwise should have been on the Benghazi issue a moment when Romney could have hit it out of the park. But instead he took the step too far. Crowley came in as sort of the voice of neutrality and took the victory away from Romney." [46]

It was precisely because Crowley was the so-called voice of neutrality who moderated a very tilted panel of so-called undecided voters that Obama was awarded a dirty-trick win.

On ABC the morning after, former Bush pollster Matthew Dowd taunted Crowley's critics as losers and implied the facts were somehow not worth considering: "I think what this may lead to is a bunch of conservatives and Republicans attacking Candy Crowley, and when that happens, that is a sure sign that President Obama won this. When you start attacking the ref, or start attacking the umpire, it means you left a lot of plays on the field, and when you see that, you know they know they lost." [47]

The networks settled on another Romney gaffe as well, that Romney said he had "binders full of women" when he was choosing female appointees for his state government in Massachusetts. Despite Romney's record of appointing women to his administration, liberals went nuts on that phrase on Twitter, and the liberal media followed obediently. [48]

The Big Three networks gave the faux-furor over the "binders" comment a whopping twenty-two mentions from Tuesday night through Friday morning. Yet when Vice President Joe Biden, on that Thursday, told an audience member that Republican "young guns" like vice presidential nominee Paul Ryan had "bullets" aimed at him, the networks delivered just a scant two total mentions, one each on CBS and NBC. ABC skipped the gaffe entirely. [49]

On the morning after the debate, ABC's Elizabeth Vargas, on *Good Morning America*, singled out the binders: "You remember the Big Bird line that dominated the conversations online and around the water cooler, in essence, after the first debate? Last night, it was another Romney comment, 'binders full of women' that caused the heat to turn on." [50]

In a forum with former CBS reporter Marvin Kalb after the election, with three of the moderators (which Crowley missed), Bob Schieffer said the town-hall format should be dumped. "It just seems not to work in my view as well. It gives them a chance to put too much show business into it. You know, you get the candidates kind of performing and walking over and getting in the other guy's space sometimes." [51]

## The Final Debate: Everyone Shrinks from Libya

The last presidential debate was moderated by Bob Schieffer, a forty-three-year veteran of CBS News who was chosen to moderate for the third election cycle in a row. Both the moderator and the candidates in this foreign policy debate were clearly affected by Candy-gate.

Schieffer's first question was on Benghazi, but it was directed at Romney and not at President Obama. It refrained from any finding of fact to the killers: "Questions remain. What happened? What caused it? Was it spontaneous? Was it an intelligence failure? Was it a policy failure? Was there an attempt to mislead people about what really happened?"

Romney, after suffering from Crowley's fractured "fact check," barely touched on Libya. Now it was his camp's turn to be stunned in disbelief. After a half minute of thank-yous and courtesies, he asserted that "terrorists" caused the murders, and moved on to Mali and other hot spots. Schieffer didn't ask Obama about Susan Rice bizarrely blaming a YouTube video on five Sunday news shows, including his own *Face the Nation*. He merely tossed the question to him with a "Mr. President?"

The only utterance of Benghazi came when the president boasted about the end of Libyan dictator Muammar Qaddafi: "Got rid of a despot who had killed Americans and as a consequence, despite this tragedy, you had tens of thousands of Libyans after the events in Benghazi marching and saying America is our friend. We stand with them." [52]

Overall, Schieffer stuck to a Jim Lehrer formula, keeping questions brief and letting the candidates be the main focus. But on this first round, Schieffer made no real attempt to advance the Benghazi story or hold the president accountable for Susan Rice's fake claims. Schieffer's restraint in the final debate also included failing to ask the president about his promise to end the custody of terrorist suspects at Guantanamo Bay in Cuba.

On June 9, 2005, on MSNBC's *Imus in the Morning*, Schieffer had raged, "This isn't just a boil. It's a cancer. This thing is not doing anybody any good." On June 19, 2006, he led off the *CBS Evening News* with angry editorializing: "Has the U.S. prison for terror suspects at Guantanamo become more trouble than it's worth? Even those who created it have to be asking that question tonight." [53] But Schieffer failed to sustain that outrage and ask a single Gitmo question to Obama in this debate.

Some Obama fans in the liberal media were crowing about an Obama win. When Romney charged "our Navy is smaller now than at any time since 1917," Obama shot back, "Well, Governor, we also have fewer horses and bayonets, because the nature of our military's changed." NBC anchor Brian Williams was especially fond of that line: "David Gregory, we always try to look for the phrase or expression that will live forever out of these. Tonight has to be 'horses and bayonets.' . . . A very sharp comeback from the President." [54] This, obviously, quickly became false. When President Obama traveled to Norfolk, Virginia, in February to dramatize the damage a sequester would cause the military, Williams and everyone else failed to remember the president's mockery of the decline of navy ships.

But just before that quip from Obama, he uncorked this lie about the sequester: "First of all, the sequester is not something that I've proposed. It is something that Congress has proposed. It will not happen." [55]

In his book *The Price of Politics*—published on September 11, six weeks before the October 22 debate—Bob Woodward reported that Obama personally approved of a plan for his chief of staff Jack Lew and congressional liaison Rob Nabors to propose the sequester to Senate Majority Leader Harry Reid. [56] Team Obama never protested Woodward's account. But now he was claiming before before 60 million people that his team never proposed the sequester. Unless he was playing Bill Clinton word games—see, *he* didn't propose the sequester, but his aides did. Nobody in the media—including Woodward—seemed to notice this before the election.

# CHAPTER 12

# Backing Away from Benghazi

Pay no attention to the failures and lies before you vote.

The media could never believe Ronald Reagan won because people agreed it was time to try conservative ideas. Over time, they all became enamored with the "October Surprise" conspiracy theory to explain why Jimmy Carter lost the 1980 election. Somehow, Carter didn't lose because he was inept in dealing with the economy and inept in ending the Iranian hostage crisis. He must have lost because Reagan's campaign made a dastardly attempt to delay the release of the hostages who had been held in Iran since November 1979. This conspiracy theory was never substantiated, no matter how hard the likes of ABC's Ted Koppel tried to prove it.

In every election cycle, the media have tried to focus their persuasive powers in the last weeks of a campaign on preventing an "October surprise" that would hurt Democratic incumbents (or challengers). On the other hand, if they could unleash or abet a dirty-trick last-minute surprise on the Republican incumbents, they have done so with impunity. Ends justify means.

So when seventeen American sailors died from an al-Qaeda suicide-bomb attack on the USS *Cole* in Yemen on October 12, 2000, the media labored mightily to disassociate the incident from President Clinton and Vice President Al Gore, the Democratic nominee for president. Conversely, in the fall of 2004, the media worked hard to find scandals that would ruin Bush's standing as commander in chief and prevent his reelection, starting most notoriously in September with Dan Rather's bumbling reliance on phony National Guard documents to suggest the president's Vietnam-era evasion of military service.

In the last week, they were still pushing new story lines attempting to dent the Bush advantage. On October 24, the front page of *The New York Times* pushed the headline "Huge Cache of Explosives Vanished from Site in Iraq." The story was dutifully pushed to the top of the three broadcast network evening newscasts. Dan Rather trumpeted at the start of the *CBS Evening News*: "Eight days to go till America elects a president, and disturbing news from Iraq is again dominating the campaign. The White House acknowledged today that a huge stockpile of ultra-high explosives is inexplicably missing from an Iraqi weapons site. Senator John Kerry called this a quote, 'great blunder' by President Bush and his administration." [1]

The next night, CBS reporter John Roberts noted the story had Team Bush "way off message today and losing in the headlines, and in danger of losing momentum at the worst possible time." In contrast, after running four soundbites from what CBS's Byron Pitts described as Kerry's "impassioned critique" of Bush policy, Pitts relayed: "said one [Kerry] aide today, 'The headlines this week are in our favor, and for now the wind is at our back.'" [2]

The *Times* was spooked into publishing this "early," since they were working with the *60 Minutes* crew at CBS, which wanted to break this story on the night of Halloween, just two days before the election. (Ironically, this worked in reverse with Rathergate: the National Guard story was scheduled to land on the eve of the election but CBS was concerned its partner, *The New York Times*, was going to skunk the network, so CBS rushed it out early.)

That malodorous last-minute media sandbag would not be dropped on the Obama administration when the U.S. consulate in Benghazi was attacked on September 11, 2012. A large group of terrorists armed with rocket launchers murdered U.S. Ambassador Chris Stevens and State Department officer Sean Smith at the consulate. Ty Woods and Glen Doherty later died defending the CIA annex after it came under attack from the same terrorists.

When that terrible day began, *CBS This Morning* brought on former *New York Times* reporter Kurt Eichenwald to pounce on. . . . George W. Bush. Eichenwald was promoting his book *500 Days*, accusing the Bush administration of ignoring warnings about a possible terrorist strike as early as May 2001. Eichenwald claimed that "the CIA did a spectacular job. . . . [T]he White House and others said, 'Well, they didn't tell us enough.' No, they told them everything they needed to know to go on a full alert, and the White House didn't do it."[3]

*The New York Times* didn't put the 9/11 attacks back on its front page but it gave its old reporter a pathway to CBS with an op-ed titled "The Deafness Before the Storm," a stale rerun blaming Bush for ignoring the warning contained in his August 6, *2001*, presidential daily briefing that Osama bin Laden might be readying an attack on the United States.[4]

On September 12, 2012, as the bad news of the Benghazi massacre streamed in, the *Times* suggested it had a different sense of holding Obama accountable. While Benghazi and other Mideast unrest was published on page A4 the day after the attack, this was on page A1: "Dissecting Romney's Vietnam Stance at Stanford." Reporter Michael Wines found that in November 1965, young Romney and his friends cared more about college spirit than geopolitics, as he "stayed true to his chinos and the Vietnam War."[5]

In the first hours after the Benghazi attack news broke, incredibly, it was Romney who was placed in the media spotlight, and it was harsh. On the 9/11 anniversary, the U.S. embassy was breached in Cairo, and Republicans were buzzing about the State Department's astonishing response: "The Embassy of the United States in Cairo condemns the continuing efforts by misguided individuals to hurt the religious feelings of Muslims—as we condemn efforts to offend believers of all religions." After the embassy's invaders pulled down the U.S. flag and put up an Islamic flag, the embassy said on Twitter, "This morning's condemnation (issued before protest began) still stands. As does our condemnation of unjustified breach of the Embassy." (The tweet was later deleted.)

This spurred Romney to put out a statement that evening around 10:30 Eastern time: "I think it's a terrible course for America to stand in apology for our values. That instead, when our grounds are being attacked and being breached, that the first response of the United States must be outrage at the breach of the sovereignty of our nation. An apology for America's values is never the right course."[6]

Romney was entirely correct in his broadside against the administration for its gutless response to an attack against Americans on American soil. Obama's allies in the press knew the embassy's response was preposterous and indefensible. How then to turn this segment against Romney? The answers came a few hours later.

News of four Americans dying in Benghazi came out around 7 A.M. the next day, so Romney decided to hold a brief press conference to comment on his Cairo-embassy statement in light of the new information. Reporters weren't looking for information. They wanted Romney to apologize for daring to play politics with the government response in Egypt and the charge that President Obama's team showed weakness. *"How could he be so heartless while Americans are dying in Benghazi?!"*

The Right Scoop website posted video with an open microphone that showed the liberal reporters on the Romney beat boldly, if quietly coordinating their line of questions to attack Romney. They were seeking a rhetorical retreat:

> JAN CRAWFORD, CBS: That's the question. . . . Yeah that's the question. I would just say "Do you regret your question?"
> ARI SHAPIRO, NPR: "Your question?" Your statement?
> CRAWFORD: I mean "your statement." Not even "your tone," because then he can go off on—
> SHAPIRO: And then if he does, I think we can just follow up and say "but this morning your answer is continuing to sound"—

Then the feed is cut off. Moments later, Crawford adds, "No matter who he calls on, we're covered on the one question." A man (not Shapiro) utters, "Do you stand by your statement or regret your statement?" [7]

There's nothing undemocratic or even unprofessional about journalists working together if the goal is to arrive at the most appropriate line of questioning. But that story line can turn out to be a very biased, politicized line—one designed to trip, to embarrass, to hurt the target. That is unethical. Reporters sometimes mock the idea of a media "conspiracy." This was not a conspiracy. It was open collusion.

## Romney's Manners Were the Big Scoop

The perversity of this situation was that Romney was attempting to be forthcoming. He called a press conference in the morning and took questions. And was hammered for it. Should he have behaved like Obama? The president of the United States made a statement without taking questions and hopped on a jet for a fundraiser in Las Vegas. "Mr. Obama and his team have learned from experience that the political costs of campaigning amid crises can be minimal," reported Jim Rutenberg in *The New York Times*.[8] The optics might have seemed terrible, but the president had confidence that the network spinners would take care of him. And did they ever. While the commander in chief palled around with his rich friends, the "news" media pounced on Romney.

On that Benghazi-dominated first night of evening news coverage, a Media Research Center analysis found the rude-Romney angle received nearly ten minutes of coverage on the Big Three newscasts (9 minutes, 28 seconds), versus just 25 seconds questioning Obama's Middle East policies.[9] Time spent covering Obama's shameful fundraising during a national crisis? Zero.

NBC's Brian Williams spoke for the media in pronouncing that Obama's line of national unity would win the spin cycle: "Romney is taking fire tonight for the way he went on the attack politically. . . . Somehow [Romney] wanted today to be about America apologizing for its values, even after it became clear today was about the death of an American ambassador and others in one of two attacks on American interests on 9/11, no less. And instead of backing away, Romney doubled down on his position."

This might sound shameless—that this was supposed to be a day of national unity and mourning, while the president flew to Las Vegas for a whoop-whoop campaign rally. (Only NBC's Chuck Todd even briefly mentioned Obama had an event in Vegas.) But the networks were true to Obama, cuing up this Obama lectured to Romney from an interview Obama granted that day to Steve Kroft of *60 Minutes*, one of his favorite softball specialists.

"There is a broader lesson to be learned here. You know, Governor

Romney seems to have a tendency to shoot first and aim later. And as president, one of the things I have learned is you can't do that. That it is important for you to make sure that the statements that you make are backed up by the facts and that you have thought through the ramifications before you make them." [10]

(If Obama were a Republican, Kroft might have mocked him for using "shoot first" language after the administration failed to offer military assistance of any kind to the scattered security personnel in Benghazi. But Obama isn't a Republican.)

CBS added a few more seconds, with Kroft following up with the typical softball, asking for Romney to feel shamed: "Do you think it was irresponsible?" Obama replied: "I'll let the American people judge that." [11] He'd let the people decide—after the networks had driven home his narrative. For her story, Jan Crawford displayed exactly what she wanted, Romney defending himself against a series of reporters demanding that he apologize for being inappropriate:

CRAWFORD: Do you think, though, coming so soon after the events really had unfolded overnight, was appropriate? To be weighing in on this as this crisis is unfolding in real time? . . .

UNIDENTIFIED FEMALE: What did the White House do wrong, then, Governor Romney, if they put out a statement saying they disagreed with it? . . .

UNIDENTIFIED MALE: You talk about mixed signals. The world is watching. Isn't this itself a mixed signal, when you've criticized the administration at a time that Americans are being killed? Shouldn't politics stop for this? [12]

But on that first night, CBS reporter David Martin, one of the few serious and knowledgeable journalists left in the business, set down a marker: this was a terrorist attack. "U.S. officials say this was not an out-of-control demonstration, but a well-executed attack by a well-armed band of thugs." After listing all the (belated) military deployments, he concluded his report: "Bottom line: This is a terrorist hunt."[13]

But by Friday the fourteenth, press secretary Jay Carney shifted the White House line into blaming "protests . . . in reaction to a video that had spread to the region," a cheesy, amateurish YouTube video slamming the prophet Muhammad called "The Innocence of Muslims." "We have no evidence of a pre-planned attack," claimed Carney.[14] (Candy Crowley, call your office.) On that day, President Obama and Secretary of State Hillary Clinton welcomed the caskets of the four lost Americans at Andrews Air Force Base. For media liberals, this became another chance to celebrate these two liberal leaders, formerly at loggerheads in the 2008 primaries, grieving for America.

On MSNBC's *Hardball*, Chris Matthews was tingling away. It was an "amazing ceremony," he insisted. After an Obama clip, he said "there was a moment in American history right there. Last week, when Obama spoke at the Democratic National Committee down in Charlotte, he said, 'I am the president.' Well, this week, he showed what it means to be president." He told Willie Brown, the former mayor of San Francisco and Speaker of the California State Assembly, "The wonderful moment when the secretary of state reached over to grab his hand after those remarks, it is something else. I am a sentimentalist, I will admit it. But I can't think of a better way to celebrate our Americanism than the way we did it just then."[15]

If George W. Bush had been president, the arrival of these four caskets would have been painted as a sickening sign of failure and incompetence, of public servants needlessly losing their lives because the White House couldn't piece together their intelligence reports. Matthews would have railed against the Bush people for failing to protect their diplomats in unstable Arab nations. Now it was time to tingle over the unified Democrats instead.

*NBC Nightly News* made no mention of Romney or Republicans.

NBC's Andrea Mitchell properly celebrated the men who died as "idealists" who "loved service and thrived on adventure." Then their haloes were rubbed on Team Obama. Mitchell ran long, loving soundbites from Hillary describing the good qualities of the deceased. NBC ran a quote of the president quoting from the gospel of John that "greater love hath no man than this, than a man lay down his life for his friends." Like a good publicist, Mitchell added that "U.S. officials insist there was no prior intelligence about the attack in Libya." [16]

Two days later, the administration sent out its ambassador to the United Nations, Susan Rice, to enunciate the same line on five networks, like this on *Meet the Press*: "This is a response to a hateful and offensive video that was widely disseminated throughout the Arab and Muslim world. . . . This is a spontaneous reaction to the video." [17]

Unlike the furor over Romney, the network response was muted, neither endorsing nor attacking the new Obama blame-the-video line. But that narrative began collapsing within days. On September 20, Jay Carney conceded the assault on the U.S. consulate was a "terrorist attack." Even then, network reporters seemed to want to spread confusion. NBC's Mitchell began that night by announcing, "Tonight, the White House confirmed the attack was an act of terror," and then reported that Carney conceded during a flight on Air Force One, "I think it's self-evident that what happened in Benghazi was a terrorist attack." But she also showed Obama failing to concede that day: "What we do know is that the natural protests that arose because of the outrage over the video were used as an excuse by extremists to see if they can also directly harm U.S. interests." Faced with this double-talk, Mitchell concluded, "U.S. officials say that this could have been a long-planned attack, taking the opportunity of a protest, or no protest at all. They are now investigating all possibilities." [18]

On *Face the Nation* on September 23, a week after the Susan Rice Sunday show tour, CBS News political director John Dickerson could see trouble brewing for Team Obama—but not from the media. It was a refreshing moment of candor. "Well, now they are calling it a terrorist attack. 'What went wrong there?' 'What did you get wrong in the first place?' 'Why weren't you securing the embassy the way you should have been?' These are points that a Republican could make, that Mitt Romney needs to make, because he knows the press isn't necessarily going to make that case for him."[19]

One of the reasons the networks may have been restrained is that President Obama himself was so slow to give up the unfactual line that a YouTube video caused the Benghazi attack. He unspooled it on the Letterman show on September 18, repeated it on a Univision town hall on September 20, and he also declined to call it a terrorist attack on ABC's *The View* on September 24.

The anchors of ABC and NBC each were granted an interview with Obama, and neither was interested in asking more than a single question about it for the public. On the October 10 *World News*, ABC's Diane Sawyer began her interview with four solid minutes of channeling liberal angst over his lackluster performance in the first debate. She also allocated more than a minute to encouraging Obama to denounce a lawyerly Mitt Romney utterance that he planned on abortion legislation if he were elected. Sawyer prompted Obama with a harsh assessment of Romney: "Is it a lie?"

The word or concept of "Libya" was not even uttered in the Sawyer-Obama segment. Viewers had to wait until the next story, by Jake Tapper, on a House committee hearing that laid out the administration's failures to provide security for the diplomats in Libya. ABC viewers got a whopping twenty seconds from the White House interview—more than half of that consumed by Obama's defense and assurance he'll "fix" anything that wasn't done properly.

TAPPER: Diane Sawyer asked the President about the White House's initial claims that the incident began with a protest against that anti-Muslim video.

OBAMA: As information came in, information was put out. The information may have not have always been right the first time. . . . Look, Diane, these are people I know. And if there's something to be fixed, it'll get fixed.[20]

Notice there's no room in this clip for an actual Sawyer question, so viewers didn't see her purported angst over four dead Americans. But they did see her upset over Obama's blown debate.

Two weeks later, on October 24, *NBC Nightly News* anchor Brian Williams aired a taped interview with the president. These are the questions the public was supposed to find most newsworthy.

First, "How is it that with—what, 13 days to go, you're fighting for your life in a 47/47 [percent, tied] race?" Williams was shocked it wasn't a landslide yet.

Second, on the same theme, "So after the excitement of '08, given the power of incumbency, you got bin Laden, you did not expect to be sitting on a more substantial race than we are as we sit here today?"

In an interview segment aired on Wednesday night and again on Thursday morning, Williams also wondered: "What's the dynamic like between you and Mitt Romney? . . . You don't appear to like each other very much." Despite his campaign's particularly nasty attacks on Romney, Obama replied: "I don't think that any relationship between me and Mitt Romney is different from previous presidential campaigns."[21]

Then on Thursday's *Nightly News*, Williams touted Obama's endorsement for the second time by former Bush secretary of state Colin Powell, as if a second endorsement somehow rises to the level of national news. He then took the familiar route of challenging Obama to be more boldly liberal. "Mr. President, the subject of rape has been in the public discourse this campaign year unlike any time I can remember it in American public life. You were asked about it last night, you've inserted a line in your speech, I noted, about women's health. Is that as far as you're comfortable going for now?"

Williams also lamented the election process and imagined Obama as a benevolent despot: "If you could fix either the Electoral College or the fact that we're going to spend a billion dollars electing a president, and Lord knows what cancer cure that might have started us down the road on, which would you do most urgently if you had unlimited powers?"

In none of these programs did Williams raise Libya. During a twenty-minute interview with President Obama aired on the October 25 *Rock Center*—a show in the 10 P.M. Eastern time hour that drew 3.7 million viewers—Williams devoted a total of one minute and thirty-six seconds to the subject of the terrorist attack in Libya—and used it as an opportunity to shield his hero from blame. He treated President Obama as a victim of faulty intelligence work:

"Have you been happy with the intelligence, especially in our post 9/11 world? The assessment of your intelligence community, as we stand here, is that it still was a spontaneous terrorist attack and were you happy with what you were able to learn as this unfolded? It went on for several hours."

Obama replied with the usual still-waiting-for-answers spin: "Well, as I've said, Brian, we're going to do a full investigation. Obviously, when four Americans are killed, you know, you have to do some soul searching in terms of making sure that all our systems are where they need to be. And that's what we are going to find out." [22]

Williams was letting Obama imply he was curious for new information. Neither of them was. Williams completely ignored a breaking story two nights earlier, wherein CBS reporter Sharyl Attkisson reported on e-mails sent directly to the White House and other government agencies in real time as the Benghazi consulate came under attack from armed jihadists. It underlined that Team Obama wasn't as confused about YouTube-inspired killers as he—and Williams—wanted people to believe. [23]

* * *

Even on CBS, the Attkisson report was treated as completely irrelevant to voters evaluating the honesty of Obama. The same CBS newscast featured reporter Nancy Cordes showing Obama drawing cheers in Florida as he "relentlessly stayed on offense," saying Romney was an untrustworthy flip-flopper: "The person who leads this country—you've got to have some confidence that he or she means what he or she says. . . . Florida, you know me! You can trust that I say what I mean!"[24]

Then came more information. On October 26, Fox News reporter Jennifer Griffin dropped a Little Boy atomic bomb. She reported that "sources claim officers at the nearby CIA annex in Benghazi were twice told to stand down when they requested to help those at the consulate. They later ignored those orders. Fox News was also told that a subsequent request for back-up when the annex came under attack was denied as well."[25]

In apparent defiance of these orders, two former Navy SEALs left the CIA annex to rescue several Americans from the consulate. Ty Woods and Glen Doherty later died defending the CIA annex. The administration had turned its back on its own consulate and four men, including a U.S. ambassador, had died as a result. The networks ignored this story.

Not every reporter avoided it. On the same day that Fox relayed this shocking new development, a local reporter in Denver, Colorado, named Kyle Clark did manage to ask President Obama about it during a campaign stop on October 26. "Were the Americans under attack at the consulate in Benghazi, Libya denied requests for help during that attack, and is it fair to tell Americans that what happened is under investigation, and we'll all find out after the election?" Imagine the president's shock that a local reporter would be so impertinently substantive.

Obama responded that "the minute I found out what was happening, I gave three very clear directives. Number one, make sure that we are securing our personnel and doing whatever we need to. . . . I guarantee you that everyone in the State Department, our military, the CIA, you name it, had number one priority making sure that people were safe."[26] Yet Fox's report—that help was requested and denied—clearly contradicted that claim.

The networks had no interest in testing Obama's claims—questionable (at best)—and ignored the Denver interview. The only coverage of these claims came when Republican guests mentioned them on the October 28 Sunday shows. Former CEO and Republican Senate candidate Carly Fiorina slammed Obama's Libya response ten minutes into NBC's *Meet the Press*: "That attack went on for seven hours . . . [with the] Secretary of Defense saying he denied requests for help over that seven hours." Gregory cut her off: "We'll get to Libya a little bit later." Unsurprisingly, NBC never did. Fiorina's brief mention was the last word on Libya during the hour-long program.[27]

On ABC's *This Week,* Newt Gingrich harped on Secretary of Defense Leon Panetta's failure to send any help to Benghazi and whacked at Obama scheduling choices: "He's canceling trips over the hurricane [Sandy]. He did not cancel trips over Benghazi." ABC host George Stephanopoulos changed the subject.[28]

On the October 28 *Fox News Sunday*, Brit Hume commented that "the mainstream organs of the media—that would be after this like a pack of hounds, if this were a Republican President—have been remarkably reticent. . . . A lot of the media, who are a combined potent force, have not done their job."[29]

Unlike their thrill over televising self-described "grieving Gold-Star mother and militant activist" Cindy Sheehan in 2004 as she protested President Bush for months, the networks were not interested in interviewing relatives of the Benghazi victims. Ty Woods's father, Charles, appeared on Fox News Channel's *Hannity* on October 29. He pleaded: "There are people in the White House—whoever it was—that [were] in that room watching that video of my son dying, their cries for help. Their order, 'Don't help them at all, let them die,' whoever that might be, it might be numerous people—you have the blood of my son. You have the blood of an American hero on your hands. I don't know who you are, but one of these days, the truth will come out. I still forgive you, but you need to stand up." [30]

It was heartbreaking.

The last outrage of Benghazi interviews surfaced very quietly on the Sunday before the election. The chronology here is very important. On September 12, the first day after the attack, Steve Kroft had interviewed the president about Libya, and CBS offered a soundbite that allowed Obama to trash Romney for shooting first and aiming later, with Kroft asking Obama if Romney was irresponsible.

Fuller interviews with Obama and with Romney aired on September 23. But only on November 4, almost two months after Benghazi, did the *60 Minutes* website post new video of Kroft asking directly if it was a terrorist attack. [31] Remember that CBS reported later they knew in real time that a terrorist group was responsible:

STEVE KROFT: Mr. President, this morning you went out of your way to avoid the use of the word "terrorism" in connection with the Libya attack. Do you believe that this was a terrorism attack?

PRESIDENT OBAMA: Well it's too early to tell exactly how this came about, what group was involved, but obviously it was an attack on Americans. And we are going to be working with the Libyan government to make sure that we bring these folks to justice, one way or the other.

KROFT: But there are reports that they were very heavily armed with grenades; that doesn't sound like your normal demonstration.

OBAMA: As I said, we're still investigating exactly what happened; I don't want to jump the gun on this.

Wait a minute. As was reported on October 20, fifteen days before this interview surfaced, and reported by CBS's own Sharyl Attkisson, Team Obama knew in real time on September 11 that Benghazi was most certainly a terrorist attack. So for the commander in chief to declare to Kroft the next day, "We're still investigating exactly what happened, I don't want to jump the gun on this" shows an astonishing detachment and an administration that was beyond inept—or the president was lying again. Either way, releasing that exchange the day after the Candy Crowley debate on October 17 would have displayed how Obama and his advisers were trying to rewrite history.

It could have been huge news and absolutely devastating news for the Obama campaign. Instead, CBS sat on it for another two weeks, while ABC and NBC also refused to call the president out for his misstatement.

It bears repeating. That quiet little release was only online. It wasn't even on the air. It didn't hit the air until the *CBS Evening News* on November 16—ten days after the election. During a story about ex-CIA director David Petraeus testifying that he never doubted that the attack was an act of terrorism, correspondent David Martin added: "Yet President Obama refrained from calling it a terrorist attack when he spoke with Steve Kroft of *60 Minutes* that afternoon."

They had successfully submerged Benghazi from emerging as a defining moment for judging Obama's competence or honesty. Compare that contrast—wanting to crush Bush's reelection on the Sunday before the 2004 election, to delaying, delaying, and then almost imperceptibly releasing information that underlined Obama's deceit on a national debate stage. They had turned a checkmate for Romney into a checkmate against him.

# EPILOGUE

## Some Steps to Combat and Persuade the Media

Did the national media deliver the election to Barack Obama? The question invites a level of analysis that is admittedly subjective in nature. What cannot be denied is their bias and their political agenda. As we've documented, it is there, unequivocally and overwhelmingly. Any journalist denying this is flirting with felony ignorance. The real question drills deeper and is more debatable: Were they believed? Did the media succeed in selling this bill of goods called "objective" "news" "reporting"—or did the public see through the charade?

The polling data point to a public that has grown skeptical, to say the least.

On September 21, just two months shy of the elections, the Gallup organization released some remarkable findings. They asked a simple question of the public: *How much trust do you have in the mass media—such as newspapers, TV and radio—when it comes to reporting the news fully, accurately and fairly—a great deal, a fair amount, not very much, not at all?* The results were eye-opening. A full 60 percent of the public has little or no trust in the news media, the highest negative on this question ever recorded by Gallup. Conversely, only 8 percent had a "great deal" of trust in the press.

On Election Night, at our behest, the McLaughlin Associates polling firm asked some questions along these lines in their omnibus survey.

The first question we wanted answered was the degree to which the public believed the news media had helped to reelect Barack Obama versus those who believed they were helping elect Mitt Romney. Take out those who believed the press was neutral, or who had no opinion and you're left with: *Obama 84.8 percent, Romney 15.2 percent.*

Did they succeed? We wanted to know—remember, we were anticipating a GOP victory—if the media might have cost Romney the election, had the public believed them. We asked Romney voters this: *"If you had accepted the liberal media's news reporting as factual, truthful and objective, would you have voted for Barack Obama?"*

The numbers stunned even veterans like us. A full 22.8 percent of Romney voters acknowledged they would have voted for the incumbent had they believed the liberal press. Another 6 percent stated they *might* have.

What, exactly, do those numbers mean? We conducted an exercise that, admittedly, is not entirely scientific, but it's proximate enough to make the necessary point. We took that 22.8 percent number out of the Romney camp and moved it into the Obama total, in every state.

On Election Night, Obama won with 51.4 percent of the popular vote, winning 28 states and registering a 332–206 electoral vote margin of victory.

Now, give him another 22.8 percent and his vote total would have risen by 13 million, to 62.5 percent. He would have won all but five states (Idaho, Wyoming, Utah, Oklahoma, and Arkansas). He would have captured 512 electoral votes. It might have cost the Republicans the three Senate seats they did finally manage to pick up. If so, the new total would be 58 Democrats, 42 Republicans, an insurmountable 16-seat advantage. The House? That may have tipped to the Democrats.

It would have been a Democrat landslide of epic proportions. Obama would declare a national mandate for his socialist transformation. His Democratic majorities would support it, and there's not a bloody thing Republicans could do to prevent it.

So, was this doomsday scenario avoided because the public didn't believe the news media? Because of this educated electorate, was the end of Western Civilization prevented? An exaggeration? Assuredly. What cannot be dismissed, however, is that 22.8 percent number. No matter how it ultimately might have been distributed, that vote switch would have been enormous. It is absolutely unquestionable that those who fought to expose the political agenda of the liberal press, be they organizations such as the Media Research Center, or conservative voices like Limbaugh, and Hannity and Levin, had a significant impact leveling the playing field.

But it is fanciful, even preposterous, to suggest the news media had *no* impact. It is far more reasonable to conclude they provided four points for Obama—his margin of victory.

In this book, we have provided you with hundreds of examples documenting the liberal bias that permeated the 2012 election cycle. Clearly there are thousands more.

These were the endless anecdotes—the sentence here, the phrase there—advancing the righteousness of Obama and/or the failings of Romney et al.

It was the constant, infuriating examples of the soft voice, the look of awe, reverence even, just being in the presence of Obama; the harsh, accusatory question, the piercing look of disbelief, even the guffaw, as the Romney camp was summarily dismissed, time after time.

It was the focus on the positive, always the positive regarding the Obama message, even if that message was incorrect, incoherent, or as was so often the case, dishonest. It was the obsession with the negative, always the negative aimed at Romney, savaging his message as incorrect, incoherent, or as so often the case, dishonest.

Most important, it was the deliberate decision to downplay, even withhold from the public the kind of news and information that might harm the reelection prospects of the incumbent, no matter how newsworthy and, ultimately, necessary for the electorate to make an informed decision: Fast and Furious, Benghazi, the assault on religious freedom, the monumental and disastrous debt created, the wasted trillions, the corruption, the handouts of billions of federal dollars in questionable (at best) federal contracts to contributors. The arrogance, the opulence, the hypocrisy, the lies.

And with the challenger? They made things up.

Obama was the most vulnerable incumbent in modern times. His performance on the economy was (and continues to be) disastrous, by any objective measurement. The United States is on the precipice of a fiscal and monetary collapse. He has done nothing to arrest, even slow the slide. Indeed, because of his excesses the country seems primed to go over the cliff. On social policy he declared war on everyone of faith with his (anti-)religious mandate, while advancing the most radical policies on key issues, from abortion to gays. On foreign policy, after being touted as the necessary antidote for the worldwide damage caused by the anti-Bush poison, he turned out to be even *less* popular.

Barack Obama was a disaster.

And he won reelection, handily.

The media's determination to project the false image of Barack Obama and his potential successor to the presidency as competent and honest public servants was underlined after the election, when the CBS *60 Minutes* butler Steve Kroft was summoned to a "historic joint interview" with Obama and Hillary Clinton. Obama announced he had commanded this airspace on CBS to thank Mrs. Clinton for her diligent service. Dutifully, the network complied.

All of that classic *60 Minutes* aggression was conserved for the next segment, directed at the competitive bicyclist Lance Armstrong. At the end of that piece, Armstrong's fiercest critic, Trevor Tygart of the U.S. Anti-Doping Agency, suggested this was Armstrong's plan: "Cheat your way to the top, and if you get too big and too popular and too powerful—if you do it that well, you'll never be held accountable."

Obama's reliance on the performance-enhancing media is like doping in politics. Kroft & Co. helped Obama cheat his way to the top, and after he reached that pinnacle of power, they never held him to account for his actions.

Liberal media bias is not new. The press has tilted liberal for decades, has it not? Yes, but never have the news media performed as they did in 2012, and if conservatives don't recognize this and commit themselves to changing the equation, they will not win again—at least not any time soon. With the real possibility that the days are numbered for this country's freedoms, it is not just a problem, it is a crisis.

Let's go back a second in time, just thirty-five years ago, and examine the media landscape then. There were the three broadcast networks along with PBS. All were liberal. There were three major magazines, *Time, Newsweek,* and *U.S. News & World Report.* Two were decidedly liberal, the third a fraction less so. There was a vibrant newspaper business; every publication with a national audience was liberal. There were two wire services; both were liberal. Liberals had a complete monopoly on the national news business in America.

Conservatives had no news outlets. Their commentary outlets were almost nonexistent as well. They had no Fox, no political talk radio, and no Internet. Conservatives controlled a handful of polemical publications, but all registered comparatively minuscule audiences. Bill Buckley could challenge liberals on his *Firing Line* show on PBS, but it was watched only by intellectuals, a fraction of a fraction of the population. Conservatives had no outlet for mass communications. Our Pony Express in the world of communications was direct mail, one step more advanced than smoke signals.

The news media were dominated by the Walter Cronkites, Dan Rathers, Peter Jennings, Tom Brokaws, Ed Bradleys, Mike Wallaces, etc.—all liberals, all routinely denounced by the right for their excesses. Entire movements were launched to stop them, with organizations formed exclusively for the purpose. We hit them for their leftist ideology, their support of centralized government and opposition to the free enterprise system; for their embrace of international leftism and rejection of American exceptionalism; for their promotion of a libertine, morally relative culture at the expense of a moral code grounded in Judeo-Christian values.

And we'd give anything to have them back.

Yesterday's journalists were liberals, not today's radical leftists, much in the same vein that their political standard bearers, like George McGovern, were several degrees to the right of the socialist presently occupying 1600 Pennsylvania Avenue. Yesterday's journalists attempted, at least on some level, sometimes, maybe once every solar eclipse or so, to strive for objectivity. Today's journalists make no such effort. They reject a code of ethical conduct if it interferes with their political mission. Yesterday's journalists by and large were educated, not just in the liberal arts, but in journalism. Today's journalists make a mockery of the word. They are naive, even sometimes downright stupid. They are undisciplined, not just in the preparation but in the delivery of news. They cannot, or just will not distinguish between news and information. They are pawns for misinformation and practiced in disinformation. They are loud, condescending, arrogant, dishonest, foolish, incompetent, mean-spirited—and dangerous.

How can this problem, this epidemic of unfairness in the national media, be cured? Let's be blunt. In a clinical sense it can't. It's a free country—at least, for now, mostly—and the national news media have the freedom to present Obama as the finest naked emperor that's ever lived. We must also salute that freedom, and defend it always. Any attempt to control the news media through government fiat must be resisted, fiercely. It is a direct challenge to democracy.

But how ironic that the opposite is equally true. A "free press" controlled by a special interest in furtherance of an agenda which necessitates public support, which support can be achieved only through the practice of censorship, of planted obfuscation and outright distortion, is in equal measure a threat to democracy and should be resisted with similar fervor.

Conservatives must put an end to this. It can be done.

How critical is this to conservatives? There is nothing more important. The 2012 cycle was not an aberration, it is the new normal. It is now an established reality that the "news" media will do anything and everything to distort and discredit any conservative imperative that challenges leftist orthodoxy. Unless and until this situation is corrected, not only will conservatives be thwarted, they will continue to lose ground as their policy prescriptions are ever more vilified. If this isn't a top-shelf concern for a conservative leader or organization, he is condemned to political death and—frankly, at some point we must say it—deservedly so.

Ironically, in a very real way they need us more than we need them. Theirs is an industry in an audience free fall, victims of technological advances, competition, and their own biases. Their monopoly is shattered. The conservative movement has virtually unlimited options now.

The broadcast networks have lost more than half their audience since 1980. The Pew Research Center's Project for Excellence in Journalism found the network newscasts drew 52.1 million viewers per night when Reagan was running against Carter. In the November 2012 sweeps period, the networks attracted just 24.1 million viewers. The contrast is starker when you consider population growth. In 1980, the networks captured 52.1 million out of an American population of 227 million, around 23 percent. In November 2012, the networks grabbed 24.1 million out of almost 314 million Americans—down to 7.6 percent.

CNN, once a serious source of news, is now an Anderson Cooper–Kathy Griffin–Eliot Spitzer–Soledad O'Brien–Piers Morgan laughingstock. The "stars" come, they go—and no one cares. *Time* magazine is on life support. *The New York Times* is gasping for breath. *Newsweek* is gone. Meanwhile, conservative talk radio continues as strong as ever, new television outlets like Fox News provide a balanced approach, and the Internet is ablaze. It is this last item that trumps all others. The Internet is the future, like it or not. The era of news is giving way to the information age. Journalism is no longer a prized endeavor for the privileged and trained few. In the era of blogging, everyone is a pamphleteer.

Conservatives must become far more educated about the industry, selective in their choices, and confrontational when attacked. And they must learn to park their publicity-seeking egos in the garage.

The research is there for anyone to recognize who will and won't be fair, and how he should be treated. Piers Morgan is not going to conduct a civilized interview and with his minuscule audience is irrelevant. So why consent to be interviewed and give him oxygen? *The New York Times* is going edit mercilessly in order to present you in the worst possible light. Why expect otherwise? Conservatives are ammo for Bill Maher, Jon Stewart, and Stephen Colbert. Why agree to be made a fool? There is nothing, absolutely nothing of value on MSNBC for a conservative. Why on earth does anyone accept any invitation for any show for any reason?

There is a world of difference between the taped and live interview. The former lends itself to shenanigans; with the latter, it's more difficult. Conservatives should always insist on a live format, if at all possible, and if in the process the interviewer pulls a fast one, with either incorrect statements, or some other exercise in Gotcha Journalism designed to embarrass the guest, the guest should pounce, and hit right back. It's national television, it's live, and they can't stop you. Embarrass them this way, and Brian Williams & Co. will never try that again. If it's taped and later manipulated, the conservative should publicly denounce the network or print outlet, fully discredit the entity, and refuse ever to participate again unless a clarification, correction, or apology—whatever the offense called for—is issued.

Conservatives should understand there are outlets that aren't biased against them and generate major audiences, even larger ones than most liberal entities. Through conservative talk radio they can reach tens of millions—daily. There is Fox, and *The Wall Street Journal* and other sources that may not be conservative, but aren't activist liberal, either. And then there's the mother lode: the Internet.

Conservatives must understand that in the information age the cultural trumps the political. It is a lesson learned by the left years ago, and one they've perfected, projecting their vision to tens of millions of people daily, nightly, using entertainment television, movies, music, digital media—all the media formats where celebrities they've recruited, not politicians, champion the cause *du jour*. They are our society's royalty. They are the Pied Pipers and their legions of adoring fans will follow blindly, but obediently. When the culture is changed, the political battle is a mop-up operation, simply codifying the new cultural norm into law. They've succeeded with gay rights, made critical advances with environmental issues, reignited momentum for abortion, created a new national outcry for immigration "reform," and now are using it to go for the political Holy Grail, gun control.

Why conservatives ignore the popular culture is puzzling, to say the least. Naïveté? Laziness? Intimidation? Arrogance? Take your pick—but until they focus their energies on the cultural media, where many, many times more people can be found than in the public policy arena, and make their voice heard loudly in the popular culture conversation, they will never succeed. The opposite also holds true: should conservatives choose to enter this arena, the results could be electrifying.

Which is not to say they haven't. Think about the hundreds, the thousands of discussions surrounding Jesus Christ. Now remember the movie, *The Passion of the Christ*. Which had a greater impact? Think about all the dissertations on liberty. Now watch *Braveheart*. Which resonated more? Flawed as he was, Mel Gibson understood that there is no reason, none whatsoever, that conservatives can't be as successful as liberals, more so even when you consider the logical footing on which the conservative argument rests.

Finally, conservatives must commit to devoting the necessary resources to the technologies of the future. Social media is here to stay and the right has been AWOL. What do Facebook, Twitter, Tumblr, Pinterest, and so many other formats have in common? They are interactive, they are enormously popular, and, most important for this discussion, they are free, absolutely free of liberal control. Conservatives can now communicate directly, instantaneously with millions upon millions of people, directing their messages, their way, when they want, where they want, and with whom they want. And by this time next year there will be a half-dozen new vehicles to transport our ideas.

The work of winning hearts and minds for America's original constitutional recipe is a daily grind, and there are few final victories.

But we have no choice if we wish to transmit the spirit of 1776 to a tercentennial celebration, and beyond. A free and balanced media is crucial to the health of this country. Journalists should feel the duty—as outlined in the Society of Professional Journalists' Code of Ethics—to "distinguish between advocacy and news reporting," that "[a]nalysis and commentary should be labeled and not misrepresent fact or context." They pledged to further democracy by "seeking truth and providing a fair and comprehensive account of events and issues." But any honest examination of the national media in 2012 would say these trampled and forgotten pledges of professionalism should be stowed away in Washington, D.C., as an educational artifact in the "Newseum."

# NOTES

## Chapter 1

1. Alexander Burns, "Barack Obama's 2012 plan: 'Kill Romney,'" *Politico*, August 9, 2011, http://www.politico.com/news/stories/0811/60929.html.
2. Lawrence O'Donnell, on *The Last Word with Lawrence O'Donnell*, MSNBC, August 9, 2011.
3. "President Obama Job Approval," realclearpolitics.com, http://www.realclear politics.com/epolls/other/president_obama_job_approval-1044.html.
4. Tim Graham, "Thomas Friedman Says GOP Looking for Someone as 'Smart and Mellifluous' as Obama," NewsBusters, December 27, 2011, http://newsbusters .org/blogs/tim-graham/2011/12/27/thomas-friedman-says-gop-looking-some one-smart-and-mellifluous-obama.
5. Scott Whitlock, "NYT's Joe Nocera Spews Venom at 'Terrorist' Tea Partiers for Strapping on 'Suicide Vests,'" NewsBusters, August 3, 2011, http://newsbusters .org/blogs/scott-whitlock/2011/08/03/nyts-joe-nocera-spews-venom-terrorist -tea-partiers-strapping-suicide.
6. Rich Noyes, "Latest Notable Quotables: Deriding the Tea Party as Terrorists 'Strapped with Dynamite,'" NewsBusters, August 8, 2011, http://newsbusters .org/blogs/rich-noyes/2011/08/08/latest-notable-quotables-deriding-tea-party -terrorists-strapped-dynamite.
7. Jack Cafferty and Nancy Gibbs, quoted in "Bloodthirsty GOP No Longer the 'Party of Life'?," Notable Quotables (October 3, 2011), http://www.mrc.org/ node/8742.
8. Scott Whitlock, "Chris Matthews: Southern 'Secessionists' Want to 'Kill' Obama . . . 'Politically,'" NewsBusters, August 3, 2011, http://newsbusters.org/ blogs/scott-whitlock/2011/08/03/chris-matthews-southern-secessionists-want -kill-obamapolitically.
9. Transcript, "One on One with Bill Maher," *Piers Morgan Tonight*, CNN, July 15, 2011.

10. Brent Bozell, "Bozell Column: Airing Anti-Palin Bilge at NBC," NewsBusters, September 20, 2011, http://newsbusters.org/blogs/brent-bozell/2011/09/20/bozell -column-airing-anti-palin-bilge-nbc.

11. Noel Sheppard, "ABC World News Investigates Bachmann Clinic: 'Where You Can Pray Away The Gay?,'" NewsBusters, July 11, 2011, http://newsbusters.org/blogs/ noel-sheppard/2011/07/11/abc-world-news-investigates-bachmann-clinic -where-you-can-pray-away-g.

12. Brent Bozell, "Bozell Column: Fear and Loathing of Bachmann," NewsBusters, August 16, 2011, http://newsbusters.org/blogs/brent-bozell/2011/08/16/bozell -column-fear-and-loathing-bachmann.

13. FunnyorDie.com, http://www.funnyordie.com/slideshows/65c6b11c2e/alternate -michele-bachmann-newsweek-covers#slide7.

14. Rich Noyes, "MRC's Notable Quotables: Slashing Rick Perry, 'the Human Tornado,'" NewsBusters, August 22, 2011, http://newsbusters.org/blogs/rich-noyes/ 2011/08/22/mrcs-notable-quotables-slashing-rick-perry-human-tornado.

15. Matthew Balan, "CBS Uses Cartoon to Spread Liberal Anti-Perry Talking Points," NewsBusters, September 13, 2011, http://newsbusters.org/blogs/matthew-balan/ 2011/09/13/cbs-uses-cartoon-spread-liberal-anti-perry-talking-points.

16. Brent Bozell, "Bozell Column: Rick's Rock vs. Reverend Wright," NewsBusters, October 4, 2011, http://newsbusters.org/blogs/brent-bozell/2011/10/04/bozell -column-ricks-rock-vs-reverend-wright.

17. Tim Graham, "WaPo's Ombudsman Makes Excuses for Very Anonymously-Sourced 'N-head' Scoop on Rick Perry," NewsBusters, October 10, 2011, http:// newsbusters.org/blogs/tim-graham/2011/10/10/wapos-ombudsman-makes -excuses-very-anonymously-sourced-n-head-scoop-rick.

18. Hugh Hewitt, "Washington Post's Drive-By Slander of Rick Perry," Real Clear Politics, October 2, 2011, http://www.realclearpolitics.com/2011/10/02/washington _post039s__drive-by_slander_of_perry_264625.html.

19. Tim Graham, "WaPo Slams Herman Cain As a Store-Closing, 'Tough-Talking Thug,'" NewsBusters, October 19, 2011, http://newsbusters.org/blogs/tim-gra ham/2011/10/19/wapo-slams-herman-cain-store-closing-tough-talking-thug.

20. Brent Bozell, "Bozell Column: Herman's High-Tech Lynching," NewsBusters, November 3, 2011, http://newsbusters.org/blogs/brent-bozell/2011/11/03/bozell -column-hermans-high-tech-lynching.

21. Noel Sheppard, "Ann Coulter Calls Politico's Herman Cain Hit Piece 'Another High-Tech Lynching,'" NewsBusters, October 31, 2011, http://newsbusters.org/ node/51414.

22. Tom Blumer, "Leftist ProPublica Questions Politico's Decision to Publish Cain Allegations," NewsBusters, October 31, 2011, http://newsbusters.org/blogs/tom -blumer/2011/10/31/leftist-propublica-questions-politicos-decision-publish -cain-allegations.

23. Kyle Drennen, "Networks Pile On Cain: Will 'Bizarre' Response to Harassment

Claims 'Derail' His Campaign?," NewsBusters, November 1, 2011, http://news busters.org/blogs/kyle-drennen/2011/11/01/networks-pile-cain-will-bizarre -response-harassment-claims-derail-his-.

24. Scott Whitlock, "Defensive Networks Devote 84 Stories to Herman Cain Scandal, Hit Him for 'Lashing Out,'" NewsBusters, November 7, 2011, http://newsbusters .org/blogs/scott-whitlock/2011/11/07/defensive-networks-devote-84-stories -herman-cain-scandal-hit-him-las.

25. Scott Whitlock, "Network Deluge: 99 Stories on Cain Harassment Charges in Less than Nine Days," NewsBusters, November 8, 2011, http://newsbusters.org/ blogs/scott-whitlock/2011/11/08/network-deluge-99-stories-cain-harassment -charges-less-nine-days.

26. Scott Whitlock, "Networks Hit Cain with 117 Stories; ABC: Accusers Seek 'Safety in Numbers' From Cain," NewsBusters, November 9, 2011, http://newsbusters.org/ blogs/scott-whitlock/2011/11/09/networks-hit-cain-177-stories-abc-accusers -seek-safety-numbers-cain.

27. Brent Bozell, "Bozell Column: Herman's High-Tech Lynching," NewsBusters, November 3, 2011, http://newsbusters.org/blogs/brent-bozell/2011/11/03/bozell -column-hermans-high-tech-lynching.

28. Brent Bozell, "Bozell Column: Let's Kill Cain's Campaign," NewsBusters, November 29, 2011, http://newsbusters.org/blogs/brent-bozell/2011/11/29/bozell -column-lets-kill-cains-campaign.

29. Scott Whitlock, "Stephanopoulos Gloats: Will My Interview with New Accuser 'Spell the End' for Cain?," NewsBusters, November 30, 2011, http://newsbusters .org/blogs/scott-whitlock/2011/11/30/stephanopoulos-gloats-will-my-interview -new-accuser-spell-end-cain.

30. Scott Whitlock, "Irony Alert: Ex-Clinton Operative Stephanopoulos Attacks Cain's 'Honesty' and 'Judgment,'" NewsBusters, November 30, 2011, http://news busters.org/blogs/scott-whitlock/2011/11/30/irony-alert-ex-clinton-operative -stephanopoulos-attacks-cains-honest.

31. Geoffrey Dickens, "Matthews Rages: Newt Gingrich Looks Like a 'Car Bomber' Who 'Loves Torturing!,'" NewsBusters, March 2, 2011, http://newsbusters.org/ blogs/geoffrey-dickens/2011/03/02/matthews-rages-newt-gingrich-car-bomber -looks-he-loves-torturing.

32. RealClearPolitics.com, "Matthews: Gingrich Has Made Politics 'Nastier, More Feral' And Uglier," November 29, 2011, http://www.realclearpolitics.com/video/ 2011/11/29/matthews_gingrich_has_made_politics_nastier_more_feral_and _uglier-co mments.html.

33. Scott Whitlock, "Smarmy Brian Ross Touts His 'January Surprise,' Eagerly Digs for Gingrich's 'Skeletons,'" NewsBusters, January 20, 2012, http://newsbusters .org/blogs/scott-whitlock/2012/01/20/smarmy-brian-ross-touts-his-october -surprise-eagerly-digs-gingrichs-.

34. Transcript of Brian Ross, "Tricky Business," ABC's *20/20*, January 4, 2008.

35. Tim Graham, "Rachel Maddow Slams Newt by Comparing Him to 'Google San-torum' Smear," NewsBusters, November 13, 2011, http://newsbusters.org/blogs/tim-graham/2011/11/13/rachel-maddow-slams-newt-comparing-him-google-santorum-smear.

36. Tim Graham, "The Same Newsweek That Trashed Bachmann Puffed Gloria Steinem as Florence Nightingale," NewsBusters, August 11, 2011, http://news busters.org/blogs/tim-graham/2011/08/11/same-newsweek-trashed-bachmann-puffed-gloria-steinem-florence-nightingal.

37. Nancy Hass, "Before Karen Met Rick," thedailybeast.com, January 16, 2012, http://www.thedailybeast.com/newsweek/2012/01/15/mrs-santorum-s-abortion-doctor-boyfriend.html.

38. Tim Graham, "Fox's 'Special Report' Passes Along MRC Finding: OWS-Loving Networks Again Skipped 'March for Life,'" NewsBusters, January 27, 2012, http://newsbusters.org/blogs/tim-graham/2012/01/27/foxs-special-report-passes-along-mrc-finding-ows-loving-networks-again-s.

39. Brent Bozell, "Newsweek's Senators to Watch," MRC.org, January 5, 2005, http://www.mrc.org/node/4200.

# Chapter 2

1. Brent Bozell, "Bozell Column: Brian Williams, from Musketeer to Mouse-keteer," NewsBusters, August 31, 2010, http://newsbusters.org/blogs/brent-bozell/2010/08/31/bozell-column-brian-williams-musketeer-mouseketeer.

2. Noel Sheppard, "Chris Matthews: 'Obama Is the Perfect Father, the Perfect Hus-band, the Perfect American,'" NewsBusters, July 17, 2012, http://newsbusters.org/blogs/noel-sheppard/2012/07/17/chris-matthews-obama-perfect-father-perfect-husband-perfect-american.

3. Jonathan Alter, "Obama Miracle Is White House Free of Scandal," Bloomberg.com, October 27, 2011, http://www.bloomberg.com/news/2011-10-27/obama-miracle-is-white-house-free-of-scandal-commentary-by-jonathan-alter.html.

4. Kyle Drennen, "WaPo's Capehart on NBC's 'Today': Obama Administration 'Re-markably Free of Scandal,'" NewsBusters, October 31, 2011, http://newsbusters.org/blogs/kyle-drennen/2011/10/31/wapos-capehart-nbcs-today-obama-admin istration-remarkably-free-scandal.

5. Brent Baker, "WashPost's Milbank Claims: 'Media Would Love to Have an Obama Scandal to Cover,'" NewsBusters, June 24, 2012, http://newsbusters.org/blogs/brent-baker/2012/06/24/washpost-s-milbank-claims-media-would-love-have-obama-scandal-cover.

6. Dana Milbank, "Fast and Furious: The scandal Republicans have been waiting for?," washingtonpost.com, November 8, 2011, http://www.washingtonpost.com/

opinions/fast-and-furious-the-scandal-republicans-have-been-waiting-for/2011/11/08/gIQAk1Q32M_story.ht ml.

7. Tim Graham and Geoffrey Dickens, "The Media's Obama Miracle: How Journalists Pretend There Aren't Any White House Scandals," MRC.org, August 8, 2012, http://www.mrc.org/node/40820.

8. Ibid.

9. Ibid.

10. Ibid.

11. "The Liberal Media's Newest Hero," Notable Quotables newsletter, August 29, 2005, http://www.mrc.org/node/8595.

12. Graham and Dickens, "The Media's Obama Miracle."

13. Carrie Johnson, "Holder: 'More Work to Do' Before Term Is Over," NPR.org, April 27, 2012, http://www.npr.org/2012/04/27/151529652/holder-more-work -to-do-before-term-is-over.

14. "Transcript: President Obama's Remarks at Univision Town Hall, Fox News Insider, September 20, 2012, http://foxnewsinsider.com/2012/09/20/transcript -president-obamas-remarks-at-univision-town-hall/.

15. Geoffrey Dickens, "ABC, CBS & NBC Blackout! Major New Findings in Fast & Furious Scandal Ignored," NewsBusters, October 1, 2012, http://newsbusters.org/blogs/geoffrey-dickens/2012/10/01/abc-cbs-nbc-blackout-major-new-findings -fast-furious-scandal.

16. Tim Graham, "Mass Amnesia Over Mass Clinton Firings," Media Reality Check newsletter, March 14, 2007, http://archive.mrc.org/realitycheck/2007/fax 20070314.asp.

17. Matthew Boyle, "Emails Reveal Justice Dept. Regularly Enlists Media Matters to Spin Press," Daily Caller, September 18, 2012, http://dailycaller.com/2012/09/18/emails-reveal-justice-dept-regularly-enlists-media-matters-to-spin-press/.

18. Mary Chastain, "At Least Jimmy Kimmel Gets What DC Elite Forgets: Fast & Furious Scandal," Breitbart.com, April 30, 2012, http://www.breitbart.com/Big -Hollywood/2012/04/30/At-Least-Jimmy-Kimmel-Gets-What-DC-Elite-Forgets -Fast-and-Furious-Scandal.

19. Brent Baker, "Correspondents' Dinner Headliner Kimmel Insists: 'It's Hard to Make Fun' of 'Cool Character' Obama," NewsBusters, April 25, 2012, http://news busters.org/blogs/brent-baker/2012/04/25/correspondents-dinner-headliner -kimmel-insists-it-s-hard-make-fun-cool-.

20. Andy Sullivan, "Analysis: Obama's 'Green Jobs' Have Been Slow to Sprout," Reuters.com, April 13, 2012, http://www.reuters.com/article/2012/04/13/us-usa -campaign-green-idUSBRE83C08D20120413.

21. Julia Seymour, "Networks Hardly Criticize Obama Green Jobs Flop," NewsBusters, August 22, 2011, http://newsbusters.org/blogs/julia-seymour/2011/08/22/net works-hardly-criticize-obama-green-jobs-flop.

22. Graham and Dickens, "The Media's Obama Miracle."

23. Ibid.

24. Eric Lipton and John M. Broder, "E-Mail Shows Senior Energy Official Pushed Solyndra Loan," *New York Times*, October 7, 2011, http://www.nytimes.com/2011/10/08/us/politics/e-mail-shows-senior-energy-official-pushed-solyndra-loan.html.

25. Carol D. Leonnig and Joe Stephens, "Energy Dept. Loan Chief Warned Staff That Personal E-mail Could Be Subpoenaed," *Washington Post*, August 14, 2011, http://articles.washingtonpost.com/2012-08-14/politics/35490043_1_personal-e-mail-e-mails-email.

26. Brent Bozell, "Bozell Column: Transparently Biased Against Disclosure," News-Busters, October 9, 2012, http://newsbusters.org/blogs/brent-bozell/2012/10/09/bozell-column-transparently-biased-against-disclosure.

27. Transcript of the vice presidential debate, Commission on Presidential Debates, October 11, 2012, http://www.debates.org/index.php?page=october-11-2012-the-biden-romney-vice-presidential-debate.

28. Alter, "Obama Miracle."

29. Noel Sheppard, "John McLaughlin: New Solyndra Revelations 'Will Become Damaging to Obama's Reelection,'" NewsBusters, August 5, 2012, http://newsbusters.org/blogs/noel-sheppard/2012/08/05/john-mclaughlin-new-solyndra-revelations-will-become-damaging-obamas.

30. Michael Isikoff, "Corzine, Top Obama Fundraiser, Under FBI Investigation," NBC News.com, November 2, 2011, http://firstread.nbcnews.com/_news/2011/11/02/8599414-corzine-top-obama-fundraiser-under-fbi-investigation?lite.

31. Graham and Dickens, "The Media's Obama Miracle."

32. Ibid.

33. Terry Keenan, "Corzine Shows There's No Justice on Wall St.," *New York Post*, May 26, 2012, http://www.nypost.com/p/news/business/corzine_shows_there_no_justice_on_EdUwVFlpOR4966IyltGvBN.

34. Jamila Trendle and Aaron Lucchetti, "House GOP Raps Corzine Over MF," *Wall Street Journal*, November 14, 2012, http://online.wsj.com/article/SB10001424127887324735104578119103238887208.html.

35. Lymari Morales, "Americans' Confidence in Television News Drops to New Low," Gallup.com, July 10, 2012, http://www.gallup.com/poll/155585/americans-confidence-television-news-drops-new-low.aspx.

36. "Top Twenty Stories of 2011," Tyndall Report, undated, http://tyndallreport.com/yearinreview2011/.

# Chapter 3

1. Tim Graham, "Team Obama Cries 'Bull(bleep)' Against Billion-Dollar Campaign Estimates," NewsBusters, December 31, 2011, http://newsbusters.org/blogs/tim-graham/2011/12/31/team-obama-cries-bullbleep-against-billion-dollar-campaign-estimates.

2. Tim Graham, "Comcast Employees Top Donors to Obama and 'Victory Fund,'" NewsBusters, August 26, 2011, http://newsbusters.org/blogs/tim-graham/2011/08/26/abc-tattles-nbc-comcast-top-corporate-donor-obama-victory-fund.

3. Ed Morrissey, "Obama Campaign Manager: Billion-Dollar Campaign Is BS," Hot Air, December 29, 2011, http://hotair.com/archives/2011/12/29/obama-campaign-manager-billion-dollar-campaign-is-bs/.

4. Kenneth P. Vogel and Dan Berman, "Team Obama Raises $1 billion," *Politico*, October 25, 2012, http://www.politico.com/news/stories/1012/82909.html.

5. Noel Sheppard, "Jamie Foxx: 'Our Lord and Savior Barack Obama,'" NewsBusters, November 26, 2012, http://newsbusters.org/blogs/noel-sheppard/2012/11/26/jamie-foxx-calls-obama-our-lord-and-savior.

6. Barbra Streisand, "Obama vs. Romney: A Clear Choice," *Huffington Post*, September 18, 2012, http://www.huffingtonpost.com/barbra-streisand/obama-vs-romney-a-clear-c_b_1894001.html.

7. "Contributions from Celebrities," Open Secrets, http://www.opensecrets.org/pres12/celebs.php.

8. Noel Sheppard, "Bill Maher Gives $1 Million to Obama Super PAC," NewsBusters, February 24, 2012, http://newsbusters.org/blogs/noel-sheppard/2012/02/24/bill-maher-gives-1-million-obama-super-pac.

9. Matthew Balan, "Santorum Fires Back at CBS's 'Gotcha,' Raises Rev. Wright Double Standard," NewsBusters, February 17, 2012, http://newsbusters.org/blogs/matthew-balan/2012/02/17/santorum-fires-back-cbss-gotcha-raises-rev-wright-double-standard.

10. Tim Graham, "Kirsten Powers Rebuts Maher's NY Times Op-ed: 'Please START Apologizing,'" NewsBusters, March 24, 2012, http://newsbusters.org/blogs/tim-graham/2012/03/24/kirsten-powers-rebuts-mahers-ny-times-op-ed-please-start-apologizing.

11. Noel Sheppard, "Laura Ingraham Schools George Stephanopoulos: 'Did Obama Give That Money Back to Bill Maher?,'" NewsBusters, May 20, 2012, http://newsbusters.org/blogs/noel-sheppard/2012/05/20/laura-ingraham-schools-george-stephanopoulos-did-obama-give-money-bac.

12. "Meet the Gaffe Seekers: Inside the Political Industry Built on Blunders," Rock Center, September 14, 2012, http://rockcenter.nbcnews.com/_news/2012/09/14/13866355-meet-the-gaffe-seekers-inside-the-political-industry-built-on-blunders?lite.

13. Tim Graham, "Newsweek Hails Bill Maher, Testament to the American Dream," NewsBusters, November 18, 2011, http://newsbusters.org/blogs/tim-graham/2011/11/18/newsweek-hails-bill-maher-testament-american-dream.

14. Brent Baker, "Sawyer's Flub: Claims Wall Street Protests Have 'Spread to More than a Thousand Countries,'" NewsBusters, October 11, 2011, http://news busters.org/blogs/brent-baker/2011/10/11/diane-sawyer-claims-wall-street-pro tests-have-spread-more-thousand-coun.

15. Geoffrey Dickens, "A Tale of Two Protests: Media Cheer Wall Street Occupiers but Jeered Tea Partiers," MRC.org, October 13, 2011, http://www.mrc.org/media -reality-check/tale-two-protests-media-cheer-wall-street-occupiers-jeered-tea -partiers.

16. Geoffrey Dickens, "Occupier Outrages Omitted," MRC.org, November 7, 2011, http://www.mrc.org/media-reality-check/occupier-outrages-omitted.

17. Noel Sheppard, "OWS Supporter Michael Moore Lies on National Television About His Wealth: No I'm Not Worth Millions," NewsBusters, October 26, 2011, http://newsbusters.org/blogs/noel-sheppard/2011/10/26/ows-supporter-michael -moore-lies-national-television-about-his-wealth.

18. Brent Bozell, "Bozell Column: Obama Courts the Glitz Elite," NewsBusters, February 4, 2012, http://newsbusters.org/blogs/brent-bozell/2012/02/04/bozell -column-obama-courts-glitz-elite.

19. Tina Daunt, "Obama Addresses Hollywood: Reelection Won't Be as Sexy as His First Campaign," *Hollywood Reporter*, October 24, 2011, http://www.holly woodreporter.com/news/obama-reelection-will-smith-james-lassiter-magic -johnson.

20. Tina Daunt and Matthew Belloni, "President Obama Holds Secret Meet-and-Greet with Hollywood Execs and Influencers (Exclusive)," *Hollywood Reporter*, October 25, 2011, http://www.hollywoodreporter.com/news/president-obama -hollywood-meeting-253151.

21. "Obama White House on Press Access: A Nixonian Quality," *San Francisco Chronicle*, October 25, 2011, http://www.sfgate.com/opinion/editorials/article/ Obama-White-House-on-press-access-a-Nixonian-2325483.php.

22. "President Obama Continues His West Coast Swing," Nexis transcript of NBC's *Today* show, October 25, 2011.

23. Kyle Drennen, "Network Morning Shows Tout 'Comedian in Chief' Obama Mocking GOP on Leno," NewsBusters, October 26, 2011, http://newsbusters.org/ blogs/kyle-drennen/2011/10/26/network-morning-shows-tout-comedian-chief -obama-mocking-gop-leno.

24. Marie Cunningham, "With Obama in Town, Protestors Rally to Fight Big Money in Politics," *Culver City Patch*, February 15, 2012, http://culvercity.patch.com/ articles/protesters-rally-wednesday-to-fight-big-money-in-politics.

25. "For February 15, 2012, CBS," Nexis transcript of *CBS This Morning*, February 15, 2012.

26. "Obama on Fundraising Tour of West Coast," Nexis transcript of *NBC Nightly News*, February 15, 2012.

27. "Your Voice Your Vote: Fundraising with the Stars," Nexis transcript of ABC *World News*, May 10, 2012.

28. "President Obama arrives in Seattle for three big-ticketfundraisers with donors in favor of his announcement in support of same-sex marriage," Nexis transcript of *NBC Nightly News*, May 10, 2012.

29. "For May 11, 2012," Nexis transcript of *CBS This Morning*, May 11, 2012.

30. Brent Baker, "On Maher, Rob Reiner Equates Tea Party to Hitler: 'All They're Selling Is Fear and Anger and That's All Hitler Sold,'" NewsBusters, October 23, 2010, http://newsbusters.org/blogs/brent-baker/2010/10/23/maher-rob-reiner-equates-tea-party-hitler-%E2%80%98all-theyre-selling-fear-and-.

31. Jordan Zakarin, "'The Daily Show' Spoofs President Obama–George Clooney Hollywood Fundraiser (Video)," *Hollywood Reporter*, May 11, 2012, http://www.hollywoodreporter.com/live-feed/daily-show-riffs-president-obama-clooney-gay-marriage-fundraiser-323480.

32. Brent Bozell, "The Washington Post Bullies Romney," NewsBusters, May 15, 2012, http://newsbusters.org/blogs/brent-bozell/2012/05/15/bozell-column-washington-post-bullies-romney.

33. Noel Sheppard, "CBS President Says at Obama Fundraiser 'Partisanship Is Very Much a Part of Journalism Now,'" NewsBusters, June 7, 2012, http://newsbusters.org/blogs/noel-sheppard/2012/06/07/cbs-president-says-obama-fundraiser-partisanship-very-much-part-journ.

34. Brent Bozell, "Partisanship Reigns at CBS," NewsBusters, June 12, 2012, http://newsbusters.org/blogs/brent-bozell/2012/06/12/bozell-column-partisanship-reigns-cbs.

35. "Obama: George Clooney a 'Good Friend,'" CBSNews.com, August 20, 2012, http://www.cbsnews.com/8301-207_162-57496165/obama-george-clooney-a-good-friend/.

36. Kyle Drennen, "Today Show Groupies Fawn over 'Crooner-in-Chief' Obama: 'He Could Be on The Voice,'" NewsBusters, January 29, 2012, http://newsbusters.org/blogs/kyle-drennen/2012/01/20/today-show-groupies-fawn-over-crooner-chief-obama-he-could-be-voice.

37. Michael Moynihan, "Ribbing on Romney's Rich Donors," *Washington Post*, July 9, 2012, http://www.washingtonpost.com/blogs/right-turn/post/ribbing-on-romneys-rich-donors/2012/07/09/gJQAielDYW_blog.html.

38. Associated Press, "Democrats Want Romney to Explain Offshore Accounts," Foxnews.com, July 8, 2012, http://www.foxnews.com/us/2012/07/08/democrats-want-romney-to-explain-offshore-accounts/.

39. Michael Barbaro, "Romney Mines the Hamptons for Campaign Cash," NYTimes.com, July 8, 2012, http://www.nytimes.com/2012/07/09/us/politics/romney-mines-the-hamptons-for-campaign-cash.html.

40. Maeve Reston, "Protesters Raise Cloud of Sand as Romney Raises $3 Million in N.Y.," LATimes.com, July 8, 2012, http://articles.latimes.com/2012/jul/08/nation/la-na-romney-protests-20120709.

41. Jeremy W. Peters, "Obama Visits New York for Star-Studded Fundraisers," NYTimes.com, June 14, 2012, http://www.nytimes.com/2012/06/15/us/politics/obama-visits-new-york-for-star-studded-fund-raisers.html.

42. Jeremy W. Peters, "Power Is Always in Vogue," NYTimes.com, June 16, 2012, http://www.nytimes.com/2012/06/17/fashion/for-anna-wintour-power-is-always-in-vogue.html.

43. Scott Whitlock, "ABC, NBC Tout 'Star-Studded' Obama Fund-Raisers for 'Prez in the City,'" NewsBusters, June 15, 2012, http://newsbusters.org/blogs/scott-whitlock/2012/06/15/abc-nbc-tout-star-studded-obama-fund-raisers-prez-city.

44. Tim Graham, "Hollywood Worries Obama's 'Increasing Reliance on Stars' Could Backfire," NewsBusters, June 22, 2012, http://m.newsbusters.org/blogs/tim-graham/2012/06/22/hollywood-worries-obamas-increasing-reliance-stars-and-celebrity-contest.

45. Ben Feller, "Obama to Celebrities: 'You're the Ultimate Arbiter of Which Direction This Country Goes,'" Associated Press, June 14, 2012, http://cnsnews.com/news/article/obama-celebrities-youre-ultimate-arbiter-which-direction-country-goes.

46. Mark Landler, "Beyoncé and Jay-Z host Obama Fund-Raiser," *New York Times*, September 18, 2012, http://thecaucus.blogs.nytimes.com/2012/09/18/beyonce-and-jay-z-host-obama-fund-raiser/.

47. Toby Harnden, "Speaking to the 47%: The $105,000 Champagne Tower Featured at Obama Fundraiser Hosted by Jay-Z and Beyoncé," *London Daily Mail*, http://www.dailymail.co.uk/news/article-2205541/280-000-champagne-tower-Obama-fundraiser-Jay-Z-Beyonce-Manhattan-night-club.html.

48. Matthew Daly, "Obama: As President You Represent Entire Country," Associated Press, http://bigstory.ap.org/article/obama-responds-romneys-victims-comments.

49. Jason Mattera, *Hollywood Hypocrites* (New York: Threshold Editions, 2012), p. 223.

# Chapter 4

1. Brent H. Baker, *How to Identify, Expose, & Correct Liberal Media Bias* (Alexandria, VA: Media Research Center, 1994), p. 25.

2. Walter Hickey, "How Barack Obama Made His Fortune," Finance.yahoo.com, September 11, 2012, http://finance.yahoo.com/news/how-barack-obama-made-his-fortune.html.

3. Joe Klein, "The Fresh Face," Time.com, October 15, 2006, http://www.time.com/time/magazine/article/0,9171,1546362-3,00.html.

4. Geoffrey Dickens, "Chris Matthews Compares Obama to Mark Twain," News-Busters, March 13, 2008, http://newsbusters.org/blogs/geoffrey-dickens/2008/03/13/chris-matthews-compares-barack-barack-obama-mark-twain.

5. Barack Obama, *Dreams from My Father* (New York: Crown, 2007), p. xvii.

6. Kyle Drennen, "NBC Decides Trump Has 'Overshadowed' Romney Clinching GOP Nomination," NewsBusters, May 30, 2012, http://newsbusters.org/blogs/kyle-drennen/2012/05/30/nbc-decides-trump-has-overshadowed-romney-clinching-gop-nomination.

7. Janny Scott, "The Story of Obama, Written by Obama," *New York Times*, May 18, 2008, http://www.nytimes.com/2008/05/18/us/politics/18memoirs.html.

8. Brent Bozell, "Bozell Column: Obama Lies About His Mom, Networks Yawn," NewsBusters, July 20, 2011, http://newsbusters.org/blogs/brent-bozell/2011/07/20/bozell-column-obama-lies-about-his-mom-networks-yawn.

9. Janny Scott, "Obama's Young Mother Abroad," NYTimes.com, April 20, 2011, http://www.nytimes.com/2011/04/24/magazine/mag-24Obama-t.html.

10. David Axelrod's appearance at the University of Chicago Institute of Politics.

11. Jack Deligter, "David Maraniss on Interviewing Obama—and Bringing Up the President's Ex-Girlfriend—for His New Biography," VanityFair.com, May 2, 2012, http://www.vanityfair.com/online/daily/2012/05/david-maraniss-barack-obama-genevieve-cook.

12. Michio Kakutani, "The Young Dreamer, with Eyes Wide Open," NYTimes.com, June 5, 2012, http://www.nytimes.com/2012/06/05/books/barack-obama-the-story-by-david-maraniss.html.

13. David Maraniss, *Barack Obama: The Story* (New York: Simon & Schuster, 2012), footnote on page 603.

14. Scott Whitlock, "Networks Hype 'Steamy' Details from Obama's Ex-Girlfriend, Downplay False 'Composite' Relationship," NewsBusters, May 3, 2012, http://newsbusters.org/blogs/scott-whitlock/2012/05/03/networks-hype-steamy-details-obamas-ex-girlfriend-downplay-compressi.

15. Maraniss, *Barack Obama*, pp. 499–501.

16. Ibid, p. 499.

17. Ibid., pp. 484–85.

18. Jack Deligter, "David Maraniss on Interviewing Obama."

19. Maraniss, *Barack Obama*, p. xx.

20. "David Maraniss Discusses New Book 'Barack Obama: The Story,'" transcript from Nexis of NBC's *Today*, June 18, 2012.

21. T. J. Stiles, "A Generational Biography in 'Barack Obama: The Story,' by David Maraniss," WashingtonPost.com, June 4, 2012, http://www.washingtonpost.com/opinions/a-generational-biography-in-barack-obama-the-story-by-david-maraniss/2012/06/04/gJQAnLnGEV_st ory.html.

22. David Maraniss's Twitter account, June 5, 2012, https://twitter.com/davidmaraniss/status/210009320857939969.

23. Noel Sheppard, "Washington Post Publishes 5,500 Word Front Page Sports Story on 'Obama's Basketball Love Affair,'" NewsBusters, June 10, 2012, http://newsbusters.org/blogs/noel-sheppard/2012/06/10/washington-post-publishes-5500-word-front-page-sports-story-obamas-ba.

24. Maraniss, *Barack Obama*, pp. 293–94.

25. Tim Graham, "WashPost 2007–08 Coverage of Obama's Punahou School Years? Mostly Gooey Basketball Patter," NewsBusters, May 11, 2012, http://newsbusters.org/blogs/tim-graham/2012/05/11/washpost-2007-08-coverage-obamas-punahou-school-years-mostly-gooey-baske.

26. Maraniss, *Barack Obama*, p. 175.

27. Lynn Sweet, "Obama's Selma Speech. Text as Delivered," suntimes.com, March 5, 2007, http://blogs.suntimes.com/sweet/2007/03/obamas_selma_speech_text_as_de.html.

28. Rich Noyes, "For Third Straight Weeknight, NBC Continues to Obsess Over Sarah Palin's Revere Tale," NewsBusters, June 7, 2011, http://newsbusters.org/blogs/rich-noyes/2011/06/07/third-straight-weeknight-nbc-continues-obsess-over-sarah-palin-s-revere-.

29. Rich Noyes, "Obama's Margin of Victory: The Media," MRC.org, August 20, 2008, http://www.mrc.org/special-reports/obamas-margin-victory-media?page=4.

30. Wil Haygood, "Inauguration Will Cement Ties Between Obama, Martin Luther King Jr.," WashingtonPost.com, January 15, 2013, http://articles.washingtonpost.com/2013-01-15/politics/36385982_1_civil-rights-bill-inauguration-day-president-barack-obama.

31. Brent Bozell, "Bozell Column: Obama's Stump Speech Myths," NewsBusters, July 10, 2012, http://newsbusters.org/blogs/brent-bozell/2012/07/10/bozell-column-obamas-stump-speech-myths.

32. Tim Graham, "Syrupy Minutes: How CBS's 60 Minutes Works Overtime for the Obama Left," MRC.org, September 23, 2010, http://archive.mrc.org/specialreports/2010/SyrupyMinutes/ExecSum.aspx.

33. "State of Corruption; Iraq's Main Corruption Fighter, Judge Radhi al-Radhi, Forced to Leave Iraq," CBS transcript of *60 Minutes*, April 13, 2008.

34. Noel Sheppard, "Rezko Sentenced to 10½ Years, Media Ignore It and/or His Ties to Obama," NewsBusters, November 23, 2011, http://newsbusters.org/blogs/noel-sheppard/2011/11/23/rezko-sentenced-10-years-media-ignore-it-andor-his-ties-obama.

# Chapter 5

1. Brent Bozell, "Diane Sawyer vs. 'Too Rich' Romney," NewsBusters, April 17, 2012, http://m.newsbusters.org/blogs/brent-bozell/2012/04/17/bozell-column-diane-sawyer-vs-too-rich-romney.

2. Michael Walker, "A Conversation with David Axelrod," University of Chicago, November 26, 2012, http://uchicagopolitics.tumblr.com/post/37412938570/a -conversation-with-david-axelrod.

3. Noel Sheppard, "Charles Blow: Mitt Romney 'Is Not a Person'—'Just a Robot' with 'Not Even a Heart,'" NewsBusters, July 18, 2012, http://newsbusters.org/ blogs/noel-sheppard/2012/07/18/charles-blow-mitt-romney-not-person-just -robot-not-even-heart.

4. Charisse Jones, "Volunteers Search for Missing Girl, 14, in Party Underworld," *New York Times,* July 12, 1996, http://www.nytimes.com/1996/07/12/nyregion/ volunteers-search-for-missing-girl-14-in-party-underworld.html, and "Missing Teen-Ager Found in New Jersey," *New York Times*, July 13, 1996, http://www.ny times.com/1996/07/13/nyregion/missing-teen-ager-found-in-new-jersey.html.

5. Jason Horowitz, "Mitt Romney's Prep School Classmates Recall Pranks, but also Troubling Incidents," *Washington Post*, May 10, 2012, http://articles.washing tonpost.com/2012-05-10/news/35456919_1_school-with-bleached-blond-hair -mitt-romney-george-romney.

6. Kathleen Parker, "A Gay Marriage Proclamation? Bullying? Much Ado About the Wrong Things," *Washington Post*, May 11, 2012, http://articles.washingtonpost .com/2012-05-11/opinions/35457918_1_gay-marriage-equal-marriage-rights -mitt-romney.

7. Joe Newby, "Family of Alleged Romney Bullying Victim Says Portrayal Is 'Factu-ally Incorrect,'" Examiner.com, May 11, 2012, http://www.examiner.com/article/ family-of-alleged-romney-bullying-victim-says-portrayal-is-factually-incorrect.

8. Scott Whitlock, "ABC Breathlessly Hypes Romney's 'Troubling' 'Teenage Bully-ing'; Did he Go 'Too Far?,'" NewsBusters, May 11, 2012, http://newsbusters.org/ blogs/scott-whitlock/2012/05/11/abc-breathlessly-hypes-romneys-troubling -teenage-bullying-did-he-go-.

9. Matt Hadro, "Should Romney Issue Bigger Apology for 'Harrowing' Prep School Incident, Asks Soledad O'Brien," NewsBusters, May 11, 2012, http://newsbusters .org/blogs/matt-hadro/2012/05/11/soledad-obrien-asks-if-romney-should-issue -bigger-apology-harrowing-prep.

10. Tim Graham, "WashPost Ombudsman Upholds Romney Hair 'Scoop' as Paper Shamelessly Admits Pro-Obama Story Timing," NewsBusters, May 12, 2012, http://m.newsbusters.org/blogs/tim-graham/2012/05/12/washpost-ombudsman -upholds-romney-hair-scoop-paper-shamelessly-admits-pr.

11. Harry Jaffe, "Merida on Obama: Both of Us Are New at This," *Washingtonian*, February 11, 2009, http://www.washingtonian.com/blogs/capitalcomment/post -watch/merida-on-obama-both-of-us-are-new-at-this.php.

12. Lois Romano, "Effect of Obama's Candor Remains to Be Seen," *Washington Post*, January 3, 2007, http://www.washingtonpost.com/wp-dyn/content/article/ 2007/01/02/AR2007010201359.html.

13. Tim Graham, "Did the WashPost Report a 5,000-Word Expose on Obama's

Cocaine Use in the Last Cycle? Of Course Not," NewsBusters, May 10, 2012, http://newsbusters.org/blogs/tim-graham/2012/05/10/did-washpost-report -5000-word-expose-obamas-cocaine-use-last-cycle-cours.

14. CNN Political Unit, "Axelrod's Tweet Worse than His Bite," January 30, 2012, http://politicalticker.blogs.cnn.com/2012/01/30/axelrods-tweet-worse-than-his -bite/.

15. Tim Graham, "NPR Host Smears Romney as 'Michael Vick of Presidential Candidates,'" NewsBusters, January 15, 2012, http://newsbusters.org/blogs/ tim-graham/2012/01/15/npr-host-smears-romney-michael-vick-presidential -candidates.

16. On The Media, "About" page, http://www.onthemedia.org/about/.

17. Gail Collins, "Time for Him to Go," New York Times, November 22, 2008, http:// www.nytimes.com/2008/11/22/opinion/22collins.html.

18. Clay Waters, "Crate-Gate Continues; Collins Calls Cain, Other GOP Candidates 'Nutjobs,'" Times Watch, December 1, 2011, http://www.mrc.org/articles/crate -gate-continues-collins-calls-cain-other-gop-candidates-nutjobs.

19. Gail Collins, "The March of the Non-Mitts," New York Times, January 5, 2012, http://www.nytimes.com/2012/01/05/opinion/collins-the-march-of-the-non-mitts .html.

20. Gail Collins, "Dogging Mitt Romney," New York Times, March 7, 2012, http:// www.nytimes.com/2012/03/08/opinion/collins-dogging-mitt-romney.html.

21. Clay Waters, "NYTimes Columnist Gail Collins Takes Her 'Seamus' Obsession to Letterman Show," NewsBusters, March 22, 2012, http://newsbusters.org/ blogs/clay-waters/2012/03/22/nytimes-columnist-gail-collins-takes-her-seamus -obsession-letterman-sho.

22. Jim Treacher, "Obama Bites Dog," Daily Caller, April 17, 2012, http://dailycaller .com/2012/04/17/obama-bites-dog/.

23. Gail Collins, "Obama's Wonderful Town," New York Times, May 5, 2012, http:// www.nytimes.com/2012/05/05/opinion/collins-obamas-wonderful-town.html.

24. Tim Graham, "NY Times Lays It on Thick: Obama as 'Everyman,' Romney as Mr. and Mrs. Cadillac," NewsBusters, March 24, 2012, http://newsbusters .org/blogs/tim-graham/2012/03/24/ny-times-lays-it-thick-obama-everyman -romneys-mr-and-mrs-cadillac.

25. Mark Leibovich, "Obama Seizes Chance to Score as an Everyman," New York Times, March 22, 2012, http://www.nytimes.com/2012/03/23/us/obama-seizes -chance-to-score-as-an-everyman.html.

26. Paul Farhi, "Michelle Obama's Target Trip: Critics Take Aim," Washington Post, Oc-tober 2, 2011, http://www.washingtonpost.com/lifestyle/style/michelle-obamas -target-trip-critics-take-aim/2011/10/02/gIQATrMLGL_story.html.

27. Kyle Drennen, "NBC's Today Swoons Over Michelle Obama Shopping at Target," NewsBusters, September 30, 2011, http://newsbusters.org/blogs/kyle-drennen/ 2011/09/30/nbcs-today-swoons-over-michelle-obama-shopping-target.

28. Matthew Balan, "Juan Williams Blasts Ann Romney as a 'Corporate Wife' on Fox News," NewsBusters, August 29, 2012, http://newsbusters.org/blogs/matthew-balan/2012/08/29/juan-williams-blasts-ann-romney-corporate-wife-fox-news.

29. Noel Sheppard, "Katey Sagal AKA Peggy Bundy Trashes Ann Romney: Mom That Doesn't Cook, Clean or 'Make Any Money,'" NewsBusters, August 13, 2012, http://newsbusters.org/blogs/noel-sheppard/2012/08/13/katey-sagal-aka-peggy-bundy-slams-ann-romney-mom-doesnt-cook-clean-or.

30. Trip Gabriel, "In Rarefied Sport, a View of the Romneys' World," New York Times, May 26, 2012, http://www.nytimes.com/2012/05/27/us/politics/ann-romneys-hobby-spotlights-world-of-dressage.html?pagewanted=all&_r=0.

31. Trip Gabriel, "Romney Horse Wins Spot on Olympic Dressage Team," New York Times, June 16, 2012, http://www.nytimes.com/2012/06/17/us/politics/horse-co-owned-by-ann-romney-earns-a-spot-on-the-olympic-dressage-team.html.

32. "Alice Elizabeth Simon Is Married to Trip Gabriel," New York Times, June 30, 1985, http://www.nytimes.com/1985/06/30/style/alice-elizabeth-simon-is-married-to-trip-gabriel.html.

33. Michelle Cottle, "The Gray Lady Wears Prada," New Republic, April 17, 2006, http://www.newrepublic.com/article/books-and-arts/the-gray-lady-wears-prada#.

34. Clay Waters, "NYT Devotes Front of Home Section to Romney-Bashing from the Candidate's Snotty Liberal Neighbors," NewsBusters, June 7, 2012, http://newsbusters.org/blogs/clay-waters/2012/06/07/nyt-devotes-front-home-section-romney-bashing-candidates-snotty-liberal.

35. "Mitt Romney's Neighbors Tell All," NBCNews.com, June 7, 2012, http://www.nbcnews.com/id/45755883/ns/msnbc-the_last_word/vp/47731177#47731177.

36. Chris Cillizza, "Mitt Romney Is the Republican Nominee. Now What?," Washington Post, April 9, 2012, http://www.washingtonpost.com/blogs/the-fix/post/mitt-romney-is-the-republican-nominee-now-what/2012/04/09/gIQAN6fU6S_blog.html.

# Chapter 6

1. Axelrod at the University of Chicago's Institute of Politics.

2. "Lawrence O'Donnell and the Plain Dealer's Connie Schultz Among Planned Parenthood's 2011 Maggie Award Winners for Media Excellence," Planned Parenthood.org, July 15, 2011, http://www.plannedparenthood.org/about-us/newsroom/press-releases/lawrence-odonnell-plain-dealers-connie-schultz-among-planned-parenthoods-2011-maggie-award-winn-37323.htm.

3. Matthew Balan, "Study: Media Go to Bat for Abortion Giant, Ignore Catholics vs. Obama Controversy," NewsBusters, February 6, 2012, http://newsbusters.org/

blogs/matthew-balan/2012/02/06/study-media-go-bat-abortion-giant-ignore
-catholics-vs-obama-controver.

4. Brad Wilmouth, "MSNBC's O'Donnell: Planned Parenthood Head Should Be
Ambassador to U.N., Komen May Not Survive," NewsBusters, February 7, 2012,
http://newsbusters.org/blogs/brad-wilmouth/2012/02/07/msnbcs-odonnell
-planned-parenthood-head-should-be-amassador-un-komen-.

5. MSNBC.com staff, "Catholic TV Network Sues US over Birth Control Mandate," NBCNews.com, February 9, 2012, http://usnews.nbcnews.com/_news/
2012/02/09/10365739-catholic-tv-network-sues-us-over-birth-control-mandate
?lite.

6. Brent Bozell, "Bozell Column: Obama vs. Catholics," NewsBusters, January 24,
2012, http://newsbusters.org/blogs/brent-bozell/2012/01/24/bozell-column
-obama-vs-catholics.

7. Julie Rovner, "Administration Stands Firm on Birth Control Coverage," NPR
.org, January 20, 2012, http://www.npr.org/blogs/health/2012/01/20/145535551/
administration-stands-firm-on-birth-control-coverage.

8. Matthew Balan, "CBS Turns to Top Catholic Bishop on ObamaCare Mandate
Scandal, ABC Punts," NewsBusters, February 9, 2012, http://newsbusters.org/
blogs/matthew-balan/2012/02/09/cbs-turns-top-catholic-bishop-obamacare
-mandate-scandal-abc-punts.

9. Joan Frawley Desmond, "HHS Ends Contract with Church Program for Trafficking Victims, Stressing Need for Contraception," National Catholic Register, October 17, 2011, http://www.ncregister.com/daily-news/hhs-ends-contract-with
-church-program-for-trafficking-victims-stressing-nee/.

10. NB Staff, "Fury Spreads: Catholic Leaders Join MRC Outrage over Network
Silence on Catholics vs. Obama Lawsuit," NewsBusters, May 23, 2012, http://
newsbusters.org/blogs/nb-staff/2012/05/23/fury-spreads-catholic-leaders-join
-mrc-outrage-over-network-silence-cathol.

11. Tim Graham, "CBS Leads Evening News with Catholics—The Accused Abusers,
Not the Obama Litigants," NewsBusters, May 24, 2012, http://newsbusters.org/
blogs/tim-graham/2012/05/24/cbs-leads-evening-news-catholics-accused-abusers
-not-obama-litigants.

12. Kyle Drennen, "After Spiking Catholic Lawsuit Against Obama, Networks Unleash Avalanche of Stories Hyping Vatican 'Scandal,'" NewsBusters, May 31, 2012,
http://newsbusters.org/blogs/kyle-drennen/2012/05/31/after-spiking-catholic
-lawsuit-against-obama-networks-unleash-avalanch.

13. House Committee on Oversight and Government Reform, "Lines Crossed: Separation of Church and State. Has the Obama Administration Trampled on Freedom of Religion and Freedom of Conscience?," Oversight.house.gov, February 16,
2012, http://oversight.house.gov/hearing/lines-crossed-separation-of-church-and
-state-has-the-obama-administration-trampled-on-freedom-of-religion-and
-freedom-of-conscience/.

14. J. Lester Feder, "Carolyn Maloney, Eleanor Holmes Norton Walk out of Contraception Hearing," *Politico*, February 16, 2012, http://www.politico.com/news/stories/0212/72971.html.

15. Brent Baker, "Bill Maher Slurs Sarah Palin as a 'Dumb Twat,'" MRCTV.org, March 6, 2012, http://mrctv.org/videos/bill-maher-slurs-sarah-palin-dumb-twat.

16. Tim Graham, "Will MSNBC Suspend Ed Schultz for Calling Laura Ingraham a 'Right-Wing Slut' and 'Talk Slut,'?" http://newsbusters.org/blogs/tim-graham/2011/05/25/will-msnbc-suspend-ed-schultz-calling-laura-ingraham-right-wing-slut-and.

17. Jenna Johnson, "Georgetown President Defends Sandra Fluke, Blasts Rush Limbaugh," WashingtonPost.com, March 2, 2012, http://articles.washingtonpost.com/2012-03-02/local/35447751_1_sandra-fluke-rush-limbaugh-health-insurance.

18. Angela Morabito, "Sandra Fluke Does Not Speak for Me," *College Conservative*, March 2, 2012, http://thecollegeconservative.com/2012/03/02/sandra-fluke-does-not-speak-for-me/.

19. Gregory Gwyn-Williams, Jr., "$9: Price for a Month's Supply of Birth Control Pills at Target 3 Miles from Georgetown Law," CNSNews.com, March 5, 2012, http://cnsnews.com/news/article/9-price-months-supply-birth-control-pills-target-3-miles-georgetown-law.

20. Stephen Gutowski, "Sandra Fluke, Gender Reassignment, and Health Insurance," MRCTV.org, March 5, 2012, http://www.mrctv.org/blog/sandra-fluke-gender-reassignment-and-health-insurance.

21. Susan Jones, "Sandra Fluke: Paul Ryan 'Would Allow Pregnant Women to Die in Our Emergency Rooms,'" CNSNews.com, September 6, 2012, http://cnsnews.com/news/article/sandra-fluke-paul-ryan-would-allow-pregnant-women-die-our-emergency-rooms.

22. Clay Waters, "NYT's Rosenthal Compares Pre-Abortion Ultrasound to Rape, but It's the Counterarguments That Are 'Deranged'?," NewsBusters, February 23, 2012, http://newsbusters.org/blogs/clay-waters/2012/02/23/nyts-rosenthal-compares-pre-abortion-ultrasound-rape-its-counterargumen.

23. Scott Whitlock, "Liberal Joy Behar Trashes Virginia: State's Abortion Law Is like 'the Taliban,'" NewsBusters, February 16, 2012, http://newsbusters.org/blogs/scott-whitlock/2012/02/16/left-wing-joy-behar-smears-va-states-abortion-law-taliban#ixzz2NbyfbQ2P.

24. Ken Shepherd, "MSNBC's Luke Russert Asks Democratic State Legislator: Are Mandated Abdominal Ultrasounds a Sort of 'Sex Crime'?," NewsBusters, February 23, 2012, http://newsbusters.org/blogs/ken-shepherd/2012/02/23/msnbcs-luke-russert-asks-democratic-state-legislator-are-mandated-abdo#ixzz2Nbz2a6jJ.

25. Jack Coleman, "Liberal Shill Jumps Shark, Hypervents That GOP Favors 'Letting Women Die,'" NewsBusters, February 27, 2012, http://newsbusters.org/blogs/

jack-coleman/2012/02/27/liberal-shill-jumps-shark-hypervents-gop-favors-letting
-women-die#ixzz2NcOmGZUU.

26. "Accused Gunman Ripped Family Research Council Policies Before Opening
Fire, Sources Say," Foxnews.com, August 16, 2012, http://www.foxnews.com/
us/2012/08/16/alleged-gunman-in-family-research-council-shooting-expected
-in-court-thursday/#ixzz2Nc2qhp9w.

27. Tim Graham, "Only ABC Offers Full Story on Shooting at FRC; CBS, NBC Blow
It Off With Tiny Reports," NewsBusters, August 15, 2012, http://newsbusters.org/
blogs/tim-graham/2012/08/15/only-abc-offers-full-story-shooting-frc-cbs-nbc
-blow-it-tiny-reports.

28. Matt Hadro, "It Took Only 20 Hours: CNN Upholds 'Hate Group' Label
for FRC," NewsBusters, August 16, 2012, http://newsbusters.org/blogs/matt
-hadro/2012/08/16/it-took-only-20-hours-cnn-upholds-hate-group-label-frc.

29. Katie Yoder, "Networks Ignore FRC Shooter's Use of SPLC 'Hate Map,'" News-
Busters, February 7, 2013, http://newsbusters.org/blogs/katie-yoder/2013/02/07/
networks-ignore-frc-shooter-s-use-splc-hate-map.

30. Ann E. Marimow, "Family Research Council Shooter Pleads Guilty to Three
Felonies," WashingtonPost.com, February 6, 2013, http://articles.washingtonpost
.com/2013-02-06/local/36940774_1_firearm-sales-floyd-lee-corkins-ii-ammu
nition-across-state-lines.

# Chapter 7

1. Adam Nagourney, Jim Rutenberg, and Jeff Zeleny, "Near-Flawless Run Is
Credited in Victory," New York Times, November 5, 2008, http://www.nytimes
.com/2008/11/05/us/politics/05recon.html.

2. Geoffrey Dickens, "Matthews: McCain Sounds like Herbert Hoover," News-
Busters, September 15, 2008, http://newsbusters.org/blogs/geoffrey-dickens/
2008/09/15/matthews-mccain-sounds-herbert-hoover.

3. Brent Baker, "NBC Raises 9/11 & Pushes Quote to Hurt McCain, ABC Ties in
Iraq," NewsBusters, September 19, 2008, http://newsbusters.org/blogs/brent
-baker/2008/09/19/nbc-raises-9-11-pushes-quote-hurt-mccain-abc-ties-iraq.

4. Rush Limbaugh, "Obama: 'The Private Sector Is Doing Fine,'" transcript on rush
limbaugh.com, June 8, 2012, http://www.rushlimbaugh.com/daily/2012/06/08/
obama_the_private_sector_is_doing_fine.

5. Kyle Drennen, "NBC's Curry Argues Obama's 'Fine' Gaffe 'Taken Out of Context,'" NewsBusters, June 11, 2012, http://newsbusters.org/blogs/kyle-drennen/
2012/06/11/nbcs-curry-argues-obamas-fine-gaffe-taken-out-context.

6. Felicia Sonmez, "White House on 'Private Sector Is Doing Fine': We're for 'Good
Reporting Filled with Context,'" Washington Post, June 11, 2012, http://www

.washingtonpost.com/blogs/post-politics/post/white-house-on-private-sector
-is-doing-fine-were-for-good-reporting-filled-with-context/2012/06/11/gJQA
rdxUVV_blog.html.

7. Jackie Calmes, "Six Words From Obama, and a Barrage in Return From the
   G.O.P.," *New York Times*, June 8, 2012, http://www.nytimes.com/2012/06/09/us/
   politics/six-words-from-obama-and-a-barrage-from-republicans.html.

8. Transcript of *World News with Diane Sawyer*, January 9, 2012.

9. Matthew Balan, "Schieffer on CBS: Romney Firing Remark Just Shy of Saying
   'Herbert Hoover Is My Hero,'" NewsBusters, January 10, 2012, http://m.news
   busters.org/blogs/matthew-balan/2012/01/10/schieffer-cbs-romney-firing-re
   mark-just-shy-saying-herbert-hoover-my-.

10. Ari Shapiro, "Romney Tries to Dig Out from 'Poor' Comment," NPR, Febru-
    ary 2, 2012, http://www.npr.org/2012/02/02/146265419/romney-tries-to-dig-out
    -from-poor-comment.

11. Geoffrey Dickens, "ABC, CBS & NBC Wait Five Days to Report Obama's 'You
    Didn't Build That' Attack on Business," NewsBusters, July 18, 2012, http://news
    busters.org/blogs/geoffrey-dickens/2012/07/18/abc-cbs-nbc-wait-five-days
    -report-obamas-you-didnt-build-attack-bu.

12. Ed Morrissey, "Videos: Romney on the Attack After Obama's 'You Didn't Build
    That' Remark," Hot Air, July 17, 2012, http://hotair.com/archives/2012/07/17/
    videos-romney-on-the-attack-after-obamas-you-didnt-build-that-remark/.

13. Trip Gabriel and Peter Baker, "Romney and Obama Resume Economic Attacks,
    Despite a Few Diversions," *New York Times*, July 17, 2012, http://www.nytimes
    .com/2012/07/18/us/politics/romney-and-obama-resume-economic-attacks
    .html.

14. Matthew Balan, "CBS Defends Obama's 'You Didn't Build That' Remarks; Invokes
    'It Takes a Village,'" NewsBusters, July 26, 2012, http://newsbusters.org/blogs/
    matthew-balan/2012/07/26/cbs-defends-obamas-you-didnt-build-remarks
    -invokes-it-takes-village.

15. Tim Graham, "NPR Puts Obama's 'You Didn't Build That' in 'Context'—With
    Think Progress Anti-Romney Spin," NewsBusters, http://newsbusters.org/blogs/
    tim-graham/2012/07/26/npr-puts-obamas-you-didnt-build-context-think
    -progress-anti-romney-spin.

16. Tim Graham, "Networks Bury Obama's 'Polish Death Camp' Gaffe, but ABC and
    NBC Find Time to Mock a Romney Misspelling," NewsBusters, May 31, 2012,
    http://newsbusters.org/blogs/tim-graham/2012/05/31/networks-bury-obamas
    -polish-death-camp-gaffe-abc-and-nbc-find-time-mock-.

17. Scott Whitlock, "Networks That Fawned over Obama's World Tour Mock Rom-
    ney's International 'Blunders,'" MRC.org, August 2, 2012, http://www.mrc
    .org/media-reality-check/networks-fawned-over-obamas-world-tour-mock
    -romneys-international-blunders.

18. Chris Cillizza, "Who Had the Worst Week in Washington? Mitt Romney," *Washington Post*, July 27, 2012, http://articles.washingtonpost.com/2012-07-27/opinions/35486280_1_romney-campaign-mitt-romney-worst-week.

19. Matt Hadro, "CNN Absurdly Claims Romney Aide's Outburst Was 'Sort of' 'Unprovoked,'" NewsBusters, July 31, 2012, http://newsbusters.org/blogs/matt-hadro/2012/07/31/cnn-absurdly-claims-romney-aides-outburst-was-sort-unprovoked.

20. Charles Krauthammer, "Romney's Excellent Trip," *Washington Post*, August 2, 2012, http://articles.washingtonpost.com/2012-08-02/opinions/35492000_1_romney-gaffe-rick-gorka-mitt-romney.

21. Geoffrey Dickens, "ABC, CBS and NBC Bury Bumbling Biden's Most Embarrassing Moments," MRC.org, September 4, 2012, http://www.mrc.org/media-reality-check/abc-cbs-and-nbc-bury-bumbling-bidens-most-embarrassing-moments.

22. Rebecca Berg, "The Caucus; On the Trail: A Metaphor Draws Notice," *New York Times*, August 15, 2012, http://query.nytimes.com/gst/fullpage.html?res=9D02E6DA173BF936A2575BC0A9649D8B63.

23. Randy Hall, "CNN's O'Brien Continues Challenging Attempt to Spin Away 'Chains' Controversy," NewsBusters, August 16, 2012, http://m.newsbusters.org/blogs/randy-hall/2012/08/16/cnns-obrien-continues-challenging-attempt-spin-away-chains-controversy.

24. "Top Ten Biden Gaffes: A 'Stand Up' Slip-Up," Time.com, http://www.time.com/time/specials/packages/article/0,28804,1895156_1894977_1841630,00.html.

25. Ed Morrissey, "Biden Spreads His Own Special Kind of St. Paddy's Day Cheer," Hot Air, March 18, 2010, http://hotair.com/archives/2010/03/18/biden-spreads-his-own-special-kind-of-st-paddys-day-cheer/.

26. Madeleine Morgenstern, "'Don't Screw Around with Me': Biden Defends 'Rape' Comments, Gets into Heated Exchange with Reporter," *The Blaze*, October 19, 2011, http://www.theblaze.com/stories/2011/10/19/dont-screw-around-with-me-biden-defends-rape-comments-gets-into-heated-exchange-with-reporter/.

27. Matthew Balan, "Nets Punt on Biden's 'Planned Parenthood Cannot Perform Any Abortions' Gaffe; Played Up Romney 'Shift,'" NewsBusters, October 12, 2012, http://newsbusters.org/blogs/matthew-balan/2012/10/12/nets-punt-bidens-planned-parenthood-cannot-perform-any-abortions-gaff.

28. Jonathan Martin, "Mission Impossible: Managing Joe Biden," *Politico*, August 16, 2012, http://www.politico.com/news/stories/0812/79776.html.

29. Howard Fineman, "Obama Needs the Merciless Joe: Countdown Day 29," *Huffington Post*, October 8, 2012, http://www.huffingtonpost.com/howard-fineman/barack-obama-joe-biden-2012_b_1947146.html.

30. Clay Waters, "New York Times' Mark Leibovich Eagerly Embraces the 'Biden Moment,'" NewsBusters, January 30, 2013, http://newsbusters.org/blogs/clay-waters/2013/01/30/new-york-times-mark-leibovich-eagerly-embraces-biden-moment.

31. Tim Graham, "Charles Jaco Goes Wacko," NewsBusters, August 19, 2005, http://newsbusters.org/blogs/tim-graham/2005/08/19/charles-jaco-goes-wacko.

32. Charles Jaco, "Jaco Report: Full Interview with Todd Akin," Fox2Now.com, August 19, 2012, http://fox2now.com/2012/08/19/the-jaco-report-august-19-2012/.

33. Charles Jaco, "The Jaco Report: Senator Claire McCaskill," Fox2Now.com, September 9, 2012, http://fox2now.com/2012/09/09/the-jaco-report-sept-9-2012/.

34. Scott Whitlock, "Media Obsession with Akin Hits Overdrive: 96 Minutes in Just Three and a Half Days," NewsBusters, August 23, 2012, http://newsbusters.org/blogs/scott-whitlock/2012/08/23/network-obsession-over-akin-hits-overdrive-96-minutes-just-over-thre.

35. Kyle Drennen, "NBC Hypes GOP in 'Hot Water' with 'High-Profile Distractions,'" NewsBusters, August 20, 2012, http://m.newsbusters.org/blogs/kyle-drennen/2012/08/20/nbc-hypes-gop-hot-water-high-profile-distractions.

36. Kyle Drennen, "NBC Declares: 'Women's Issues Are Front and Center Again' and GOP Is 'Reeling,'" MRC.org, August 21, 2012, http://www.mrc.org/node/40962.

37. Scott Whitlock, "Howard Fineman: 'Todd Akin Is the Paul Ryan of Missouri,'" NewsBusters, August 20, 2012, http://m.newsbusters.org/blogs/scott-whitlock/2012/08/20/howard-fineman-todd-akin-paul-ryan-missouri.

38. Brent Baker, "'Fed Up' Gingrich Calls Out Media Refusal to Discuss Extremism Among Democrats,'" NewsBusters, September 2, 2012, http://newsbusters.org/blogs/brent-baker/2012/09/02/fed-gingrich-calls-out-media-refusal-focus-extremism-democratic-platfor.

39. Noel Sheppard, "Joy Behar: People like Romney and Ryan Are 'Trying to Kill Us,'" NewsBusters, August 29, 2012, http://dev.newsbusters.org/blogs/noel-sheppard/2012/08/29/joy-behar-people-romney-and-ryan-are-trying-kill-us.

40. Scott Whitlock, "All Three Networks Hype 'Controversial' GOP Senate Candidate and His 'Ties' to Romney," NewsBusters, October 24, 2012, http://newsbusters.org/blogs/scott-whitlock/2012/10/24/all-three-networks-hype-controversial-gop-senate-candidate-and-his-t.

41. Scott Horsley, "President Obama Stops in Chicago to Vote Early," NPR, October 26, 2012, http://www.npr.org/2012/10/26/163687995/obama-stops-in-chicago-to-vote-early.

42. Alexander Burns, "Obama Airing Mourdock-Themed Radio Ads," Politico, November 1, 2012, http://www.politico.com/blogs/burns-haberman/2012/11/obama-airing-mourdockthemed-radio-ads-147956.html.

43. Tim Graham, "Liberal Radio Hosts Cheer On Tough Questions from Reporters—to Romney About Mourdock," NewsBusters, October 27, 2012, http://newsbusters.org/blogs/tim-graham/2012/10/27/liberal-radio-hosts-cheer-tough-questions-reporters-romney-about-mourdoc.

44. Clay Waters, "New York Times Eager to Paint Mourdock Rape Comment as 'Dilemma' Making It 'Difficult' for Romney," NewsBusters, October 25, 2012, http://

newsbusters.org/blogs/clay-waters/2012/10/25/new-york-times-eager-paint
-mourdock-rape-comment-dilemma-making-it-diff.

45. Brent Bozell, "Bozell Column: The News Squashers," NewsBusters, October 30, 2012, http://newsbusters.org/blogs/brent-bozell/2012/10/30/bozell-column-news -squashers.

46. Matt Hadro, "Dem Senate Candidate Insulted CNN's Candy Crowley, but CNN Hasn't Reported It," NewsBusters, October 25, 2012, http://newsbusters.org/ blogs/matt-hadro/2012/10/25/dem-senate-candidate-insulted-cnns-candy -crowley-cnn-hasnt-reported-it.

47. Matthew Balan, "Mainstream Media Ignore Obama's Radical Abortion Record," NewsBusters, October 10, 2008, http://newsbusters.org/blogs/matthew-balan/ 2008/10/10/mainstream-media-ignore-obama-s-radical-abortion-record.

48. John McCormack, "Audio: Obama Says 'That Fetus or Child' Was 'Just Not Coming Out Limp and Dead,'" *Weekly Standard*, August 23, 2012, http://www .weeklystandard.com/blogs/audio-obama-says-fetus-or-child-was-just-not -coming-out-limp-and-dead_650611.html.

# Chapter 8

1. "We're Not Biased, Fox News Is," Notable Quotables, February 17, 2006, http:// www.mrc.org/notable-quotables/notable-quotables-02272006.

2. Tim Graham, "NPR Claims Romney Seeks 'Friendly Confines' of Fox, but Obama's Comedy Show Was Not 'Friendly,'" NewsBusters, September 19, 2012, http://newsbusters.org/blogs/tim-graham/2012/09/19/npr-claims-romney-seeks -friendly-confines-fox-obamas-comedy-show-was-not.

3. Clay Waters, "NYT Cheers 'Media Critic in Chief' Obama as He Complains About 'False Balance,'" NewsBusters, August 8, 2012, http://newsbusters.org/blogs/clay -waters/2012/08/08/nytimes-nods-along-media-critic-chief-obama-excoriates -press-false-bala.

4. Keith Koffler, "Obama Abolishes the Press Conference," White House Dossier, May 4, 2012, http://www.whitehousedossier.com/2012/05/04/obama-abolishes -press-conference/.

5. Authors' review of White House website section on press briefings, http://www .whitehouse.gov/briefing-room/press-briefingswhitehouse.gov.

6. Paul Farhi, "Obama Keeps Newspaper Reporters at Arm's Length," Washington post.com, February 10, 2013, http://www.washingtonpost.com/lifestyle/style/ obama-keeps-newspaper-reporters-at-arms-length/2013/02/10/3638c5ae-7082 -11e2-ac36-3d8d 9dcaa2e2_story.html.

7. Brent Bozell, "White House Press Zombies," MRC.org, March 13, 2003, http:// archive.mrc.org/BozellColumns/newscolumn/2003/col20030313.asp.

8. Tim Graham and Rich Noyes, "Still Liberal, Still Biased: How Big Media Helped the Left and Hurt the Right in 2003," MRC.org, January 2004, http://archive.mrc .org/specialreports/2004/report0104_p2.asp.

9. Scott Whitlock, "ABC's Terry Moran: For Obama, Presidency Is a 'Step Down,'" NewsBusters, February 20, 2009, http://newsbusters.org/blogs/scott-whitlock/ 2009/02/20/abcs-terry-moran-compares-visionary-obama-george-washington.

10. Scott Whitlock, "ABC's Terry Moran Raves Over President's Press Conference: 'An Obama Smackdown,'" NewsBusters, November 15, 2012, http://newsbusters.org/ blogs/scott-whitlock/2012/11/15/abcs-terry-moran-raves-over-presidents-press -conference-obama-smackd.

11. Jim VandeHei and Mike Allen, "Obama the Puppet Master," *Politico*, February 18, 2013, http://www.politico.com/story/2013/02/obama-the-puppet-master-87764 .html.

12. Tim Graham, "Pro-Carney Reporter Asks: 'Is Obama Too Mean to the Media, or Are Reporters Just Whiny?' He Picks (B)," NewsBusters, February 22, 2013, http://newsbusters.org/blogs/tim-graham/2013/02/22/pro-carney-reporter-asks -obama-too-mean-media-or-are-reporters-just-whin.

13. Todd Purdum, "Next Question? The silly season doesn't usually come in February, but complaints by the White House press corps about lack of access miss the point," *Vanity Fair*, February 2013, http://www.vanityfair.com/politics/purdum/ 2013/02/president-obama-white-house-reporters-access.

14. Scott Whitlock, "Barbara Walters' Slobbering Interview with Obama: What Super Power Do You Want?," NewsBusters, December 23, 2011, http://newsbusters.org/ blogs/scott-whitlock/2011/12/23/barbara-walters-slobbering-interview-obama -what-super-power-do-you-w.

15. Scott Whitlock, "Barbara Walters Slams 'Uninformed' Sarah Palin: Many Find the Idea of You as President 'Scary,'" NewsBusters, December 9, 2010, http:// newsbusters.org/blogs/scott-whitlock/2010/12/09/barbara-walters-slams-unin formed-sarah-palin-many-find-idea-you-pres.

16. Tim Graham, "Barbara Walters Pushes Michelle Obama to Run for Office: 'You'd Be a Very Popular Candidate,'" NewsBusters, May 29, 2012, http://newsbusters .org/blogs/tim-graham/2012/05/29/barbara-walters-pushes-michelle-obama -run-office-youd-be-very-popular-ca.

17. Ryan Robertson, "ABC's 'The View' Crew Had Some Puffy Questions for Obamas," NewsBusters, September 26, 2012, http://newsbusters.org/blogs/ryan -robertson/2012/09/26/abcs-view-crew-piled-puffy-questions.

18. Tim Graham, "ABC 'View' Crew Went Soft on Obamas, but Thumped Ann Romney with Abortion, Contraception, and Draft Evasion," NewsBusters, October 18, 2012, http://newsbusters.org/blogs/tim-graham/2012/10/18/abc-view -crew-went-soft-obamas-thumped-ann-romney-abortion-contraception.

19. Scott Whitlock, "Robin Roberts Awed by Obama's Gay Marriage Stand: I

Get 'Chills' When I Hear It," NewsBusters, May 10, 2012, http://newsbusters
.org/blogs/scott-whitlock/2012/05/10/abcs-robin-roberts-awed-obamas-gay
-marriage-stand-i-got-chills-when-.

20. Tim Graham, "ABC Admits Team Obama Picked Robin Roberts Due to Her
Race, Age, and Previous (Soft) Interviews," NewsBusters, May 10, 2012, http://
newsbusters.org/blogs/tim-graham/2012/05/10/team-obama-says-out-loud-it
-picked-abcs-roberts-due-her-race-age-and-pre.

21. Tim Graham, "NPR Snubs Interview with the President, So It Airs on Fox
News," NewsBusters, September 26, 2007, http://newsbusters.org/blogs/tim
-graham/2007/09/26/npr-snubs-interview-president-so-it-airs-fox-news.

22. Scott Whitlock, "Robin Roberts, Who Got 'Chills' From Obama, Pushes Ann
Romney: 'Why Not Release' Taxes?," NewsBusters, July 19, 2012, http://news
busters.org/blogs/scott-whitlock/2012/07/19/robin-roberts-who-got-chills
-obama-pushes-ann-romney-why-not-release.

23. Brent Bozell, "CBS: Still Lazy with the Obamas After All These Years," News
Busters, July 18, 2012, http://newsbusters.org/blogs/brent-bozell/2012/07/18/
bozell-column-cbs-still-lazy-obama-after-all-these-years.

24. Matthew Balan, "Charlie Rose Boosts 'Enormously Successful' ObamaCare in
Softball Interview of President, Mrs. Obama," NewsBusters, July 16, 2012, http://
newsbusters.org/blogs/matthew-balan/2012/07/16/charlie-rose-boosts-enor
mously-successful-obamacare-softball-intervie.

25. Jodi Kantor, The Obamas (New York: Little, Brown, 2012, ), p. 42.

26. Brent Bozell, "David Limbaugh's Devastating Book," MRC.org, June 5, 2012,
http://www.mrc.org/bozells-column/david-limbaughs-devastating-book.

27. Noel Sheppard, "Michele Bachmann Greeted with 'Lyin' A—B—ch' by Jimmy
Fallon's Band," NewsBusters, November 22, 2011, http://newsbusters.org/blogs/
noel-sheppard/2011/11/22/michele-bachmann-greeted-lyin-b-ch-jimmy-fallons
-band.

28. Brent Baker, "After Hitting GOP Candidates from Left, NBC's Williams Presses
Obama from Left," MRC.org, September 13, 2011, http://www.mrc.org/bias
-alerts/after-hitting-gop-candidates-left-nbcs-williams-presses-obama-left.

29. Brent Baker, "NBC Debate Moderators Pepper Republicans with Questions from
the Left," MRC.org, September 8, 2011, http://www.mrc.org/bias-alerts/nbc
-debate-moderators-pepper-republicans-questions-left.

30. Kyle Drennen, "NBC's Williams in Awe of Obama's 'Even Keel' During Bin
Laden Killing," NewsBusters, May 3, 2012, http://newsbusters.org/blogs/kyle
-drennen/2012/05/03/nbcs-williams-awe-obamas-even-keel-during-bin-laden
-killing.

31. Kyle Drennen, "NBC's Morales Demands Ann Romney Be 'Transparent' and Release More Tax Returns," NewsBusters, August 16, 2012, http://newsbusters.org/
blogs/kyle-drennen/2012/08/16/nbcs-morales-demands-ann-romney-be-trans
parent-and-release-more-tax-re.

# Chapter 9

1. James Bennet, "'Nightline' Pulls the Plug on Convention Coverage," *New York Times*, August 15, 1996, http://www.nytimes.com/1996/08/15/us/nightline-pulls-the-plug-on-convention-coverage.html.

2. Keach Hagey, "Online Media Will Star at the Conventions," *Wall Street Journal*, August 19, 2012, http://online.wsj.com/article/SB10000872396390444233104577597870434505042.html.

3. Margaret Hartmann, "Ann Romney's Speech Bumped for Hawaii Five-O Rerun," *New York*, August 23, 2012, http://nymag.com/daily/intelligencer/2012/08/ann-romneys-speech-bumped-for-hawaii-five-o.html.

4. "Coddling Democrats & Discrediting Republicans," MediaWatch, September–October 1988, http://archive.mrc.org/mediawatch/1988/watch19880901study.asp.

5. Rich Noyes, "The Media vs. the GOP: Intolerant, Anti-Women, and Always Too Conservative," NewsBusters, August 27, 2012, http://newsbusters.org/blogs/rich-noyes/2012/08/27/media-vs-gop-intolerant-anti-women-and-always-too-conservative.

6. "Network TV Convention Disparities," MediaWatch, September 1992, http://archive.mrc.org/mediawatch/1992/watch19920901.asp#Study.

7. Adam Nagourney, "A Party of Factions Gathers, Seeking Consensus," *New York Times*, August 26, 2012, http://www.nytimes.com/2012/08/27/us/politics/republicans-worry-about-keeping-factions-reined-in.html.

8. Brent Bozell, "Republicans, Torn Apart in Factions?," NewsBusters, August 28, 2012, http://newsbusters.org/blogs/brent-bozell/2012/08/28/bozell-column-republicans-torn-apart-factions.

9. Ibid.

10. Scott Whitlock, "Frenzied Media Give Four Times More Coverage to Akin Flap than Biden's 'Chains' Smear," NewsBusters, August 22, 2012, http://newsbusters.org/blogs/scott-whitlock/2012/08/22/frenzied-media-give-four-times-more-coverage-akin-flap-bidens-chains.

11. David Bauder, "Chris Matthews Took Home Trophy as Most Over-the-Top Pundit," Associated Press, September 1, 2012, http://cnsnews.com/news/article/chris-matthews-took-home-trophy-most-over-top-pundit.

12. Matthew Sheffield, "Yahoo Bureau Chief David Chalian: Romneys 'Happy to Have a Party with Black People Drowning,'" NewsBusters, August 29, 2012, http://newsbusters.org/blogs/matthew-sheffield/2012/08/29/abc-news-romneys-happy-have-party-when-black-people-drown.

13. Matthew Sheffield, "Gwen Ifill Stands Up for Fired David Chalian: 'God's Gift to Political Journalism,'" NewsBusters, August 29, 2012, http://newsbusters.org/blogs/matthew-sheffield/2012/08/29/liberal-pbs-journo-gwen-ifill-stands-disgraced-david-chalian.

14. Geoffrey Dickens, "Brian Williams to Valerie Jarrett: Positive Media Coverage for Obama Will Be a 'Tall Order,'" NewsBusters, September 7, 2012, http://news busters.org/blogs/geoffrey-dickens/2012/09/07/brian-williams-valerie-jarrett -positive-media-coverage-obama-will-.

15. Kyle Drennen, "NBC's Lauer Cites Obama Flack to Question if Paul Ryan Gave an 'Honest Speech,'" NewsBusters, August 30, 2012, http://newsbusters.org/blogs/ kyle-drennen/2012/08/30/nbcs-lauer-cites-obama-flack-question-if-paul-ryan -gave-honest-speech#ixzz2Nj0pDiZf.

16. Matt Hadro, "George Stephanopoulos Relays E-Mail from 'Top Democrat' Ripping Ryan's Speech," NewsBusters, August 30, 2012, http://newsbusters.org/blogs/ matt-hadro/2012/08/30/george-stephanopoulos-relays-e-mail-top-democrat -ripping-ryans-speech.

17. Transcript of *CBS This Morning*, September 4, 2012.

18. Kyle Drennen, "NBC's Lauer: Romney Questioned 'The Very Legitimacy of the President of the United States's Citizenship,'" NewsBusters, August 28, 2012, http://newsbusters.org/blogs/kyle-drennen/2012/08/28/nbcs-lauer-romney questioned-very-legitimacy-president-united-statess-.

19. Jake Tapper, "Obama Campaign Uses Romney 'Birther' Joke to Raise Funds, Question GOPer's Fitness for Office," ABCNews.com, August 24, 2012, http://abcnews .go.com/blogs/politics/2012/08/obama-campaign-uses-romney-birther-joke-to -raise-funds-question-gopers-fitness-for-office/.

20. Kyle Drennen, "NBC's Guthrie Invites Elizabeth Warren to Label Romney 'Personification' of 'Wall Street Greed and Excess,'" NewsBusters, September 4, 2012, http://newsbusters.org/blogs/kyle-drennen/2012/09/04/nbcs-guthrie-invites -elizabeth-warren-label-romney-personification-wal.

21. Brent Baker, "CBS's Pelley Presses Mitt Romney: 'I Wonder How You Would Explain This Republican Party to Your Father?,'" NewsBusters, August 27, 2012, http://newsbusters.org/blogs/brent-baker/2012/08/27/cbs-s-pelley-presses-mitt -romney-i-wonder-how-you-would-explain-republi.

22. Brent Baker, "Pelley Trumpets Obama's 'Remarkable Moment of Candor' in What Makes the 'Sacrifices Worth It,'" NewsBusters, September 15, 2012, http:// newsbusters.org/blogs/brent-baker/2012/09/15/pelley-trumpets-obama-s -remarkable-moment-candor-what-makes-sacrifices-.

23. Transcript of *CBS Evening News*, September 5, 2012.

24. Tim Graham, "Bill Press Hails Democratic 'Truth' Convention, Compared to 'Pale Male Stale' GOP Convention of 'Lies,'" NewsBusters, September 7, 2012, http://newsbusters.org/blogs/tim-graham/2012/09/07/bill-press-hails-demo cratic-truth-convention-compared-pale-male-stale-go.

25. Matt Vespa, "Daily Beast's Tomasky Calls 2012 RNC Convention Racist," NewsBusters, August 28, 2012, http://newsbusters.org/blogs/matt-vespa/2012/08/28/ daily-beasts-tomasky-calls-2012-rnc-convention-racist.

26. Rosalind S. Helderman and Jon Cohen, "As Republican Convention Emphasizes Diversity, Racial Incidents Intrude," *Washington Post*, August 29, 2012, http://articles.washingtonpost.com/2012-08-29/politics/35490241_1_latino-voters-convention-stage-party-with-black-people.

27. Ibid.

28. FoxNews.com staff, "Mia Love Wikipedia Page Vandalized with Slurs," FoxNews.com, August 29, 2012, http://www.foxnews.com/politics/2012/08/29/mia-love-wikipedia-page-vandalized-with-slurs/.

29. David A. Graham, "Charlotte Swag: 'Once You Vote Black You Never Go Back' and More," *The Atlantic*, September 4, 2012, "http://www.theatlantic.com/politics/archive/2012/09/charlotte-swag-once-you-vote-black-you-never-go-back-and-more/261934/.

30. Geoffrey Dickens, "NBC's Brian Williams Obnoxiously Presses Rubio About GOP's 'Rape Debate,'" NewsBusters, August 28, 2012, http://newsbusters.org/blogs/geoffrey-dickens/2012/08/28/nbcs-brian-williams-obnoxiously-presses-rubio-about-gops-rape-deba.

31. Brent Baker, "Chuck Todd: 'Technically Factual' Ryan 'Distorted the Truth,'" NewsBusters, August 30, 2012, http://newsbusters.org/blogs/brent-baker/2012/08/30/todd-claims-ryan-distorted-truth-must-concede-ryan-technically-factual-.

32. Scott Whitlock, "Networks Pound Rubio on Anti-Hispanic GOP, Deride Paul Ryan," NewsBusters, August 29, 2012, http://newsbusters.org/blogs/scott-whitlock/2012/08/29/networks-pound-rubio-anti-hispanic-gop-paul-ryan-hitting-mitt-romney.

33. Ibid.

34. *PBS NewsHour* transcript, August 29, 2012, http://www.pbs.org/newshour/bb/politics/july-dec12/rubio_08-29.html.

35. Matt Hadro, "ABC Hosts GOP-Bashing Univision Anchor Over Airing Susana Martinez's RNC Speech," NewsBusters, August 29, 2012, http://newsbusters.org/blogs/matt-hadro/2012/08/29/abc-hosts-liberal-univision-anchor-over-airing-susana-martinezs-rnc-spee.

36. Transcript of CBS News live convention coverage, August 29, 2012.

37. Geoffrey Dickens, "On NBC: Williams and Brokaw Use Condi Rice Speech to Depict Republicans as Narrow-Minded," NewsBusters, August 30, 2012, http://newsbusters.org/blogs/geoffrey-dickens/2012/08/30/nbc-williams-and-brokaw-use-condi-rice-speech-depict-republicans-n.

38. Ted Robbins, "GOP Rising Star: Gov. Martinez Is a Former Democrat," NPR.org, August 29, 2012, http://www.npr.org/2012/08/29/160227100/gop-rising-star-gov-martinez-is-a-former-democrat.

39. Transcript of *CBS This Morning*, August 30, 2012.

40. "Woodruff vs. First Lady," MediaWatch, September 1992, http://archive.mrc.org/mediawatch/1992/watch19920901.asp#FiveB.

41. "Team Clinton: The Starting Line-Up of the Pro-Clinton Press Corps," Media Research Center, August 1, 1996, http://archive.mrc.org/specialreports/1996/clinton/woodruff.asp.

42. Brent Baker, "Brian Williams Reprimands Ann Romney for Saying Mitt Romney 'Is Going to Save America,'" NewsBusters, August 29, 2012, http://newsbusters.org/blogs/brent-baker/2012/08/29/brian-williams-reprimands-ann-romney-saying-mitt-romney-going-save-amer.

43. Michelle Obama Democratic National Convention speech, *Chicago Sun-Times*, August 26, 2008, http://blogs.suntimes.com/sweet/2008/08/michelle_obama_democratic_conv.html.

44. Scott Whitlock, "Brian Williams to Michelle Obama: 'What Makes You Angriest' at GOP?,'" NewsBusters, August 28, 2008, http://newsbusters.org/blogs/scott-whitlock/2008/08/28/brian-williams-michelle-obama-what-makes-you-angriest-gop.

45. Tim Graham, "Jane Pauley's 'Unusual Empathy' for Liberals," MRC.org, February 20, 2003, http://www.mrc.org/media-reality-check/jane-pauleys-unusual-empathy-liberals.

46. Whitlock, "Brian Williams to Michelle Obama: 'What Makes You Angriest' at GOP?".

47. Brent Baker, "Pelley and Williams Zinged Mrs. Romney from Left, but Avoid Contentious Politics with Mrs. Obama," NewsBusters, September 6, 2012, http://newsbusters.org/blogs/brent-baker/2012/09/06/pelley-and-williams-zinged-mrs-romney-left-avoid-contentious-politics-m.

48. Ibid.

49. Brent Baker, "Pelley Pushes Ann Romney on 'Whether Republicans Have Women's Best Interests at Heart?,'" NewsBusters, August 28, 2012, http://newsbusters.org/blogs/brent-baker/2012/08/28/pelley-pushes-ann-romney-whether-republicans-have-women-s-best-interest.

50. 2008 Democratic National Party Platform, http://www.presidency.ucsb.edu/ws/index.php?pid=78283.

51. Julien Pecquet and Pete Kasperowicz, "After Three Votes, Dems Put Jerusalem, God Back into Party Platform," TheHill.com, September 5, 2012, http://thehill.com/video/campaign/247747-dems-reinstate-language-on-jerusalem-god-in-their-party-platform.

52. Lauren Markoe, "Dems Under Fire for Removing 'God' from Platform, but 'faith' Is Named 11 Times," *Salt Lake City Tribune*, September 5, 2012, http://www.sltrib.com/sltrib/lifestyle/54835555-80/platform-god-faith-democratic.html.csp.

53. "Revised Platform Elicits Boos at DNC in Charlotte," NPR, *Talk of the Nation*, September 6, 2012, http://www.npr.org/2012/09/06/160686513/revised-platform-elicits-boos-at-dnc-in-charlotte.

54. Brent Baker, "ABC Spikes Democrats Forced to Make Embarrassing Platform

Fixes, Celebrates Michelle Obama's Twitter Popularity," NewsBusters, September 5, 2012, http://newsbusters.org/blogs/brent-baker/2012/09/05/abc-spikes-democrats-forced-make-embarrassing-platform-fixes-celebrates.

55. Ibid.

56. "Shields and Brooks Discuss Democratic Party Unity," *PBS NewsHour*, September 5, 2012, http://www.pbs.org/newshour/bb/politics/july-dec12/shieldsbrooks2_09-05.html.

57. Mark Landler, "Pushed by Obama, Democrats Alter Platform over Jerusalem," September 5, 2012, http://www.nytimes.com/2012/09/06/us/politics/pushed-by-obama-democrats-alter-platform-over-jerusalem.html.

58. Tim Graham, "WashPost Found 'Strong Shift to the Right' in GOP Platforms—But Democrats Achieved 'Balance,'" http://newsbusters.org/blogs/tim-graham/2012/09/05/washpost-found-strong-shift-right-gop-platforms-democrats-achieved-balan.

59. Brent Baker, "Pinkerton's Amusing Take on How Media Would Have Reacted if GOP Had Platform Dispute," NewsBusters, September 9, 2012, http://newsbusters.org/blogs/brent-baker/2012/09/09/pinkerton-s-amusing-take-how-media-would-have-reacted-if-gop-had-platfo.

60. Kyle Drennen, "NBC's Mormon Hit Piece: 'A Church Still Dealing with the Issue of Polygamy . . . Inequality,'" NewsBusters, August 24, 2012, http://newsbusters.org/blogs/kyle-drennen/2012/08/24/nbcs-mormon-hit-piece-church-still-dealing-issue-polygamyinequality.

# Chapter 10

1. Josh Barro, "Today, Mitt Romney Lost the Election," Bloomberg.com, September 17, 2012, http://www.bloomberg.com/news/2012-09-17/today-mitt-romney-lost-the-election.html.

2. David Corn, "SECRET VIDEO: Romney Tells Millionaire Donors What He REALLY Thinks of Obama Voters," *Mother Jones*, posted September 17, 2012, http://www.motherjones.com/politics/2012/09/secret-video-romney-private-fundraiser.

3. "A Conversation with David Axelrod," video posted at UChicagoNews, November 26, 2012. http://news.uchicago.edu/webcast/conversation-david-axelrod.

4. Quoted by Mike Allen in "Politico Playbook," *Politico*, November 11, 2012, http://www.politico.com/playbook/1112/playbook9441.html.

5. Geoffrey Dickens, "ABC, CBS, NBC Hype Romney Hidden Camera Tape, Bury Obama's 'Redistribution' Clip," Media Reality Check, September 21, 2012, http://www.mrc.org/media-reality-check/abc-cbs-nbc-hype-romney-hidden-camera-tape-bury-obamas-redistribution-clip.

6. "Crushing Mitt Romney with Media-Generated 'Earthquake,'" Notable Quot-

ables, October 1, 2012, http://www.mrc.org/notable-quotables/crushing-mitt
-romney-media-generated-earthquake.

7. Transcript of *CBS Evening News*, September 18, 2012.

8. Matthew Balan, "Schieffer Hypes Romney Video: 'Extraordinary Moment';
'Seems to Confirm . . . He Is Out of Touch,'" NewsBusters, September 19, 2012,
http://newsbusters.org/blogs/matthew-balan/2012/09/19/schieffer-hypes-rom
ney-video-extraordinary-moment-seems-confirmhe-out.

9. Kyle Drennen, "NBC's Scarborough Rants: Romney Having 'One of the Worst
Weeks of Any Presidential Candidate,'" NewsBusters, September 18, 2012, http://
newsbusters.org/blogs/kyle-drennen/2012/09/18/nbcs-scarborough-rants-rom
ney-having-one-worst-weeks-any-presidential-.

10. Tim Graham, "On The View, Barbara Walters Disses Hasselbeck as All Alone in
Backing Romney's 47 Percent Talk," NewsBusters, September 18, 2012, http://
newsbusters.org/blogs/tim-graham/2012/09/18/view-barbara-walters-disses
-hasselbeck-all-alone-backing-romneys-47-perc.

11. Mayhill Fowler, "Obama: No Surprise That Hard-Pressed Pennsylvanians Turn
Bitter," *Huffington Post*, April 11, 2008, http://www.huffingtonpost.com/mayhill
-fowler/obama-no-surprise-that-ha_b_96188.html.

12. Tim Graham, "Omitting for Obama: How the Old Media Censored New Media
Scoops in 2009," Media Research Center, January 25, 2010, http://www.mrc.org/
special-reports/omitting-obama?page=4.

13. Brent Bozell, "Planned Parenthood, Spiked," Media Research Center, February 8,
2011, http://www.mrc.org/bozells-column/bozell-column-planned-parenthood
-spiked.

14. Scott Whitlock, "Multi-Millionaire Chris Matthews Mocks Mitt Romney by Singing 'If I Were a Rich Man,'" NewsBusters, September 18, 2012, http://newsbusters
.org/blogs/scott-whitlock/2012/09/18/multi-millionaire-chris-matthews-mocks
-mitt-romney-singing-if-i-were.

15. Christina Romer and Jared Bernstein, "The Job Impact of the American Recovery
and Reinvestment Plan," January 9, 2009, http://www.ampo.org/assets/library/
184_obama.pdf, p. 4.

16. Josh Gerstein, "Obama: The Beginning of the End," *Politico*, February 18, 2009,
http://www.politico.com/news/stories/0209/18958.html.

17. Data retrieved from the U.S. Department of Labor, Bureau of Labor Statistics,
March 2013, http://data.bls.gov/timeseries/LNS14000000.

18. "Estimated Impact of the American Recovery and Reinvestment Act on Employ-
ment and Economic Output from January 2012 Through March 2012," Congressional Budget Office, May 2012, http://www.cbo.gov/sites/default/files/cbofiles/
attachments/05-25-Impact_of_ARRA.pdf.

19. Remarks delivered at "Fiscal Responsibility Summit," February 23, 2009, and
quoted in a White House report issued March 20, 2009, http://www.whitehouse
.gov/assets/blog/Fiscal_Responsibility_Summit_Report.pdf, p. 1.

20. Address to a Joint Session of Congress, February 24, 2009, http://www.white house.gov/the_press_office/Remarks-of-President-Barack-Obama-Address-to -Joint-Session-of-Congress.

21. ABC *World News with Charles Gibson*, February 25, 2009.

22. John Merline, "Weak Recovery Driving Deficits; Recession in the Past; Obama's Own Budgets Disprove His Claim That Slump Still to Blame," *Investor's Business Daily*, February 17, 2012.

23. ABC *World News with Diane Sawyer*, February 13, 2012.

24. *CBS Evening News*, October 19, 2012.

25. *Meet the Press* transcript for November 13, 2011, NBCNews.com, November 13, 2011, http://www.nbcnews.com/id/45276821/ns/meet_the_press-transcripts/t/ meet-press-transcript-november/#.UUO2_VeiHws.

26. News release from the United States Census Bureau, September 12, 2012, https:// www.census.gov/newsroom/releases/archives/income_wealth/cb12-172.html.

27. News release from the United States Census Bureau, September 10, 2009, http:// www.census.gov/newsroom/releases/archives/income_wealth/cb09-141.html.

28. Data from the U.S. Department of Agriculture's Food and Nutrition Service monthly program, retrieved March 2013, http://www.fns.usda.gov/pd/34SNAP monthly.htm.

29. ABC *World News with Diane Sawyer*, September 17, 2012.

30. *NBC Nightly News*, September 12, 2012.

31. Remarks in Hartford, Connecticut, June 23, 2007, as noted in "Promise Audit: Tracking President Obama's Progress on Campaign Promises," *National Journal*, http://promise.nationaljournal.com/health-care/provide-universal-health-care/.

32. Remarks by the President and Vice President at Signing of the Health Insurance Reform Bill, March 23, 2010, http://www.whitehouse.gov/the-press-office/ remarks-president-and-vice-president-signing-health-insurance-reform-bill.

33. Quoted by John Merline, "Health Premiums Up $3,065; Obama Vowed $2,500 Cut; ObamaCare Adds to Woes; 2008 Campaign Pledge Relied on Ignoring History, Optimistic Assumptions," *Investor's Business Daily*, September 25, 2012.

34. "Updated Estimates for the Insurance Coverage Provisions of the Affordable Care Act," Congressional Budget Office, March 2012, http://www.cbo.gov/sites/ default/files/cbofiles/attachments/03-13-Coverage%20Estimates.pdf.

35. ABC *World News with Diane Sawyer*, March 26, 2012.

36. "Estimates for the Insurance Coverage Provisions of the Affordable Care Act Updated for the Recent Supreme Court Decision," Congressional Budget Office, July 2012, http://cbo.gov/sites/default/files/cbofiles/attachments/43472-07-24 -2012-CoverageEstimates.pdf.

37. *NBC Nightly News*, June 28, 2012.

38. Elizabeth Mendes, "Americans Favor Keystone XL Pipeline," Gallup.com, March 22, 2012, http://www.gallup.com/poll/153383/americans-favor-keystone -pipeline.aspx.

39. *NBC Nightly News*, January 18, 2012.

40. *CBS Evening News*, January 18, 2012; *NBC Nightly News*, January 18, 2012.

41. *CBS Evening News*, March 22, 2012.

42. Art Hovey, "Heineman Says OK to Pipeline," *Lincoln (Nebraska) Journal-Star*, online article posted January 22, 2013, http://journalstar.com/news/local/govt-and-politics/heineman-says-ok-to-pipeline/article_5e1ec510-4e49-5e72-8ddf-34392cb4c475.html.

43. Speaking at Loyola University, October 19, 1998, http://www.youtube.com/watch?v=ge3aGJfDSg4.

44. Jeffrey Meyer, "Andrea Mitchell Inadvertently Admits Double Standard at MSNBC: Chuck Todd Remains Silent," NewsBusters, September 19, 2012, http://newsbusters.org/blogs/jeffrey-meyer/2012/09/19/andrea-mitchell-inadvertently-admits-double-standard-msnbc.

45. Scott Whitlock, "Unlike NBC, ABC's Jake Tapper Highlights Reverend Wright in New Video," NewsBusters, October 3, 2012, http://newsbusters.org/blogs/scott-whitlock/2012/10/03/unlike-nbc-abcs-jake-tapper-highlights-reverend-wright-new-video.

46. Matt Hadro, "Robert Gibbs Mocks CBS's Coverage of Obama Tape, Charlie Rose Changes the Subject," NewsBusters, October 3, 2012, http://newsbusters.org/blogs/matt-hadro/2012/10/03/roberts-gibbs-mocks-cbss-coverage-obama-tape-charlie-rose-changes-subjec.

47. Remarks to the National Conference of Black Mayors in Baton Rouge, Louisiana, March 5, 2007, http://www.presidency.ucsb.edu/ws/index.php?pid=77001.

48. Ed Klein, "The 'Bribe' to Silence Wright," *New York Post*, May 12, 2012, http://www.nypost.com/p/news/national/the_bribe_to_silence_wright_io9jneobl3fUF0cb7LpcNM.

49. Tim Graham and Geoffrey Dickens, "The Media's Obama Miracle: How Journalists Pretend There Aren't Any White House Scandals," MRC.org, August 8, 2012, http://www.mrc.org/node/40820.

50. Tapper, Jake, "Obama Friend Whitaker Denies Wright Allegation of Bribe," http://abcnews.go.com/blogs/politics/2012/06/obama-friend-whitaker-denies-wright-allegation-of-bribe/.

51. Jodi Kantor, *The Obamas* (New York: Little, Brown, 2012), p. 193.

52. Ibid., p. 43.

53. Ibid., p. 203.

54. NBC *Today*, September 12, 13, and 14, 2004.

55. Kitty Kelley, *The Family: The Real Story of the Bush Dynasty* (New York: Doubleday, 2004).

56. "CBS Plugged Fortunate Son," Cyber Alert, MRC.org, http://archive.mrc.org/cyberalerts/2000/cyb20000214.asp#2.

57. Pete Slover, "Publication Halted on Bush Biography; Records Indicate Author Is Felon," *Dallas Morning News*, October 22, 1999.

58. Matthew Balan, "Bob Schieffer Scorns 'Race-Baiting' Rev. Wright Attack; Obama Not a 'European Socialist,'" NewsBusters, May 22, 2012, http://newsbusters.org/blogs/matthew-balan/2012/05/22/bob-schieffer-scorns-race-baiting-rev-wright-attack-obama-not-europea.

# Chapter 11

1. Scott Whitlock, "ABC's GOP Debate Questions 6 to 1 Liberal, 25% on Contraception, Gay Rights," NewsBusters, January 9, 2012, http://newsbusters.org/blogs/scott-whitlock/2012/01/09/abcs-gop-debate-questions-6-1-liberal-25-contraception-gay-rights.
2. Brent Bozell, "Bozell Column: Say No to Feisty Liberal Moderators," NewsBusters, October 23, 2012, http://newsbusters.org/blogs/brent-bozell/2012/10/23/bozell-column-say-no-feisty-liberal-moderators.
3. Rich Noyes, "ABC's Stephanopoulos Leads Post-Debate Media Spin for Democrats," NewsBusters, October 2, 2012, http://newsbusters.org/blogs/rich-noyes/2012/10/02/abcs-stephanopoulos-leads-post-debate-media-spin-democrats.
4. Matt Hadro, "Liberal Journalist Carole Simpson Laughs at Romney, Praises Obama on CNN," NewsBusters, October 2, 2012, http://newsbusters.org/blogs/matt-hadro/2012/10/02/liberal-journalist-carole-simpson-laughs-romney-praises-obama-cnn.
5. Commission on Presidential Debates, October 3, 2012, http://www.debates.org/index.php?page=october-3-2012-debate-transcript.
6. Andrew Kirell, "Bill Maher Rips Obama's Performance Via Twitter: 'Looks Like He Does Need a Teleprompter,'" Mediaite, October 4, 2012, http://www.mediaite.com/tv/bill-maher-rips-obamas-performance-via-twitter-looks-like-he-does-need-a-teleprompter/.
7. Matthew Sheffield, "Chris Matthews Blasts Obama for Debate Performance, Urges Him to Get Talking Points from MSNBC," NewsBusters, October 3, 2012, http://newsbusters.org/blogs/matthew-sheffield/2012/10/03/msnbc-hosts-stunned-lackluster-obama-debate-performance.
8. Noel Sheppard, "Tom Brokaw: If Romney Performed like Obama Did Last Night 'It Would Have Been Over,'" NewsBusters, October 4, 2012, http://newsbusters.org/blogs/noel-sheppard/2012/10/04/tom-brokaw-if-romney-performed-obama-did-last-night-it-would-have-bee.
9. Brent Bozell, "Obama Lost So Badly Media Couldn't Spin It. . . . But Guess What's Next," NewsBusters, October 4, 2012, http://newsbusters.org/blogs/brent-bozell/2012/10/04/obama-lost-so-badly-media-couldnt-spin-itbut-guess-whats-next.
10. Matt Vespa, "Liberal on Liberal Violence: MSNBC's Fineman Slams 'Useless' Jim Lehrer," NewsBusters, October 4, 2012, http://newsbusters.org/blogs/matt

-vespa/2012/10/04/liberal-liberal-violence-msnbcs-fineman-calls-lehrer-use less.

11. Commission on Presidential Debates, October 3, 2012, http://www.debates.org/index.php?page=october-3-2012-debate-transcript.

12. Tim Graham, "Liberal Radio Has the DNC Song Sheet: Romney Only Won Because He's a 'Pathological Liar,'" NewsBusters, October 6, 2012, http://newsbusters.org/blogs/tim-graham/2012/10/06/liberal-radio-has-dnc-song-sheet-romney-only-won-because-hes-pathologica.

13. Commission on Presidential Debates, October 3, 2012, http://www.debates.org/index.php?page=october-3-2012-debate-transcript.

14. Matthew Balan, "Norah O'Donnell Jabs Romney on Big Bird Line: 'Silly Thing to Bring Up,'" NewsBusters, October 4, 2012, http://newsbusters.org/blogs/matthew-balan/2012/10/04/norah-odonnell-jabs-romney-big-bird-line-silly-thing-bring.

15. Matt Hadro, "GOP Congressman Lays Into CNN for 'Doing a Disservice' to Struggling Americans," NewsBusters, October 4, 2012, http://newsbusters.org/blogs/matt-hadro/2012/10/04/gop-congressman-lays-cnn-doing-disservice-struggling-americans.

16. Noel Sheppard, "PBS Strikes Back: 'Romney Does Not Understand the Value the American People Place on Public Broadcasting,'" NewsBusters, October 4, 2012, http://newsbusters.org/blogs/noel-sheppard/2012/10/04/pbs-strikes-back-romney-does-not-understand-value-american-people-pla.

17. Matt Hadro, "CNN Keeps Hyping Romney's Proposed PBS Cuts, PBS Host Calls It 'Attack on Children,'" NewsBusters, October 5, 2012, http://newsbusters.org/blogs/matt-hadro/2012/10/05/cnn-keeps-hyping-romneys-proposed-pbs-cuts-pbs-host-calls-it-attack-chil.

18. Brent Baker, "Journalists Decry 'Threat' to PBS from Romney for 'Targeting' Big Bird, Rally to Defense of PBS Subsidy," NewsBusters, October 8, 2012, http://newsbusters.org/blogs/brent-baker/2012/10/08/journalists-decry-threat-pbs-romney-targeting-big-bird-rally-defense-pb.

19. Tim Graham, "Will Moderator Martha Raddatz Bring Her Biased 'Budget Slasher' Talk to Paul Ryan Tonight?," NewsBusters, October 11, 2012, http://newsbusters.org/blogs/tim-graham/2012/10/11/will-moderator-martha-raddatz-bring-her-biased-budget-slasher-talk-paul-.

20. Ibid.

21. Tim Graham, "ABC's Raddatz Attended Women's Event at Biden's House—With Other Female TV Journos," NewsBusters, October 12, 2012, http://newsbusters.org/blogs/tim-graham/2012/10/12/abcs-raddatz-attended-womens-event-bidens-house-other-female-tv-journos.

22. Commission on Presidential Debates, October 11, 2012, http://www.debates.org/index.php?page=october-11-2012-the-biden-romney-vice-presidential-debate.

23. Rich Noyes, "Debate Moderator Favors Biden; ABC Colleagues Cheer: 'Martha

Raddatz for President,'" NewsBusters, October 12, 2012, http://newsbusters.org/blogs/rich-noyes/2012/10/12/debate-moderator-tilts-obama-abc-colleagues-cheer-martha-raddatz-preside.

24. Commission on Presidential Debates, October 11, 2012, http://www.debates.org/index.php?page=october-11-2012-the-biden-romney-vice-presidential-debate.

25. Tim Graham, "Smug WashPost TV Reviewer: Raddatz Favored Biden, Ryan Was Juvenile and an 'SVU' Pervert?," NewsBusters, October 12, 2012, http://newsbusters.org/blogs/tim-graham/2012/10/12/smug-washpost-tv-reviewer-raddatz-favored-biden-ryan-was-juvenile-and-sv.

26. Noyes, "Debate Moderator Favors Biden."

27. Matthew Sheffield, "Presidential Debate Co-Chair Admits Picking Candy Crowley Was 'Mistake,'" NewsBusters, February 20, 2013, http://newsbusters.org/blogs/matthew-sheffield/2013/02/20/presidential-debate-co-chair-admits-candy-crowley-was-mistake.

28. Brett LoGiurato, "Here's How the Undecided Voters Were Selected to Ask Obama and Romney Questions at Tomorrow's Debate," Business Insider, October 15, 2012, http://www.businessinsider.com/obama-romney-town-hall-debate-how-voters-were-selected-2012-10.

29. Rich Noyes, "MRC Study: By 2-to-1 Margin, Journalists Favor Liberal Questions at Town Hall Debates," MRC.org, October 16, 2012, http://www.mrc.org/node/41520.

30. Rich Noyes, "Candy Crowley Aids Obama with 2-to-1 Liberal Agenda & Validation of Libya Falsehood," MRC.org, October 17, 2012, http://www.mrc.org/node/41544.

31. Commission on Presidential Debates, October 16, 2012, http://www.debates.org/index.php?page=october-1-2012-the-second-obama-romney-presidential-debate.

32. Brent Baker, "NBC Nightly News Showcases 'Undecided Voter' Trashing Romney Hours After She Declares for Obama," NewsBusters, October 18, 2012, http://newsbusters.org/blogs/brent-baker/2012/10/18/nbc-nightly-news-showcases-undecided-voter-trashing-romney-hours-after-.

33. Commission on Presidential Debates, October 16, 2012, http://www.debates.org/index.php?page=october-1-2012-the-second-obama-romney-presidential-debate.

34. Irin Carmon, "Wage-Gap Debate Questioner Katherine Fenton 'Absolutely Not' a Feminist," Salon.com, October 17, 2012, http://www.salon.com/2012/10/17/wage_gap_debate_questioner_katherine_fenton_absolutely_not_a_feminist/.

35. Commission on Presidential Debates, October 16, 2012, http://www.debates.org/index.php?page=october-1-2012-the-second-obama-romney-presidential-debate.

36. Cristina Costaniti, "Meet Lorraine from the Presidential Debate—Or Was It

Lorena?," ABCNews.com, October 17, 2012, http://abcnews.go.com/ABC_Univi
sion/News/meet-lorraine-osorio-presidential-debate-lorena/story?id=17501899.

37. Commission on Presidential Debates, October 16, 2012, http://www.debates
.org/index.php?page=october-1-2012-the-second-obama-romney-presidential
-debate.

38. "The Issue That Goes Ignored," *New York Times*, October 18, 2012, http://www
.nytimes.com/2012/10/19/opinion/the-issue-that-goes-ignored.html.

39. Noyes, "Candy Crowley Aids Obama."

40. Commission on Presidential Debates October 16, 2012, http://www.debates
.org/index.php?page=october-1-2012-the-second-obama-romney-presidential
-debate.

41. Ibid.

42. White House Transcript, September 12, 2012, http://www.whitehouse.gov/the
-press-office/2012/09/12/remarks-president-deaths-us-embassy-staff-libya.

43. Glenn Kessler, "Fact Check: Libya Attack," *Washington Post*, October 16, 2012,
http://www.washingtonpost.com/blogs/post-politics/wp/2012/10/16/fact-check
-libya-attack/?wprss=rss_campaigns.

44. Brent Baker, "Candy Crowley Not in 'Cahoots' with Obama; He and Axelrod
Used Her," NewsBusters, October 20, 2012, http://newsbusters.org/blogs/brent
-baker/2012/10/20/candy-crowley-not-cahoots-obama-he-and-axelrod-used-her.

45. Brent Bozell, "Candy Crowley Self-Destructs," NewsBusters, October 18, 2012,
http://newsbusters.org/blogs/brent-bozell/2012/10/18/bozell-column-candy
-crowley-self-destructs.

46. Ibid.

47. Scott Whitlock, "On ABC, Matthew Dowd, Donna Brazile Target Conservatives:
Attacks on Crowley 'Sure Sign' Obama Won," October 17, 2012, http://news
busters.org/blogs/matthew-balan/2012/10/17/abc-matthew-dowd-donna
-brazile-target-conservatives-attacks-crowley-s.

48. Scott Whitlock, "Desperate ABC Hypes Romney's 'Binder Blunder'; Will It 'Halt'
GOP Gains?," NewsBusters, October 18, 2012, http://newsbusters.org/blogs/
scott-whitlock/2012/10/18/desperate-abc-hypes-romneys-binder-blunder-will
-it-halt-gop-gains.

49. Geoffrey Dickens, "Study: ABC, CBS & NBC Hype Romney's 'Binders' over
Biden's 'Bullets' by 11 to 1 Margin," NewsBusters, October 19, 2012, http://news
busters.org/blogs/geoffrey-dickens/2012/10/19/study-abc-cbs-nbc-hype
-romneys-binders-over-bidens-bullets-11-1-ma.

50. Ibid.

51. Kalb Report, January 28, 2013, https://research.gwu.edu/sites/research.gwu.edu/
files/downloads/DemocracyInAction_Transcript.pdf.

52. Commission on Presidential Debates, October 22, 2012, http://www.debates
.org/index.php?page=october-22-2012-the-third-obama-romney-presidential
-debate.

53. Tim Graham, "Will Schieffer Ask Obama About That 'Cancer' Called Guantanamo?," NewsBusters, October 22, 2012, http://newsbusters.org/blogs/tim-graham/2012/10/22/will-schieffer-ask-obama-about-cancer-called-guantanamo.

54. Geoffrey Dickens, "NBC's Williams: Obama's 'Horses and Bayonets' Zinger Will 'Live Forever,'" NewsBusters, October 23, 2012, http://newsbusters.org/blogs/geoffrey-dickens/2012/10/23/nbcs-gregory-obamas-horses-and-bayonets-zinger-was-line-night#ixzz2NpxtHJSK.

55. Commission on Presidential Debates, October 22, 2012, http://www.debates.org/index.php?page=october-22-2012-the-third-obama-romney-presidential-debate.

56. Deroy Murdock, "Obama Caught Lying About Sequester," NationalReview.com, February 26, 2013, http://www.nationalreview.com/corner/341553/obama-caught-lying-about-sequester-deroy-murdock.

# Chapter 12

1. Brent Baker, "Nets Follow NY Times and Kerry, Hype Missing Explosives Cache," Cyber Alert, October 26, 2004, http://www.mrc.org/biasalerts/nets-follow-ny-times-and-kerry-hype-missing-explosives-cache-10262004#1.

2. Brent Baker, "Like with Forged Memos, CBS Plows Forward with Explosives Story," CyberAlert, October 27, 2004, http://www.mrc.org/biasalerts/forged-memos-cbs-plows-forward-explosives-story-10272004#1.

3. Matthew Balan, "On 9/11 Anniversary, CBS Promotes Vanity Fair Editor's Blame Bush Tome," NewsBusters, September 11, 2012, http://newsbusters.org/blogs/matthew-balan/2012/09/11/911-anniversary-cbs-promotes-vanity-fair-editors-blame-bush-tome.

4. Kurt Eichenwald, "The Deafness Before the Storm," NYTimes.com, September 10, 2012, http://www.nytimes.com/2012/09/11/opinion/the-bush-white-house-was-deaf-to-9-11-warnings.html.

5. Tom Blumer, "NY Times Puts Coverage of Cairo, Benghazi Attacks on Page A4," NewsBusters, September 12, 2012, http://newsbusters.org/blogs/tom-blumer/2012/09/12/nyt-puts-story-about-cairo-benghazi-attacks-page-a4.

6. Louis Jacobson, "Did the U.S. Embassy in Cairo Make an Apology?," Politifact.com, September 12, 2012, http://www.politifact.com/truth-o-meter/article/2012/sep/12/romney-says-us-embassy-statement-was-apology-was-i/.

7. "EXCLUSIVE: Open mic captures press coordinating questions for Romney 'no matter who he calls on we're covered,'" Right Scoop, September 12, 2012, http://www.therightscoop.com/exclusive-open-mic-captures-press-coordinating-questions-for-romney-no-matter-who-he-calls-on-were-covered/.

8. Jim Rutenberg, "Despite Libyan Crisis, Obama Campaign Plans to Stay on

Schedule," *New York Times*, September 12, 2012, http://thecaucus.blogs.nytimes .com/2012/09/12/despite-libyan-crisis-obama-campaign-plans-to-stay-on -schedule/.

9. Rich Noyes, "The Media's Coverage of the Libya Attacks: From Slanted to Suppressed," NewsBusters, November 2, 2012, http://newsbusters.org/blogs/rich -noyes/2012/11/02/media-s-coverage-libya-attacks-slanted-suppressed.

10. Transcript of *NBC Nightly News*, September 12, 2012.

11. Transcript of *CBS Evening News*, September 12, 2012.

12. Ibid.

13. Ibid.

14. "Press Briefing by Press Secretary Jay Carney, 9/14/2012," Whitehouse.gov, September 14, 2012, http://www.whitehouse.gov/the-press-office/2012/09/14/press -briefing-press-secretary-jay-carney-9142012.

15. Brent Bozell, "Bozell Column: NBC and MSNBC, Networks of Wusses," September 18, 2012, http://newsbusters.org/blogs/brent-bozell/2012/09/18/bozell -column-nbc-and-msnbc-networks-wusses.

16. Ibid.

17. "September 16: Benjamin Netanyahu, Susan Rice, Keith Ellison, Peter King, Bob Woodward, Jeffrey Goldberg, Andrea Mitchell," *Meet the Press* transcript, September 16, 2012, http://www.nbcnews.com/id/49051097/ns/meet_the_press -transcripts/t/september-benjamin-netanyahu-susan-rice-keith-ellison-peter -king-bob-woodward-jeffrey-goldberg-andrea-mitchell/.

18. Transcript of *NBC Nightly News*, September 20, 2012.

19. Scott Whitlock, "CBS Concedes: Romney Better Push Libya Because the Press Won't 'Make the Case for Him,'" MRC.org, September, 2012, http://www.mrc .org/node/41332.

20. Brent Baker, "Sawyer Spends 4 Minutes Channeling Liberal Angst over Obama's Debate Performance; 20 Seconds on Libya Dissembling," NewsBusters, October 10, 2012, http://newsbusters.org/blogs/brent-baker/2012/10/10/sawyer-spends -4-minutes-channeling-liberal-angst-over-obama-s-debate-pe.

21. Kyle Drennen, "NBC's Williams Can't Understand Why Obama Isn't Winning by a Landslide," NewsBusters, October 25, 2012, http://newsbusters.org/blogs/ kyle-drennen/2012/10/25/nbcs-williams-cant-understand-why-obama-isnt -winning-landslide.

22. Brent Baker, "Incredibly, in Prime Time Interview Brian Williams Treats Obama as a Victim of Bad Intelligence on Benghazi," NewsBusters, October 26, 2012, http://newsbusters.org/blogs/brent-baker/2012/10/26/incredibly-prime-time -interview-brian-williams-treats-obama-victim-bad-.

23. Matthew Balan, "Libya E-mails Break; Morning Shows Minimize Pressure on Team Obama," NewsBusters, October 24, 2012, http://newsbusters.org/blogs/ matthew-balan/2012/10/24/libya-e-mails-break-morning-shows-minimize -pressure-team-obama.

24. Transcript of *CBS Evening News*, October 23, 2012.
25. Noyes, "The Media's Coverage of the Libya Attacks.
26. Ibid.
27. Brent Bozell, "Bozell Column: The News Squashers," NewsBusters, October 30, 2012, http://newsbusters.org/blogs/brent-bozell/2012/10/30/bozell-column-news -squashers.
28. Noyes, "The Media's Coverage of the Libya Attacks."
29. Ibid.
30. Ibid.
31. Matt Vespa, "On Eve of Election, CBS News Finally Releases Libya Excerpts of Obama Interview," NewsBusters, November 5, 2012, http://newsbusters.org/ blogs/matt-vespa/2012/11/05/eve-election-cbs-news-finally-releases-libya -excerpts-obama-interview.

# INDEX

# ABOUT THE AUTHOR

L. Brent Bozell III is the president of the Media Research Center, the leading right-wing media watchdog. Whenever the media behaves badly, Bozell and the MRC are the "go-to" group for Fox News and conservative commentators, from Rush Limbaugh to Mark Levin. They are dedicated to rebutting and forestalling the media from their mission in composing a very slanted "first draft" of history.

Tim Graham is the director of media analysis for the MRC.